States of Exception

States of Exception

Everyday Life and Postcolonial Identity

Keya Ganguly

University of Minnesota Press

Minneapolis

London

An earlier version of chapter 3 appeared as "Migrant Identities: Personal Memory and the Construction of Selfhood," *Cultural Studies* 6, no. 1 (1992): 27–50. Reprinted with permission from Routledge Press and Taylor & Francis.

Published by the University of Minnesota Press
111 Third Avenue South, Suite 290
Minneapolis, MN 55401-2520
http://www.upress.umn.edu

Library of Congress Cataloging-in-Publication Data

Ganguly, Keya.
     States of exception : everyday life and postcolonical identity / Keya
Ganguly.
          p.   cm.
     Includes index.
     ISBN 0-8166-3716-4 (hard : alk. paper) — ISBN 0-8166-3717-2 (pbk. :
alk. paper)
     1. East Indian Americans—Ethnic identity.   2. East Indian
Americans—Psychology.   3. East Indian Americans—Social life and
customs.   4. Identity (Philosophical concept)   5. Memory (Philosophy)
6. Postcolonialism—Social aspects—United States.   7. Postcolonialism—
United States—Psychological aspects.   8. United States—Ethnic
relations.   I. Title.
E184.E2 G36   2001
305.891'4073—dc21   00-010327

Printed in the United States of America on acid-free paper

The University of Minnesota is an equal-opportunity educator and employer.

11 10 09 08 07 06 05 04 03 02 01   10 9 8 7 6 5 4 3 2 1

In memory of my grandfather, P. C. Bhattacharyya, O.B.E.

and

to my grandmother, Kamala Devi

Contents

Acknowledgments

I should like to thank my parents, Bidyut and Debi Prasanna Ganguly, whose love and support have made everything possible. Their skepticism, as scientists, about what we humanists do has always been a challenge and the spur to my learning some compelling lessons in intellectual doubt. I can acknowledge only inadequately the debt owed to the members of the Indian community in southern New Jersey who participated in the ethnographic project at the core of this book. They remain, of necessity, unnamed; more than a decade later, they also remain "my" community and continue to teach me that belongingness is a matter of faith. But I should like to single out J. B. Benegal and Krishna Benegal for their help with the project and for the music, dance, many meals, and much good humor they have shared with me.

The University of Minnesota Press first approached me in 1994 with an interest in publishing this work. Through many delays and not a few reconceptualizations of the stakes involved, my editor, William Murphy, and two successive directors of the press, Lisa Freeman and Douglas Armato, maintained their confidence in the project. The Press also provided me with two extraordinarily careful, incisive, and supportive readers' reports; for their generosity with time and advice, my gratitude to Ross Chambers and Neil Larsen.

To the members of my dissertation committee at the University of Illinois, Urbana-Champaign, I owe very special thanks. Larry Grossberg supervised my dissertation with an expansiveness that belied the differences between his thinking and mine. Jim Carey has my admiration for being an exemplary intellectual as well as an important mentor and the person who, as early as the 1970s, stewarded the introduction of cultural studies in the United States. And my debts to Zohreh Sullivan cannot be expressed in words alone: She has been confidante, counselor, and fairy godmother all rolled into one and over all these years. The commitments expressed in this book may not be shared by my former teachers, but I have tried to keep in mind the training they provided in how to think against the grain.

A year spent in 1990–1991 as a postdoctoral fellow at the Pembroke Center for Teaching and Research on Women at Brown University gave me the opportunity to start rethinking my ideas about theory, practice, and scholarly engagement. I should like to thank Karen Newman and Elizabeth Weed as well as members of the Pembroke seminar for providing a forum for debating and exchanging ideas. My year at Brown brought me the friendship of Neil Lazarus, with whom I continue to share a passion for cricket, food, and dialectics. Providence also granted me an introduction to Eric Clarke—who, apart from being the closest of friends, has served as my most critical interlocutor in all matters. Much of this book was written during my years of teaching in the Program in Literary and Cultural Theory at Carnegie Mellon University. My comrades, through some difficult institutional times, were Crystal Bartolovich, Sharon Dilworth, Ronald Judy, and Paul Smith; I am better for knowing them and grateful for their continuing friendship. I also thank Peter Stearns, former dean of humanities and social sciences at Carnegie Mellon, for his personal encouragement and for two faculty development grants (in 1992 and 1995). Colin MacCabe at the University of Pittsburgh took time out of his busy schedule to smooth the rough edges of my life in Pittsburgh. I thank him for his guidance and friendship.

Since 1997 my colleagues in the Department of Cultural Studies and Comparative Literature at the University of Minnesota have provided a keen and supportive environment in which to pursue critical comparative work. I am particularly indebted to Richard Leppert and John Mowitt for their insights and encouragement. The students in my graduate seminars consistently provide a high standard of intellectual rigor to live up to, and many of my ideas on a different articulation of postcolonial scholarship, cultural studies, and continental theory were worked out in conversations with them. I must also thank Don Johnson, of the Ames Library of South Asia at the University of Minnesota, for up-to-date information on relevant scholarly literature and especially for providing me with the image for the cover illustration.

Other friends, past and present, have made my years spent in this country of expatriate uncertainty, fulfilling in different ways. For that, I thank Anthony Arnove, Anne Balsamo, Dipesh Chakrabarty, Mary Childers, Mark Douglas, Tom Haakenson, Julian Halliday, Matthew Ruben, Gayatri and Adesh Saxena, Carol Stabile, and Elayne Tobin. I have shared the most incomparably intense exchanges about politics, life and fate with Janaki Bakhle, Shashi Karpur, and Claudia Lima Costa. I know they cannot be recompensed. Stuart Hall and Edward Said have long exemplified my personal ideals of scholarly excellence (even if neither cared to recognize the influence of their thought on mine), and I thank Stuart for his various kindnesses to me over the years. The person whose ideas and engagements suffuse my own is my husband, Tim Brennan. But since discretion is the better part of valor, let me thank him only for transforming my *vie quotidienne.*

By now this book is long overdue, although the lag time between its conception and appearance was required in order for my ideas to become clear, even to me. In part this is a matter of thinking that one should only write a book when one has something to say, and in part it is a result of wrestling with the gap between empirical and theoretical questions. Not a little of the gap remains and for all unresolved problems as well as infelicities in the text, I am alone responsible.

States of Exception

INTRODUCTION

Gunga Gin and Other Anomalies

So I'll meet 'im later on
At the place where 'e is gone—
Where it's always double drill and no canteen;
'E'll be squattin' on the coals
Givin' drink to poor damned souls,
An' I'll get a swig in hell from Gunga Din!
Yes, Din! Din! Din!
You Lazarushian-leather Gunga Din!
Though I've belted you and flayed you,
By the livin' Gawd that made you,
You're a better man than I am, Gunga Din!

I first heard Rudyard Kipling's "Gunga Din," one of his *Barrack-Room Ballads,* as a child. Although the prose and poetry of the West, especially in the tradition of English literature, is very much a staple of the contemporary schooling system in India, this poem was one that I had encountered outside the formal educational processes that locate and produce middle-class, Anglicized Indian subjects like myself. "Gunga Din" had been recited to me by a civil service colleague of my grandfather's, and for many years it remained beyond recall, partitioned off in some recess of the imagination labeled "childhood." It is only in recent years that I can remember, with extraordinary clarity, the experience of sobbing at the injustice visited upon Gunga Din—at his having to serve colonial masters, only to die and go to hell and even there to be consigned forever to "givin' drink to poor damned souls." I recall as well the dismay of my grandfather's friend, who was astonished that he had rendered a five-year old disconsolate by the mere recitation of such a "classic" poem. Patrician Anglophile that he was, I suppose he had intended the poem to tell a story of nobility and steadfast servitude: sort of a hybridized combination of an indigenous ideology of *karma yoga* and a staunch Protestant work ethic embodied in the figure of the "blackfaced" water carrier to the British troops. Instead, I had misheard the tale. I could not comprehend how such a narrative of abjection could be regarded as uplifting.

The decades intervening between that encounter and this telling have taught me to recognize that the distances separating intention and effect, a story's logic and its reenactment, or indeed, ideology and consciousness require very complicated accountings. In this book, I attempt to provide such an account in terms of the experiences of an immigrant Indian community in southern New Jersey. I desire to think concretely about the crosshatched trajectories of colonization and globalization as they come to demarcate quotidian understandings of postcolonial identity, which is to say, within the recurrent practices of everyday life. So the term "practice" should be understood as modifying the quotidian or the routine—with its familiar employment in the phrase "the practice of everyday life" foregrounding the influence of Michel de Certeau's analyses in his *Arts de faire*.[1] In the subsequent volume of *The Practice of Everyday Life, Living and Cooking* (*L'invention du quotidien*, vol. 2: *Habiter, cuisiner*), Certeau gives us a framing of the concept of a cultural practice on which I have relied throughout:

> [I]t is the more or less coherent and fluid assemblage of elements that are concrete and everyday (a gourmet menu) or ideological (religious, political), at once coming from a tradition (that of a family or social group) and reactualized from day to day across behaviors translating fragments of this cultural device into social visibility, in the same way that the utterance translates fragments of discourse in speech. A "practice" is what is decisive for the *identity* of a dweller or a group insofar as this identity allows him or her to take up a position in the network of social relations inscribed in the environment.[2]

Let me suggest at the outset that an ethnographic analysis of a community's self-representation in and through the routines of daily experience has no absolute purchase on questions of subject formation or consciousness. But it is one means of connecting abstract formulations about identity with the cultural and historical exigencies that provide the often insubstantial and always contingent bases for the consolidation of what passes as the postcolonial predicament. It is not necessary to separate "theoretical" pronouncements from descriptive or "ethnographic" ones, any more than the personal anecdote with which I began needs to possess an essential or oppositional privilege. I wish to claim that *all* forms of inquiry have both determinate and provisional motivations that are sometimes contradictory and regularly unthematized. My childhood memory of Kipling's poem "Gunga Din" serves as a *mise-en-abîme* of the tensions and anxieties attached to trafficking in problems of history, memory, and identity from a position that recognizes the inescapable contradictions between teller and tale told. Moreover, the inseparable contingencies of experience that go beyond constraints of signification—the prison-houses of language and discourse, so to speak—evince the difficulty of speaking about a predicament from within it.

I shall return (in chapter 1) to the consequences of my own location as a putative "native informant" on matters postcolonial, but here I want to mark the difference between a perspective that trucks in the recovery of true history and one that presupposes a discontinuity between knowledge and truth. However daunting the epistemological problem of truth may be, we must rouse ourselves from a Nietzschean solipsism and address the somewhat less obdurate question of levels or genres of truth. At this more modest level of "realism," postcolonial inquiry is marked by a special burden because our discourse community and our governing protocols for establishing analytic truths, are incommensurable with the everyday experiences of most postcolonial subjects (who do not live as if academic talk about their predicament either validates or invalidates their convictions). In focusing on everyday life, therefore, I am mindful of the incipient risk of hypostatizing the status of experience as if the mere banality of its expressions might rescue them from being ontologized. Put more simply, despite its quotidian force in producing self-understandings, experience cannot be taken as knowledge of *being*. But if, as Marx famously pointed out in his "Theses on Feuerbach," "social life is essentially practical," it ought to be possible to say something about the practical consolidations of such life without having to make abstract, metaphysical assertions about what Theodor Adorno called "existential bombast" in his trenchant polemic against Martin Heidegger, *The Jargon of Authenticity*.[3]

Adorno's writings, along with those of other associates of the Frankfurt school, have been of paramount importance in understanding the reformulation and reification of experience in capitalist modernity. Carrying on the mode of thinking of Karl Marx, Max Weber, Georg Simmel, and Georg Lukács, the Frankfurt school critics offered crucial insights into how modern experience is atrophied or frozen in the commodity form.[4] Their critiques, still pressingly relevant four or five decades later, center on a historical materialism precisely to avoid granting any expressive autonomy to experience. They teach us that the relay between being and knowing, or between history and understanding, is, though constituted in language, less a problem of language (against poststructuralism) than of alienation (with Marx). That is why the status of experience must be interrogated in order to get closer to the core of sensuous activity frozen and disguised in the husk of everyday life. The argument about reification is hardly heretical today, but the consequences of experiential reification in modernity (including in its postcolonial cultural configurations) appear to have gotten lost in the explosion of propositions about border crossings, liminal zones, the aporia of postcoloniality, performative or strategic essentialisms, and so on. Neither an increased sensitivity to questions of otherness nor a heightened awareness of marginal and mobile identities has adequately accounted for the multiple intersections between a dominant political-economic order and articulations of cultural difference. Culturalist explanations that favor the liminality or alterity of subaltern experience seem to be the current trend. This trend has overshadowed consideration of the mutually constituting effects of a globalizing economic and cultural imperative on the one hand and the emergence of local identities locked in struggle against imperial sovereignty on the other.[5]

I hope to redirect attention away from exceptionalist discourses that categorize postcoloniality as enviably, if impossibly, other. The ensuing account is caught up in a quite different problematic of elucidating the complex and circuitous means by which the relation between a colonially inflected sense of the past and an emergent immigrant selfhood is inhabited or lived out. That this form of subjectivity is produced in and by the experience of immigration (in contrast, say, to exile or migrancy, which are not voluntary propositions) has, I argue, everything to do with the *rationalization* of identity.[6] The confluence of interests and ideas (to be described at greater length in chapter 4) shaping immigrant investments in "heritage" or "tradition" reflects the process by which an identity—emerging as a sentimental response to and refusal of an overarching narrative of bourgeois selfhood—is rationalized actively, in the sense that Weber gave to the process of self-management. Weber, we may recall in passing, was concerned with how, under forms of early capitalist social development, religious attachments (and we might add traditional customs) were revalued into materialistic ones—so that the pursuit of wealth or "worldly activity," to use his phrase, could be rationalized as ethical conduct. Then as now, the appeal to religion or tradition enabled the buttressing of conscience, particularly "good conscience," less as the stuff of authentic piety or purity than as "one of the means of enjoying a comfortable bourgeois life."[7]

This is not to suggest that immigrant preoccupations are inauthentic or that forms of identity articulated by the "base" economic imperatives of immigration are somehow less than real. Rather, the crisis of postcolonial identity stems from one of authority: a problem analogous to the diagnosis of bourgeois modernity that Antonio Gramsci captured by his phrase "The old is dying and the new cannot be born." Postcoloniality represents those "morbid symptoms" *(fenomeni morbosi)* that Gramsci sees as appearing in the interregnum between a colonial past and a postcolonial present.[8] Forms of social experience produced in this interregnum accordingly have far more to do with expressing the logic of capital than with ontological uncertainties about the melancholia of radical alterity.

If, therefore, postcolonial narratives are exemplary, it is because they are culturally particular instances of the ways that the articulation of postcolonial experience runs up against received understandings about otherness. As self-consolidating acts, such narratives resist a dominant bourgeois sociality characteristic of North American existence, even as they betray anxieties about propriety and about "fitting in." It bears reemphasizing that nothing inherently subversive attaches to the dislocations and transmutations undergone by immigrant subjects caught up in their own embourgeoisement. On the contrary, the self-production of an identity located and locatable in the U.S. context as "immigrant" puts pressure on the extent to which it is possible to remain outside this culture's insistently assimilationist and instrumental forms of social valorization. In saying this, I mean to indicate the local, contextual transactions by which forms of identity reproduce, as well as fail to reproduce *exactly,* mainstream ideologies about what is valued and valuable. My interest lies in the quotidian remainders—what one might call the exceptions—within the dictates of a hegemonic narrative of identity through which the logic of capital seeks universalization.[9]

The itinerary of such exceptions are, as I have already indicated, provisional and contingent rather than given either as historical essences or methodological a prioris. What I have to say, then, proceeds from the supposition that any stocktaking of experience depends upon these provisionalities and contingencies of circumstance, which Raymond Williams called "accidents of society." This is to say that some of the most powerful insights into the meaning of particular actions or experiences are made possible only by chance or happenstance. As Marcel Proust's *À la recherche de temps perdu* brilliantly laid out in fictional form, insight is sometimes produced only in retrospect: light cast on a previously unilluminated matter. The theoretical counterpart of Proust's portrayal of such retroactive mechanisms of perception are, we know, given their most complex, even confounding elaboration in Freud's concept of *Nachträglichkeit,* or "deferred action." My reach cannot extend to settling disputes over Freud's use of the concept of deferred action (which appeared in his writings from 1895 onward), but it is worth noting what Freud himself wrote to Wilhelm Fliess (on December 6, 1896):

> I am working on the assumption that our psychical mechanism has come into being by a process of stratification: the material present in the form of memory-traces being subjected from time to time to a *re-arrangement* in accordance with fresh circumstances—to a *re-transcription.*[10]

Whereas Freud seems to underline the mechanism of "retranscription" (with its allied sense of a preexisting "transcript"), Jacques Derrida, by contrast, has popularized a reading of Freud that regards deferral as irreducible. In *Writing and Difference* Derrida appropriates Freud's conception of deferral for his own claims about *différance:*

> The unconscious text is already a weave of pure traces, differences in meaning and force are united—a text nowhere present consisting of archives which are *always already* transcriptions.... Everything begins with reproduction. Always already: repositories of a meaning which was never present, whose signified presence is always reconstituted by deferral, *nachträglich,* belatedly, *supplementarily:* for the *nachträglich* also means *supplementary.*[11]

In rendering the complications of retroactivity inevitable—the incantation of the "always already"—Derrida effects a hostile takeover of Freud's more rigorously specified ideas about the status of the past and remands them to the temporal abyss of the "scene of writing." The contingent in Freud becomes primary in Derrida (with the accompanying reproof against confusing this with anything originary or a priori).

If we were to remain faithful to Freud's own inclinations about the process (however speculative) of history, we might read the recollection of my childhood introduction to Kipling's poem as a momentary though concrete remembrance of things past, a remembrance whose significance emerged much later against the backdrop of my initial experiences as an assistant professor. On taking up my first teaching position, I found myself wondering how to teach courses prepackaged under the rubric of "postcolonialism." For my own part, I thought it was more important for students to learn about the historical and political consequences of colonialism in the contemporary world system: to learn that there is nothing so "post" about colonialism, as it were. So I resisted the pedagogic emphasis on the grandly ontologizing (as well as periodizing) gestures of postcolonial theory and its privileging of literary texts as truths about the so-called Third World.[12] Reminded of Williams's ironical question, "When Was Modernism?" I wanted to ask in the wake of the disciplinary scramble to colonize postcolonial studies: "When Was the Postcolonial?"[13]

The answer to this question unfolded very much in the manner of a return of the repressed (to continue the Proustian/Freudian metaphor of latency). One evening a few months into teaching a course on "alterity and representation," I went to a local restaurant with a colleague. That night the establishment was fairly busy, and we were seated next to a party of diners who watched, with more than passing interest, our progress through dinner. Toward the end of the meal, a member of this adjacent party could no longer contain his curiosity and leaned over to ask me where I was from. I responded, "India"; to which he asked, "Kashmir?"

"No, Bengal," I replied.

"Are you sure?" he questioned.

"What do you mean? Of course I'm sure I'm from Bengal," I said with some irritation.

He then asserted, "I've been to India and I could swear that you were from Kashmir." After that he proceeded to demonstrate his expansive cultural knowledge by reciting, loudly and dramatically, Kipling's "Gunga Din." His rendition was distinctive in that, in his eagerness (combined, perhaps, with inebriation), he kept alluding to the poem's protagonist as "Gunga *Gin*." When he came to the bit about being "a better man than I am, Gunga Gin," my colleague and I beat a quick retreat from the restaurant.

This encounter with "Gunga Din" reengaged the very different memory of hearing the poem during my childhood in India. The two episodes (set about twenty-five years and twenty thousand miles apart) converge to reveal the difficulty and perhaps impossibility of escaping the archival effects of European constructions about India and Indians.[14] A little of what Gayatri Chakravorty Spivak has called "sanctioned ignorance" is also revealed in the habit of the Western subject who, as principal beneficiary of expanding markets and deregulated economies, comes into contact with the non-West with only a reductive attempt at interaction.[15] The Anglicized Indian from the elite "comprador" classes, who took on the burden of European representations both during and after the period of colonization, is not, in the present conjuncture, unlike the entitled American, whose sense of manifest destiny remains intact even if it is modified by liberal impulses to appear in the benign guise of assimilating (rather than dominating) the other. Thus, if the colonial maxim "not quite, not white" designated the *babu*—the impossible subject position of the Anglicized Indian in the days of the Raj—then in the context of contemporary society, the postcolonial self is riddled with the dilemmas of being "not quite, not right" because she is in danger of being both misheard and misread.[16]

My past and present encounters with the associative afterlife of Kipling's poem highlight the following structural parallel: Just as my grandfather's friend had internalized an imperial logic whereby the oppressive force of Kipling's racism simply offered itself as a literary naturalization of the nobility of the savage, decades later my intoxicated interlocutor in the restaurant asserted a muscular conviction about his cultural authority on the basis of some slight personal experience of India and his (mis)-rendering of "Gunga Din." A self-negating cultural anxiety inhabited by the former parallels a self-serving cultural authoritarianism exhibited by the latter, but both positions reveal a supra-individual relationship to the narrative of British colonialism and its discursive remains.

The multiple trails of a colonial history connect the contemporary experiences of the community I have undertaken to write about in this book. However, it is precisely as an *afterlife*—with its own dynamics, effects, and expressive capacities—that the historical narrative of colonialism must be reckoned with, since, obviously, the context of immigrant experience in the United States is not coterminous with what happened in India during (and after) British rule. The political calculus is no longer specifically colonial, insofar as the administrative form of British colonialism in India has been superseded (albeit by the less visible yet more efficient neocolonialist dynamics of the current conjuncture). In this new context, a fortuitous consequence of globalization is that the " 'will to power' of the inherent dominative mode" (as Williams paraphrased Nietzsche) has had to make room for subjects whom it has not quite been able to assimilate into its inexorable and paralyzing telos of objecthood.[17] That the imperialist drive toward objectification is inadequate accounts in good measure for the anxiety of influence underlying parapraxes such as "Gunga Gin." And ever since Freud gave us an understanding of the psychopathological function of slips of the tongue, we now know to read linguistic and mnemonic lapses as symptoms of repressed or inexpressible social anxieties.[18]

Returning once more to my encounter with "Gunga Gin," we might pause over the slippage between "Din" and "Gin" and over the ways it reinstates a colonial equivalence between native and slave: a historically sedimented construction of the other as always ready to serve, be it labor or libation. The misremembered name of the water-carrier, "Gunga Gin," brings congealed fantasies and phantasmatic desires from the past up to the surface of the present. Furthermore, the serendipitous similarity between "gin" and "djinn" (also popularly transcribed as "genie") reminds us that in such orientalist constructions as the story of Aladdin and his lamp, the Arabic word *jinnee* (meaning both slave and imp) connotes the figure of the magical servant who gloriously yet silently provides for his (white) master. An unintended lapse in memory on the part of my interlocutor in the restaurant, the slip betrays and projects the continuing force of a colonial desire for silent servitude. It also reveals the disregard with which Western subjects often perceive the other: Djinn, slave, subservient subject—all blur into a literal and metaphoric haze as a result of an accidental encounter.

On a different plane, the supplementary associations attached to "Gin" as physical intoxicant and phantom construction reflect the complex relay between history and hallucination, literary reference and fantastic image. As such, they had the energizing effect of illuminating for me the peculiar hold of past distortions on material in the present. And, finally, the parapraxis expresses the untimeliness and sense of unreality accompanying the postcolonial subject's reception within supposedly cosmopolitan cultural circles. A penumbra of misrecognition and mis-remembrance seems to surround even latter-day Western encounters with the non-West's otherness; the result is that day-to-day negotiations in, say, mainstream U.S. society are, for the Indian, regularly loaded with a quality of oddness. Such oddness, emblematized by our mutual rela-tion to the experience of continuing to be "not quite, not right," pro-vides the tacit link between members of my ethnographic community and myself. We might describe this predicament, both individual and collective, as anomalous—in the sense of looking unfamiliar and speak-ing differently, but also in the sense of never being seen to embody "nor-mal" values, be they religious, secular-cultural, political, sexual, or some-thing else.[19] The depradations of history reappear as uncanny traces and incomplete conjunctions of our singular and collective pasts caught in the glare of a dominating Western consciousness intent on melting the other into its pot of readable (if not agreeable) presences.

To this vexed problem of anomalous historical positioning we might add the epistemological anomaly of "ethnography through thick and thin." The phrase is George Marcus's, and it signals the repatriation of ethno-graphic practice on the terrain of a postreflexive pragmatism.[20] Anthro-pologists now go out of their way to refrain from referring to their ethno-graphic subjects as their possessions and to cultivate a balance in power relations between ethnographer and informant. Such acts of good in-tention are indeed praiseworthy, but let me risk a different, more ob-tuse position: My intention in this book is neither to possess the commu-nity I engage nor to fetishize my activities in it (assuming such possession was at all possible and my activities were worthy of fetishization). So when I refer, as I did in the paragraph above, to "my" ethnographic com-munity, it is as an ironic notation of its impossible status as the independent subject of an ethnographic inquiry. Thus two procedural points are in order.

First, my contention is that notwithstanding the great strides made by anthropologists in coming to terms with the effects of "writing" on "culture," the assumption is that methodological reflexivity or ethical piety gets us off the hook. It does not. And the reason is not because observers have been adequately or inadequately respectful of their observed, have learned or not learned to recognize the autonomy of their ethnographic subjects, have silenced or trusted the voices of informants, and so on. In each case, it goes without saying that it is better to respect, recognize, trust. These are all fieldwork niceties, but observing them would not obviate the fact that in every case an epistemological step continues to be "scotomized"—which, to remember Freud's lesson on fetishism, is to say *more than merely* disavowed.

Second, the perspective I want to stake out should be distinguished from the current theoretical popularity of the ontogenetic primacy of Jacques Lacan's fable of misrecognition (which, in the work of scholars like Homi Bhabha, is read as a mysterious force that both forecloses on and explodes into the social). The parasubjective cast of Lacan's understanding of force as embedded in his conception of the "mirror stage" must be revalued before it can be imported to think about the socius in which, by contrast, mechanisms of force are all too objective.[21] So I am instead drawn to the sentient forces that demarcate the quotidian and displace the workings of the unconscious onto practices of everyday life.

My focus in this introduction on the anomalies of misremembrance, misrecognition, misplacement, and misappropriation has to do with wanting to suggest the myriad difficulties attending "the actually existing" or determinate conditions of the postcolonial subject's self-fashioning. The anecdotes I relayed above work very generally, if fortuitously, to highlight a central tension crisscrossing the analysis of culture today: There is an urgent need to understand the complexity of cultural mediations given their depletions and effacements under late capitalism. And yet the very possibility of "writing culture" emerges from under the shadow of imperialist and capitalist logics of appropriation and transmogrification. The world market on the one hand and uneven development on the other have severely distorted forms of social being constituted in the face-off between decentered capital and diasporic labor. Some of the lineaments of my own thinking have already been noted, but let me repeat that the mode of dialectical inquiry to which I am committed takes its inspiration from Walter Benjamin's work, as well as that of Adorno, Lukács, Simmel, Williams, and Certeau, and from the dispersed effects of these thinkers on the British cultural studies tradition—not in itself a dialectical or systematic school of thought.

To return to the note I have struck about culture-as-instrumentality, Benjamin's famous seventh concept *(Begriff)* on history is pertinent in impressing upon us that "there is no document of civilization that is not at the same time a document of barbarism."[22] This has become an oft-cited "thesis" in pronouncements about the impossibility of culture, but the context of its utterance has been less well remarked. For Benjamin also defiantly affirmed what he called the "new poverty of experience" and proposed the need "not to grasp at the last straws of a dying culture, but to get ready to survive culture if need be."[23] For him, the impoverishment of experience resulted from the disarticulation of culture and perception and betokened conditions of modern existence as well as the decay of tradition. A concern about the cultural effects of the degeneration of experience on modes of subjective existence is what marks a coming together of Benjamin's generation of interwar Marxists (writing a conjunctural history of Europe) and the more dispersed and displaced politics of Third Worldist affirmations of cultural sovereignty and ethnic or postcolonial identities. Of particular significance to me is the Frankfurt school's insistence on reading the history of modernity *otherwise*. This reading is not, as in Freud's diagnosis of "civilization," a progressivist (though discontented) narrative of ontogeny recapitulating phylogeny; rather, it is a reading proposed through a series of dialectical negations of the logic, formula, and rationality of Enlightenment regimes of thought. Ultimately, it is the ethical and political force of Benjamin's or Adorno's critique of epistemology as well as their alternative envisioning of historical knowledge that makes their writings relevant to my consideration of postcoloniality.

If in the waning years of the twentieth century, we are witness to the intensification of a crisis of culture (and its corollary domains of subjectivity, politics, and knowledge), then the solution must in some measure reside in tackling the vexed relationship between what we term experience and where we situate culture. By this token, if the everyday appearance of contradictory narratives of history, culture, and identity construes the perverse terrain of postcoloniality, we are compelled to recognize that "the postcolonial" does not represent a preexisting *condition* (whatever may be the merits of Jean-François Lyotard's proposals about "the postmodern condition").[24] Rather, it is a mode of operating within a cultural and historical canvas of understandings and misunderstandings about the emergence of this particular subject.

The persistent and general questions about culture, instrumentality, and misrepresentation aside, abstracting any truth into a knowable one involves a certain dissolution. Any community that is the object of an ethnographic inquiry is, as far as it goes, an empirical "object" and not an empirical "reality." Ethnography, by this light, is a missed encounter with the real though not, or at least not necessarily, a missed attempt at knowing the real. Alongside other anomalous conditions at issue, let us add a definitional one: Ethnographies are anomalies in that they exist as irregularities, narrative exceptions that disturb the not-so-placid surfaces of reality. As a form of writing, ethnography is paraphrasis and defines a condition of "social inauthenticity." Even as committed an ethnographer as Claude Lévi-Strauss could not avoid recognizing the inauthenticity at the heart of the ethnographic project, despite spending the greater part of his work in attempts, as Derrida pointedly charged, to compensate for this "violence" and to efface the discontinuity between "I see yellow" and "the world is yellow."[25] To follow the import of Derrida's critique, one would have to say that the "remorse that produce[d] anthropology" has given us reflexivity as the cure for it—a strategy of containment rather than a reckoning with the possibility of how thinking overcomes its circumstances.

Although this book cannot satisfactorily tackle all or even one of the difficulties it proposes, it seems to me that, as Benjamin suggested, if we are to "survive culture," we cannot afford to abstain from addressing the problem of understanding any more than we can avoid engaging with experience on the grounds that it is ineffable, ideological, or degraded. The task is to face head-on the irreducible encounter between the petrification of experience in late capitalism and, to use one of Benjamin's preferred terms again, a "redeemed" horizon of culture. Translated into the concerns of this project, I want to reckon with the hardened, often agonizing aspects of reformulating the politics of postcolonial identity in a cultural and academic milieu in which a too-easy celebration of otherness and difference accompanies, simultaneously, an all-too-familiar neglect of the stakes for doing so.

But though the necessity, even urgency, of separating the wheat of experiential dilemmas from the chaff of pronouncements about cultural truth is transparent, it is far less clear how one might proceed with this imperative. The difficulties standing in the way of such a consideration of the incommensurabilities of experience and identity are historical as well as epistemological; the practice of ethnography is emblematic of both these difficulties in that it revokes the authority of the "purely" historical (that which happened, that which is past) as it works to consolidate a knowable present. In a radical sense, ethnographic knowledge is shot through and through with its own "meta" constitution, even if the metaethnographic is not often squared directly within the ideal of fieldwork—which takes the problematic of mediation to be secondary (rather than constitutive of the object of knowledge).

My purpose is precisely to take a stab at describing the mediations between experience and the self-representation of postcolonial subjects, not as a story of origins but as a partial attempt to articulate a collective and responsible rejoinder to the global effects of Western imperialism (as doctrine and principle of domination). Speaking of an analysis of identity as a *rejoinder* to a prior problematic—that of imperialism—allows me to draw attention to the elusiveness of historical realities without reinscribing notions of an unavailable but originary ideal of identity.[26] In other words, my concerns are not restorative or referential, nor do they arise out of some axiomatic deconstructive reflex about constitutively immanent impossibilities. Rather, I want to take a route that bypasses both a preoccupation with authentic Indianness and its obverse textualization into a fashionably appropriated fragment, the trace of the other. The engagement, then, is with the field of power relations and dynamics that produce but do not exhaust the signification of a particular form of postcolonial experience: that of the middle-class inhabitants of an immigrant Indian community in southern New Jersey. It should go without saying that the questions of signification and force raised in this book are not restricted to this community alone.

An inventory of a community's rituals of self-production must begin with locating its spatiotemporal coordinates and grounding the manner of intervening in those rituals. In my case, the ethnographic site escapes some of the ways that the idea of "the field" is fetishized, not least because it is in New Jersey. However exotic or mysterious the idea of India and Indians sounds to the American ear, it is difficult to render it so when the locale is along the arterial highway of the New Jersey Turnpike. But such a location is entirely apt for my purposes because I want to draw attention to the implications of "degraded" aspects of concrete reality—the routines of labor and living—for studying postcolonial cultures. Whereas the relationship of historical structure to linguistic or cultural expression (in, for example, literary representations of identity) is at the heart of postcolonial studies, the banal entailments of social life are seldom addressed, despite commitments to the ideas of lived experience and social reality.[27] The reinscription of exoticist, or at least hypostatic, understandings of experience continues unabatedly in the politics of literary and ethnographic representation of "emergent cultures" even when generally orientalist, specifically Indological traditions of knowledge have been rejected.[28] In contrast, I take my cue from Benjamin's insistence that a reinvigorated story of communal experience must be retrieved from the very debris of modernity and discerned within the alienated forms of labor underpinning capitalist social relations.

One of the central terms in Benjamin's various analyses of modern experience is "shock." The subject of many nuanced secondary discussions about its usage, the term ranges in meaning from the neurological "trauma" visited upon subjects whose bodies act as conductors for the thrusts and repetitions of everyday life in the modern world, to the mechanism for "absorbing" (rather than conducting) the alienation produced by a system in which money is the real measure of man.[29] Alternately posed as "distractive" or "destructive," the category of shock in Benjamin's work opens up possibilities for thinking about what happens to social ties (such as those of belonging or becoming) within processes of embourgeoisement. Miriam Hansen and Susan Buck-Morss have both pointed out (to somewhat different ends) that for Benjamin shock is related to the decay of experience and the dissipation of affect. But this relation is not one of disorder or breakdown—a diagnosis of modern subjectivity that would be far too pathological from Benjamin's contrarily utopian perspective. Rather, the relation is premised on the ways that the anesthetizing effects of modernity are counteracted through "innervation," whereby consciousness "deals with" the external world, the world, simultaneously, of sensory overstimulation and emotional impoverishment.

"Innervation" refers, broadly, to early Freudian propositions about the "conversion" of psychic energy, although, as Hansen compellingly argues, Benjamin leaned heavily on contemporary perceptual psychology, reception aesthetics, and acting theory to explore the mechanisms by which emotional effects are triggered (negatively by industrial technology and, so went the assumption, positively by aesthetic technique). Influenced at least as much by the Soviet ciné-discourse of biomechanics as by Freudian psychoanalysis, Benjamin proposed understanding modern consciousness in terms of such innervation, and I will have occasion (in chapter 1) to say more about the implications of shock for immigrant self-conceptions.[30] Here, let it suffice to indicate that as in other modes of dealing with or negotiating the limits of existence, there is in Benjamin's theorizing of shock an emphasis on the imaginative, not in the sense of recuperating the autonomy of the aesthetic but in the very anaesthetics of modern living. It is perhaps ironic that the pop psychological idiom of "culture shock"—used to describe the dislocation and disorientation of travelers to foreign lands—is not far off the mark from Benjamin's more esoteric ideas about anaesthetized perception. For the term "culture shock" not only highlights the unfamiliar and unaccustomed aspects of "coming to America" (for example, the relentlessness of anonymous apartment dwelling, fast food, glass ceilings, corporate culture, or television sitcoms); it also proposes, through an inversion, the ways that redirecting psychic and material energies in communal or cultural rituals makes it possible to keep at bay the shock of the everyday itself.

It would be remiss of me to introduce the thematic of shock and its relationship to bourgeois forms of experience if I were to leave its attribution mainly to Benjamin, or for that matter, Freud. Precisely because Benjamin was not much of a Freudian, it is significant to remember that he, like many other figures now associated with influential theorizations of value and subjectivity (Adorno, Benjamin, Ernst Bloch, Siegfried Kracauer, and Lukács, among others), took his lead in conceptualizing shock from Simmel, whose sociology, like that of Weber's, provides some defining terms for understanding modern rationality.[31] But whereas Weber's spin on how acquisitiveness receives a positive value coding in capitalist societies centered on the ideal of a Protestant ethic, Simmel gave a more phenomenological account of the rationality, or as he put it, "psychology," of acquisition. That is to say, whereas Weber's analysis of the paradoxical triumph of instrumental reason emphasized the secular returns on the religious attitude of "savings and salvation," Simmel took aim at the value system that subordinated religious attitudes in the first place. According to Simmel, the value that comes in to replace religion in modernity is money or, more accurately, the money-form.[32] One contemporary editor of Simmel's work has summarized it as "God in the **form** of belief, money in the form of the concrete abstraction."[33]

Of particular interest here is that the psychology of money that Simmel proposed is very much a *psychology*, in which the concept of innervation (or something resembling it closely) is at the core of his wide-ranging symptomization of modern life: of the "blasé" attitude of city dwellers, the drive toward "stylization" (which is Simmel's description of the pursuit of leisure), and the effect of "sheer equivalence"—the hallmark of monetary value—on the spaces, habits, and perceptions of modern subjects. As early as 1903, in his essay "The Metropolis and Mental Life," Simmel suggested that "[t]he psychological foundation, upon which the metropolitan individuality is erected, is the intensification of emotional life due to the swift and continuous shift of external and internal stimuli." Likewise, he thought that emergent modern consciousness, "metropolitan intellectuality," as he characterized it, was "the consequence of those rapidly shifting stimulations of the nerves which are thrown together in all their contrasts."[34]

A hundred years later, the point to take away from Simmel's (as well as Benjamin's or Freud's) reliance on mentalistic ideas to describe a money- or consumption-saturated existence is that, in every one of their accounts, capitalism's effects on consciousness, social imagination, and everyday life are not just ideological; they are, almost constitutively, physiological. One may well want to modify the psychologistic burden of these accounts, but we do have to reckon with the ways that forms of social being under capitalism are marked *not* by their difference from or their imaginative re-creation of some monolithic construct of modern identity but, to the contrary, in their indifference to or innervation by it.

My remarks in the section above represent an inevitably failed attempt at rebottling some part of that genie let loose by Benedict Anderson's idea of the "imagined community"—a phrase that now flows somewhat uncontrollably within discussions of national or communal identity (perhaps to Anderson's own dismay).[35] If our social-theory forebears were even partly right, then the question of identity turns less on the power of the symbolic to generate active cultural resistances to the dominant order than on the instrumentalities of administered life.[36] So to transfer my attention to the circumstances under which a dialogue of identity takes place, a dialogue seen as a consolidating as well as a capitalizing value, let me outline the particulars of the immigrant Indian community's location and the structure of my discussions in this book.

Adult members of the community from among whom I selected my informants all live within a thirty-mile radius of each other in the suburbs of southern New Jersey, about a half-hour's drive east of Philadelphia and an hour-and-a-half's drive south of New York City. New Jersey, nicknamed the Garden State, is, in this particular location at any rate, characterized by shopping malls and highways connecting the industrial and service centers of the metropolitan East Coast. But by the very token of being a commercial hub, it is also a place where, in mundane if accidental ways, the transnational flow of labor has deposited a small but significant population of immigrant Indians. Transplanted there in the early 1970s and '80s (when the revision of U.S. immigration laws permitted the entry of substantial numbers of people from the Indian subcontinent with techno-managerial expertise), these people live, work, and construct fictions of solidarity and selfhood against the setting of expensive housing developments that simultaneously disguise the surrounding ecological damage, topographical blandness, and parochialism of U.S. suburbia.

I visited and lived in this community at various times between May 1988 and July 1990. The peculiarities of my own circumstances will be taken up again in chapter 1, but let me take this moment to underscore the fact that people made their routines of daily life available to me on the basis of the presumption that I was an insider. My conclusions about problems of ethnicity, marginality, or oppositionality were only possible in the light of a post hoc theoretical working out of the issues that these abstractions aspire to name. Behind any conclusions, however, lie their bases in my unformed, daily interactions with the principals whose experiences are depicted here.

The five chapters sandwiched between this introduction and the afterword each take up the problem of immigrant subjectivity, although none of them provides a positive documentation of *ethnos;* in that sense, this is an ethnographic travesty. Nor is my intervention meant to "give voice" to anybody, certainly not to any silent subalterns. For one thing, matters of embourgeoisement are very far from subalternity; for another, dialectical inquiry (to be distinguished strictly from what passes in anthropological literature as "dialectical anthropology") cannot presuppose its object, ethnographic or otherwise. There is no voice "out there" to which we must, with appropriately good intentions, cede authority. Rather, the desire embodied in my effort is to think postcoloniality—as opposed to thinking *about* postcoloniality—from within specific kinds of immigrant experience. That experience and those immigrants exist, but a theorization of their daily lives must take some form that resists the sleights of hand of "participant-observation." If I participated and observed, I also theorized, and any claims to knowing must be staked on the last.

Chapter 1 elaborates on the construction of the field of vision as it pertains to issues of representation within the community examined. It is both a methodological statement and a critique of method; the two (method and methodology) are not the same, of course, even if in cultural studies usage the terms have come to seem interchangeable. I sketch out the practical contours of this inquiry: the locus of my ethnographic intervention and the negotiations that set its parameters. I address the limits of intersubjective agreement on the charged symbolisms of identity and subjecthood. In addition, the chapter tries to untangle the submerged connections between this particular immigrant community's maneuvers to constitute itself by capitalizing on a mythicized Indianness and disciplinary investments in such currently fashionable topics as national or ethnic identity or postcolonialism. I draw attention to the ways that forms of knowledge production, through various methodological and evidentiary measures, replicate gestures of self-authentication and self-interest. The identitarian thinking that determines my ethnographic informants' attempts to represent themselves also, if less visibly, underlies the reified "tribal" interests of academic inquiry in general.

Chapter 2 gives a provisional genealogy of the problem of experience and the antinomial character of everyday life. A conceptual detour, it halts the progress of the ethnographic moment as such, although to my mind conceptual gestures have as much legitimacy as do the gestures that usually set the stage for reporting ethnographic expeditions. As expeditions go, those into conceptuality may be less enticing but more critical if, as I indicated earlier in this introduction, reflexivity is to be anything other than a methodological chant. Attempting to expand on conceptual concerns, I turn to the epistemological problem of the separation of theory and practice. As a corrective to the incipiently empiricist belief that the real world can be grasped without mediation, I examine the paradox of everyday life and its retroactive presentation (in an ethnography of this sort, for instance). Deriving its impetus from Lukács's arguments about the reified structure of consciousness in bourgeois life, this chapter deals with difficulties in the category "experience."

Chapter 3 takes up the relationship of identity to the structures of memory. Here the focus is on specifically ethnographic details of remembrance. My attention is caught by the ways that immigrant subjects (both men and women) reveal a consciousness that is inflected by a fragmented though forceful understanding of a colonial past and of its dispersed effects on their lives. The narratives of history and memory that informants produce suggest that the very undecidability of the past constitutes the basis for shoring up the present and future. The fragility of the category of the past is an enabling condition for articulating the self, of course, but what is crucial is the past's negative valence for male immigrants versus its idealized status in women's remembrances. I also discuss how a subjective understanding of colonization, divorced from its historical moorings, retains an imaginative force in people's ways of coming to terms with their marginalization in contemporary U.S. society. So although postcolonial identity is a well-wrought fiction, it reveals its bases in inherited convictions about the vicissitudes of colonial domination and in equally unshakable beliefs about the exceptionalism of an Indian past. This past-present relation is an important site of recalcitrance against capitalist ideologies of self interest in that it enforces a tension in the daily workings of middle-class immigrants caught between traditional appeals to collective welfare or cultural solidarity on the one hand and their upwardly mobile desire to enter the West's circuit of consumerist individualism on the other.

Chapter 4 presents an argument about the logic of the habitus, the deeply sedimented elements of social or national life. Further developing the conceptual arguments in chapter 2, this is an essay on food and its implications for concepts of authenticity and taste. As I argue throughout, notions of Indianness are the imaginative re-creations of immigrant investments, but by that very token, they are significant for understanding how the contradictions of experience are inhabited and transformed into ideals of propriety and belongingness. To this end, my focus on practices of food consumption is sharpened with continuing help from Adorno and Benjamin. The discussion also follows up on the running argument between Pierre Bourdieu and Certeau on taste preferences and the consolidation of cultural capital. My purpose in this chapter is to address the problematic of consumption literally, in (and through) the practical consumption of food—less to elevate it into a subversive practice of ethnic particularity than to explicate its relationship to the specificity of the middle-class Indian lifestyle.

Chapter 5 is a meditation on visual image, storytelling, and identity. Continuing to draw on Benjamin's work, specifically his meditations on the philosophy of history, I examine dominant Western representations of a mythicized "Indian tradition." My point of departure is that any analysis of contemporary cultural formations needs to account for the Western mass media's impact on everyday experience everywhere. For Indian immigrants with an attachment to the singularity of their cultural identity, media use takes on a twofold and contradictory significance: First, the media socialize audiences into being American (or at least Americanized). But second, the media reveal processes of marginalization that also make "becoming" American an impossibility. So my concern is to investigate how immigrants negotiate the dominant culture's impulse to orientalize, particularly given that this impulse disrupts their own drive toward imagining a reconsolidated and "post"-colonial identity. If immigrant appeals to Indianness receive substantial impetus from their negation in media representations, the question is, What practical form does cultural contestation take? To attempt an answer, I turn to a particular moment in the 1990s when Indian culture was spectacularized in a number of venues—from "Raj Revival" narratives, to the Festival of India exhibition at the Smithsonian Institution and at museums around the country, to televised images found in programs such as *Masterpiece Theater*. I pick a specific case that sheds light on the mechanisms by which postcolonial subjects come to terms with their conditions of entry into mainstream culture. Through my ethnographic community's responses to public television's serialized production of director Peter Brook's adaptation of *The Mahabharata*, I explore the influence of ideals of community and cultural memory on an alternative conception of modern identity. Such a conception distinguishes itself from the norms of a narrative of the modern imposed by the globalizing if avant-garde aesthetic pretensions of dominant Western culture. My aim here, in the concluding chapter of a book that attempts to question the grounds and terms of identity, is to provide some account of the ways that the reception of narratives of experience and history enable and constrain the manifold emergences of the postcolonial subject.

The afterword provides a brief speculation on the necessity for reintegrating the question of value within discussions of identity. Though it has become critical for cultural studies to think about the production and adjudication of value, the problem continues to be engaged mainly from literary or linguistic perspectives. This is what allows Patrick McGee, for instance, to assert that "[t]he prison house of language is the structure of value." McGee, who follows Jean Baudrillard and Derrida in claiming that a critique of value makes deconstruction the strategy of responsibility, seems to think that the putative errors of historical materialism are overcome by affirming indeterminacy, general writing, the incommensurate, and so on. Far from demonstrating that "telling the other" is accomplished, usefully, on the "terrain of literary study," McGee's readings become yet another symptom in the hypertrophic body of propositions about language, or to use the preferred phrase, "the text," as the limit of value production and "the basis of a radical alterity that can neither precede nor succeed the mark of identity but must underwrite it as its nonidentity, as its trace."[37] Quite in opposition to such an approach on the grounds of both its philosophical and historical inaptitude, I broach the possibilities within postcolonial cultural studies for a reappointment with Marxist dialectics and its insights into the tensions between conceptuality and the world.

The discussions following this introduction depend upon ethnographic material to amplify the processes in and through which everyday life mediates the shifting and uncertain ground between cultural ensembles and public forms. They also testify to the difficulties facing an act of show-and-tell that takes on the burden of representing a particular narrative of identity and at the same time questions the production of abstract cultural or philosophical truths from completely contingent experiences of daily life. To me, this is the most productive burden of ethnographic representation. Though ethnography can no longer justify itself on the grounds that it produces an objectively verifiable picture of reality—certainly when the issues at stake are as obtuse and slippery as identity or subject consciousness—it has the advantage of demonstrating, in practical and often discomfiting ways, what Adorno termed the object's resistance to appropriation within conceptual categories. The challenge is to try and maintain a philosophical insistence on the "actuality" of thought so that from a dialectical point of view (about which I say more in chapter 1), one is prevented from going on about the unity of theory and practice while reinforcing their separation. I hope that the speculative and philosophical aspects of my account serve not as a ruse against accountability but as an obligation toward it.

It follows that both conceptually and methodologically the teller is responsible to the tale, its cast of characters, and constituencies of readers—outside of pious proclamations of "positionality" and defensive maneuverings around the charge of subjectivism. A pointillist relativism or an unreconstructed faith in the transparency of evidence are not the only options available to someone interested in separating the force of quotidian truths from the abyss of infinite semiosis. In the spirit of Adorno's claim that "philosophy, which once seemed obsolete, lives on because the moment to realize it was missed," I want to throw in my lot with an anthropology of experience whose object *and* mode of inquiry exceed, or better yet, undermine themselves.[38]

This book is a belated entry in the ongoing project of contested readings, belated by virtue of the fact that the history subtending it has been under way for almost three hundred years. It will take more than the *détournement* of critical readings to undermine either the disciplinary order of "the West" or the experiences of discrimination that both disable and enable the production of postcolonial consciousness in the present conjuncture. But if the epistemological hierarchy informing such ideas and ideals as "tradition," "the past," "selfhood," and "otherness" is to be challenged from within and without the confines of academic thought, it becomes all the more urgent to hold on to experiences and illuminations produced in the mediations between intellectual practice and the world at large. These readings are, therefore, possible only because of my own anomalous positioning: both within a community attempting to realize its self-identity and also in an institutional setting where the present has become highly problematic for those who want to overcome its material conditions and modes of thinking.

There is an irony attached to writing about a community whose constitutive character and preoccupation with discursive self-production are bound to be surpassed in the next generation or two, given the diluting effects of the passage of time and passing of generations. As I write, second- and third-generation constituents are growing up with different memories, experiences, and expectations than those of their parents. The difference in their horizon of expectations has to do with more than merely readjusting the meaning of social being on the basis of practical necessities. Like all Generation X-ers, the new generation of "Indian Americans" embodies a certain politics of forgetting, a cavalier disregard for history—the history of its own location no less than the provenance of older generations. To the extent that such willed and unwilled forgetting can be understood, it betokens the dominant culture's ideological insistence on assimilating everything and everyone into the mainstream, the present, the post-historical. Celebrating the immediacy of the "always already" blocks the possibility of thinking as much as it eschews hope for a transformed future. This is no less a problem for my ethnographic community than for the general predicament of theory with its presentist bias. The responsibility to choose between an idealist nostalgia for the past and a rationalized narrative of the present is one that troubles community members in the same way that it haunts academics as we try to imagine what will become of us in a "downsized" future. It is also a responsibility rejected by the younger generation of immigrants for fairly reactive and reactionary reasons having to do with continuing fantasies of social mobility, a wishful disavowal of difference, and even complacency about what the future will bring. As we know, the quest for happiness can accompany impoverished and cynical calculations about how to achieve it.

By seeking to salvage "lost tribes" from the vicissitudes of history, anthropology has traveled some way on the proverbial road paved with good intentions.[39] As an ironic riposte to those rescue operations of old-fashioned anthropology and even the more new-fangled experiments and laments of modernist writing on disappearing traditions, I focus on this immigrant community's emergence in and through the elusiveness of the present: the suspended quality of its generational struggles over being Indian and becoming American. Benjamin, in his meditations on history, evokes the "state of emergency"—literally, the "state of exception" (Ausnahmezustand)—that determines both the experiences of marginalized communities (represented for him by the doomed struggles of various antifascist groups) and the emergent possibilities for a reconfigured future. To recall his eighth thesis on the concept of history: "The tradition of the oppressed teaches us that 'the state of emergency' in which we live is not the exception but the rule."[40] The ambiguity of theorizing possibilities of emergence under a state of exception, is for him—and for me—profoundly productive. An important impetus for writing this book thus resides in my awareness that the cultural imperative to domesticate the other is likely to make everyday resistances disappear and be lost in the shadow of the commodification of experience in late capitalist society. In a very different context from the one that informed Benjamin's thinking, the following chapters are also speculations about the possibilities for an emergent political consciousness of the present.

CHAPTER ONE

Writing the Field

In its beginnings, the national bourgeoisie of the colonial countries identifies itself with the decadence of the bourgeoisie of the West. We need not think that it is jumping ahead; it is in fact beginning at the end.

—FRANTZ FANON, *The Wretched of the Earth*

Each informant, even the most sincere, experiences an "instinctive need to dissimulate particularly delicate points. He will gladly take advantage of the slightest chance to escape the subject and dwell on another." Native collaborators "lie" in jest, by venality, by desire to please, or in fear of neighbors and the gods. Forgetful informants or Europeanized informants are particularly dangerous types of "liars."

—MARCEL GRIAULE, *Méthode,* as quoted by James Clifford

Dialectical Commitments

How does one prevent a laudable commitment to interdisciplinary work from becoming more a banal and self-serving skirmish than a serious engagement with (and across) disciplinary ideas? This is not only a question that has plagued cultural studies but also, albeit less immediately, a problem for all intellectual pursuits in which who does what, how, and most important, *why,* has to be settled as a matter of procedure.[1] I raise it in the context of discussing the constitution of my "field" because it seems odd that the very quarters that have issued calls for rethinking concepts such as identity, subjectivity, and the disciplinary object have

been less than attentive to the cross-disciplinary implications of traveling lightly (to adapt Edward Said's early cautions against eliding the his-
toricity of particular theories and concepts).[2] One particular manifestation of the allusiveness with which the "idiolect" of a discipline has
been exported elsewhere is in the use of the term "native informant" to
refer to scholars from formerly colonized nations now located in the
metropolitan academy. With respect to the emergent practices of postcolonialism and the general ways that this field implicates cross-cultural
inquiry, what does it mean for us to position ourselves, however am-
bivalently, as "native informants"? Native to what and informants of
what?[3]

The seemingly obvious reponse to the last query is that postcolonial
scholars are seen to share the same cultural (and perhaps even phylogenetic) dispositions as their interlocutors, especially if the interlocution
requires other "natives." The second part of the question—"informants
of what?"—prompts an equally transparent reply, although it is perhaps a little troubled by the connotations attached to being an informant. Still, the import here too is that postcolonial scholars supply information about other cultures (usually their own) to their readership in
the Western (chiefly Anglo-American) academy. In what follows, I should
like to explore the contradictions of this emergent vision of the field
and its practitioners, particularly in terms of its impact on the constitution of postcoloniality as an object of knowledge. The interest I have
in the professional development of postcolonial studies is ultimately to
be read amid the echo of a question asked by Clifford Geertz almost
two decades ago in *Local Knowledge:* Is there a native's point of view?[4]

Within the discipline of English studies (and such subdisciplines as
cultural studies, women's studies, or ethnic studies), general responses
to questions relating to the identity and interests of the representing subject have been offered along the lines of an opposition between essentialism and antiessentialism, with Gayatri Chakravorty Spivak's now re-
pudiated proposal of "strategic essentialism" located as an intermediate
sort of *ex ante* justification.[5] These ways of characterizing the problem
of "positionality" seem to me to miss a lot, since at least within the specific
ambit of postcolonial scholarship, the crux of the matter has to do with
the following: It is not merely that the represener exemplifies the constitutive contradictions of on the one hand representing the colonized
and on the other inhabiting the structures of institutional power that

in different times and places have been responsible for the violence of colonialism. More importantly, in the very confrontation of complicity and critique, which is to say in its mediation, the object too is transformed.

To ask questions of truth and essence is to miss the crucial point, which, as Fredric Jameson famously characterized it, has to do with the "breathlessness [of] the shift from the normal object-oriented activity of the mind to . . . dialectical self-consciousness—something of the sickening shudder we feel in an elevator's fall or in the sudden dip in an airliner."[6] The "recalcitrance" of the object forces the subject to transcend an "everyday habitual mode of thought" and to account for the recognition that the relation between "thinkers and observers" and the "real" is one of contradiction rather than continuity or contiguity.[7] The categorical separation of subject and object, along with the binarism of essentialism and antiessentialism is by this dialectical light no longer adequate to the historical situation of postcolonial intellectual discourse and production.

So the agenda of inquiry ought to be less about defending the nativist credentials of the representer (does she *truly* represent her constituency? or even, as in traditional Marxism's idealization of the proletariat's consciousness, is the subject the bearer of "correct" knowledge?) than about staking out the preponderance of the object (which is at the heart of Jameson's adaptation of Theodor Adorno's dialectical thinking). In Adorno's conception of the role of critical theory, the object's force resides less in its ubiquity or quiddity than in the resistance it puts up to its appropriation by the subject. It is important to stress that the categories of subject and object are neither self-evidently given nore simply ideational. Indeed, their epistemological and historical collocation is what allows the object of representation to elude the embrace of an all-knowing, or to use a formulaic term from the ideology of anthropological fieldwork, "empathetic," subject/observer.

There are of course considerable differences among dialectical thinkers as to whether the object has a magical force of its own through which it is able to produce momentary flashes of truth about a shadowy reality (as in Walter Benjamin's conception) or, in Adorno's modernist terms, about the object's ability to break through the domination of speculative thought within a philosophical *Kraftfeld* (force field). In all its forms, however, a materialist dialectics attempts to wrest analysis away from the grounds of contemplation to those of praxis.[8] Criticism cannot be adequately ruthless, to borrow another phrase from the history of debates within Marxism, without subjecting one's concepts to the measure of their irreconcilability with reality. It is this fallibilistic impulse that lends dialectical thinking relevance and urgency in a contemporary world in which the most profound uncertainties—about the historical effects of violence, the nature of memory, the solidity of tradition, or the ephemera of everyday life under capitalist alienation—are met with inverse and ideological demands of exacting and exactable verification.

When it comes to analyzing the discursive effects of colonialism, then, a theoretical agenda concerned with the *inadequations* of subject and object presents challenges far more severe than the adjudication of whether one is authorized exclusively by dint of race, gender, or sexuality to do the right thing. "Adequation" (and its corollary, "inadequation") is a philosophical concept of some density and retains only a hint of its family resemblance with "adequacy" or "sufficiency." It is a term that the Frankfurt school critics, particularly Adorno, borrow from the phenomenology of Edmund Husserl in order to forward their critique of logical positivism and yet maintain the idea of a valid social inquiry that is not simply interpretation or hermeneutics. In Husserl's terms, adequation has to do with the possibility of covering the distance between propositions and states of affairs or things. The properly philosophical attitude requires

> the zigzag motion between focusing on things and focusing on propositions, which are then verified or falsified when they are confirmed or disconfirmed by the way things appear. Evidence is the activity of either having a thing in its direct presence or experiencing the conformity or disconformity between an empty intention and the intuition that is to fulfill it. There are degrees of evidence; things can be given more or less fully and more or less distinctly. *Adequation* occurs when an intuition fully satisfies an empty intention.[9]

But of course the Frankfurt school's dialectical positions do not simply repeat the Husserlian line on adequation, as if that were the last word on the relationship between subject and object. Rather, adequation takes on shades of its contrary, of inadequation, when, for example, Adorno is at pains to point out that "[a]ll thinking is exaggeration, in so far as every thought that is one at all goes beyond its confirmation by the given facts. Yet the difference between thought and its factual confirmation harbors the potential for delusion as well as for truth.... There are no discretely conclusive, absolutely reliable, independent criteria; the decision is taken only through a structure of complex mediations."[10]

So when I speak as I do from time to time (in this chapter and in the rest of the book) about the adequation of subject and object or concept and reality, it is on the terms of such a complication of the subject-object relationship—not only in its phenomenological givenness but in the ways that it underwrites the goals of dialectical understanding.

On this reading, an investment in the pregivenness of identities, or more precisely, in their pregiven authority to take on the burden of representation, is likely to miss the forest of symbols for the trees of referentiality because such investments rest on opinions that are in principle beyond examination. If the opposition between nativism and indeterminacy (where the former produces authentic value and the latter merely the paralysis of reflexive knowledge) is to be rejected as false, what is at stake, as Said phrased it well over a decade ago, are the "actual *affiliations* between the world of ideas and scholarship, on the one hand, and the world of brute politics, corporate and state power, and military force, on the other."[11]

The transition from filiation to affiliation, to be strictly genealogical for a moment, marks a shift from cognate relations (from the Latin *cognatus*, "of same birth or blood") to those of solidarity. And it permits one to think beyond the terms of a narrowly construed identity politics to argue, instead, for a representational practice that can take account of the discontinuities between identities, experiences, and knowledge. The key distinction here has to do with shifting the focus of representation from delegation *(Vertretung)* to designation *(Vorstellen)*: that is, from a concern with how reliably representations serve as proxies or delegates of reality to a concern with their legibility as signifying practices that cipher the politics of meaning.[12] But precisely because this new theoretical optic demands attention to the designating functions of representation—how the object both signifies and defies its categorization and construction by the subject—it also requires a different practical orientation.

Interdisciplinarity may well describe the orientation necessary when investigation moves from a relatively stable entity like literature to the messier aspects of, to call upon Said again, the "worldliness of the world." I may be forgiven my own disciplinary heresy in casting literature as a stable entity, since my purpose is not to reproduce an idealization of literature's transcendence but to note the differences that obtain *even in processes of abstraction* when the object of inquiry is, say, "the work of Shakespeare" as contrasted with "ethnic identity." The conceptual difference between these two objects is marked by the presumptive stability of the former and the instability of the latter. Notwithstanding arguments about differences in meaning and interpretation, textualist approaches assume that regardless of variations in readerly and writerly motivations, the text—for example, of *King Lear* or *The Bluest Eye*—is an object in the real world: In a given edition of *King Lear* the words on a given page are predetermined and everybody can point to them. No such certitude exists about the designation of the object "ethnic identity." The procedural upper hand possessed by literary study is that critical styles for conceptualizing and examining texts—such as interpretive communities, reader response, semantic horizons, contextual criticism, and so on—work to contain rather than transform the constitution of objects within preset disciplinary limits.[13]

Conceptual distances between forms of textual study "delegated" by disciplinary criteria and reformulations of representation-as-designation are also reflected in the defenses that those of us investigating things *like* ethnic identity have to marshal in order to justify our own fields of vision. Despite being further and further away from a Shakespearean "reality," one rarely has to justify "being" a Shakespeare scholar (if the Modern Language Association [MLA] job scenarios are anything to go by). I digress somewhat from my main theme in order to draw attention to the ontological cast of disciplinary knowledge and specialization. In contrast, the uncertainty surrounding "postcolonialism" immediately requires that the term, its objects, and their scholarly relevance be defined in disciplinary terms that usually fail to capture the range of knowledges entailed in its scope. At the same time, the postcolonialist is asked to produce an internal critique of her practice as "proof" of a somewhat tautological "self-reflexivity" (what else could one be reflexive about?) and to fend off external attacks on the study of actual, lived discourses of otherness as "politicized," or worse, "unscholarly." My point is that a rationale staked on interdisciplinarity is unlikely to get us out of this squeeze, but a commitment to dialectical thinking might, since among other things, it would require the reflexive Shakespearean to justify the simplifications entailed in the (equally factitious) construction of her disciplinary object. One might even hope that dialectics could demand that all its takers reckon with the instabilities between meaning and being.

The problem is less that interdisciplinary approaches to cultural inquiry lack "depth" than that the relay between assumptive frameworks and the real world is incommensurable. Interdisciplinary scholarship often sacrifices an insistence on this irreconcilability of subject and object and opts to admit that its claims are staked with respect to breadth over rigorousness. Alternatively, if entry into recognizable enclaves of disciplinary integrity is hard to come by (as it most often is), the justification for "multiculturalism" (read as interdisciplinarity) has been made on the parochial terms that its scholars belong to a minority or are racially and culturally authentic.[14] I, for one, do not think the ground of rigor has to be ceded to what, in something of a pun, might be called "guilded" ideas (that is, those produced within guilds either by "specialists" or, equally, by the "oppressed few" as guilded truths). Even if we could produce an algebra of lesser and greater oppressions or better and worse specializations, it is not at all clear that forms of inquiry based on such principles have much to offer other than *their* pregiven conceptual horizons and *their* conventional modes of argumentation—that is, the integrity of their identities as such. I am mindful about making purely formalistic equations between identities (between those based on class, race, or some other axis of authenticity and those predicated on membership in privileged disciplines, for example), for these are not transposable domains of value. My only interest here is to indicate the tendential effects of notions of belongingness, particularly in a cultural milieu in which "those who belong" are only accommodated within exclusionary limits. In fact, Said's emphasis on affiliation was exactly intended to overcome such tendential claims. As he put it:

> It is patently true that, even within the atomized order of disciplines and fields, methodological investigations can and indeed do occur. But the prevailing mode of intellectual discourse is militantly antimethodological, if by methodological we mean a questioning of the structure of fields and discourses themselves. A principle of silent exclusion operates within and at the boundaries of discourse; this has now become so internalized that fields, disciplines, and their discourses have taken on the status of immutable durability. Licensed members of the field, which has all the trappings of a social institution, are identifiable as belonging to a guild, and for them words like "expert" and "objective" have an

important resonance. To acquire a position of authority within the field is, however, to be involved internally in the formation of a canon, which usually turns out to be a blocking device for methodological and disciplinary self-questioning.[15]

We might say that the moment to defend interdisciplinarity against the ideology of canon formation has passed, if only as an unfortunate symptom of the victory of an identitarian logic that continues to counterpose a banalized notion of the canon or the field with the "vulgarity" of those who would dig it up in unsystematic ways. But as Said's statements remind us, the choice is not only between serious and archival specialization (studying literary periods, historical eras, or anthropological objects) and an indiscriminate casting about for vocabularies or frames of reference. There is also the option of avowing that one cannot know, ahead of time, how the concept will meet up with its object; how, in other words, the relay between terms, frameworks, and thought will be adequated in the "secular" world.[16]

My desire to rethink the possibilities of dialectics has everything to do with arguing that reflexivity is not merely a matter of affirming deconstructive vigilance or an ipso facto marshaling of evidentiary criteria. In the final analysis, neither gets us any further than saying that epistemological certainty is vain (in which case we either give up on knowable truths or pile up quantities of evidence that can only substitute for rather than enact proof). Dialectical thought is notably different from phenomenological or positivistic conceptual systems, where either "texts" or "data" provide the bedrock of evidence. It proceeds from the assumption that an epistemology that centers itself on the *principle* that its categories and criteria of evidence match the real world cannot provide the court in which the relation between subject and object is adjudicated. Contrarily enough, only the registers of everyday experience, "facts as unpleasantly common as common sense," permit us to recognize that the Husserlian principle of "phenomenological reduction" (essential to all conceptual and theoretical propositions about the world) is precisely a conceptual, not an explanatory, maneuver.[17]

The realm of the object, as distinct from subjective attempts to conquer thought, is what pushes dialectics beyond deconstructive attempts whose efficacy (if it might be called that) resides in specifying a politics of location and marking the complicity of knowledge with structures of power and meaning.[18] But as I read them, deconstructive efforts founder on the grounds of a logical contradiction: The critique of logocentrism ends up in increasing refinements of questions and their categories but brings no real illumination to the circumstances to which thought might apply itself in the world of objects. Without deprecating the contributions of deconstruction, I should nonetheless like to assert that it remains locked in the grip of a system of thought that reproduces its own conditions of thinking. The circularity of this mode of thought was, on one occasion and in a moment of self-scrutiny, described by gay studies theorist Eve Sedgwick as "kinda subversive, kinda hegemonic."[19]

If the aim of postcolonial critique is not only to redirect the gaze of the Eurocenter toward its other but also to transform the very conditions under which thinking is produced, then performative theoretical gestures—despite their claims for oppositionality—are unlikely to provide the way out. In saying this, I do not mean to take the high moral ground but merely to point out the consequences of eschewing the terms of a tradition of Marxist analysis that is far from spectral (pace Derrida).[20] It is entirely consistent within the tradition of bourgeois Western thought to conceive of criticism as a contemplative activity that does not upset the apple cart of power relations in society. Deconstructive approaches have, at least in this respect, proved to be no different in terms of their politics—notwithstanding either their rhetorical aims or the uncomprehending caricatures to which they have sometimes been subjected in a generalized anti-intellectual cultural milieu.[21]

In a scholarly environment in which critics are as subject as anybody else to the seductions of the "cultural logic of capitalism" (dubbed postmodernism or some other "post"), it is perhaps unsurprising to find that the notion of Marxism's demise is increasingly taken for granted or that Marxism is "theorized" out of existence. But as the conjunctural example of a unified Germany reveals to the discerning eye, Marxism, like the Berlin Wall, is more than an edifice. It emblematizes a body of ideas whose main force has, in a number of social and historical cases, withstood the encroachment of the Western market of ideas and cultural values. So even if the history of Marxism attests (as it must) to a history of failures, postcolonial discourse forgets at its own peril that its conditions of emergence are predicated on the paradoxical success of such failures.[22] This point about the discomfiture that Western critics feel when faced with the mutual exclusivity of their sociopolitical preferences and Marxism is reinforced if we refer back to Jameson's synthetic insights in *Marxism and Form* and to his account of the Anglo-American reception of Georg Lukács's work:

> [I]n the long run even his [Lukács's] more sympathetic Western critics turn away from him in varying degrees of disillusionment: they came prepared to contemplate the abstract idea, but in practice they find themselves asked to sacrifice too much. . . . Such discomfort is hardly surprising, for it marks the approach of Western relativism to its own conceptual limits: we conceive of our culture, indeed, as a vast imaginary museum in which all life forms and all intellectual positions are equally welcome side by side, providing they are accessible to contemplation alone. Thus, alongside the Christian mystics and the nineteenth-century anarchists, the Surrealists and the Renaissance humanists, there would be room for a Marxism that was but one philosophical system among others. . . . [T]he peculiarity of the structure of historical materialism lies in its denial of the autonomy of thought itself, in its insistence, itself a thought, on the way in which pure thought functions as a disguised mode of social behavior, in its uncomfortable reminder of the material and historical reality of spirit. Thus as a cultural object, Marxism returns against cultural activity in general to devalue it and to lay bare the class privileges and the leisure which it presupposes for its enjoyment. It thus ruins itself as a spiritual commodity and short-circuits the process of culture consumption in which, in the Western context, it had become engaged.[23]

The concrete circumstances that make postcolonial critique possible—attempts to dismantle Eurocentric and privileged norms of thinking; insistence on the power-knowledge nexus and its location in Western theoretico-political perspectives; thematizations of the incommensurability of cultural forms—all attest to historical materialism's dialectical impulse *not* to let ideas rest on the threshold of a radical but paralyzed theoretical reflexivity but, rather, to hold reflexivity as well as reflection accountable to their mistakes and betrayals in the larger world of politics, culture, and people. Indeed, what Jameson calls "culture consumption" produces a critical consumptiveness in scholars who, faced with declarations about the failure of "actually existing" socialisms, are unable to think themselves unto the alteristic and potentially transformative conjunctures often avowed in their theories. And in practice they never seem to step into the "contingencies of value" (the phrase is Barbara Herrnstein Smith's)[24] that, if only as utopian forms, shed light on what we might call anticapitalist futures.

Postcolonial studies ought not to generate for itself the predicament of theories that content themselves with resting at the borders, so to speak, of knowledge and experience, since its own conditions of possibility are premised on a material historical contingency: the emergence of postcolonial subjects from under the ideological and material domination of the West. Such material constraints on what *can* be said demand taking seriously not just abstract theoretical consciousness but also its worldly consolidations. From this perspective, the enterprise of constituting a field of inquiry or an object of analysis entails pitting concepts against reality less as an exercise in claiming correspondence or noncorrespondence than as a way of allowing us "to see what something is through the simultaneous awareness of what it is not."[25] To put this more sharply, the object does not recoil from the subject in its impenetrable separability from the latter (as if meaning were only given in difference); instead, the object's own destination and character must be understood as aleatory and protean but above all empirical and historical.

I want to be careful not to be misunderstood as suggesting that dialectical thinking is unconcerned with correspondences between meaning and being. Quite the contrary. Since the goal is to locate the mediations between knowledge and reality, dialectics represents the activity in the realm of thought to fashion imagistic, or in Benjamin's usage, "constellated," connections between available fragments of damaged life and a totality beyond the reach of the structures attempting to approximate it. Accordingly, questions about the materiality of the world and the conceptuality of its representation do not simply admit to an opposition between the two, but to a condensation of thought and experience.

Jameson's early formulations on this subject are worth revisiting because subsequent debates about his notion of "cognitive mapping" have swamped some very provocative proposals advanced in *Marxism and Form*. They had to do with moving beyond a narrowly hermeneutic model of reading texts and cultures toward something that approximates approximation—that is, toward significance, not reference. He proposed that an interdisciplinary focus must reckon with the uncertainty present in all acts of sustained thinking regarding the "uneasy suspicion that the whole teetering construction [of inquiry] stands as a monument not to new laws of nature, but rather to the rules of some private mental hobby."[26] So if something of the dialectical spirit enters interdisciplinary analysis, the *failure,* or to be more precise, inadequacy, of one's concepts can be presupposed. This is far preferable to the anxiety about producing positive knowledge. Far from compromising rigor, a dialectical approach requires following through on the consequences of anti-identitarian thinking, especially in arenas where disciplinary nativism ("speaking as an anthropologist or a literary critic") often masquerades as credentialed knowledge.

If it can be acknowledged that abstract processes of identity formation (be it within disciplinary or ethnic enclosures) are unlikely to get us closer to the truth, to the affiliations as well as the distances between conceptual horizons and their counterparts in the social and historical worlds of concrete experience, the turn to a revivified interdisciplinarity might get postcolonial scholars out of thinking that they have to assume the position of native informants. The presumption that rejecting the epistemological hubris of the self-authorizing traditional intellectual requires adopting the subject position of the native is blinkered in its reproduction of a methodological naivete. One needs only to recall that the native informant is someone who snitches on his people and then seeks to mitigate the betrayal by occasionally producing "unreliable" data for the imperializing anthropologist.[27]

The failure of identity thinking to fix the postcolonial representer as the knowing subject, expert or native, ought neither to be valorized as the mystical impossibility of representation nor (as in Judith Butler's avowal of feminism as "the subversion of identity") to be regarded as a performance, a "kind of persistent impersonation."[28] The idealization of native truths and points of view might be envisioned more productively in working out a negative dialectic that, in the terms given by Adorno, perceives that "the ideal of identity must not simply be discarded. Living in the rebuke that the thing is not identical with the concept is the concept's longing to become identical with the thing."[29] As such, a negative dialectic exemplifies a belated refusal of the persistent Enlightenment ideology of gnosticism: the imperative of positive knowledge as the basis for power or, equally, salvation.

How have these times, in which proclamations of reflexivity or affirmations of "dialecticization" (which often refer to no more than "contrast") are abundant, produced calls for the occupation of Third-World-scholar-as-native-informant?[30] One explanation might be that the corporealism often accompanying nativist pitches to authority (implying that one has to *be* one to know one) is a defensive reaction to the objectivist demands of both traditional humanist and social scientific approaches. On the opposite side of the divide, where the "strategic essentialists" live, there is also little security attached to poststructural-ism's vaunted stricture that all readings are misreadings. As I see it, a willed strategy of essentialism or an interrogative self-criticism (in an-thropological or other investigations) is served best when it is served last; that is, at the moment when it can bring its object into focus. The problem for reflexive inquiry has proved to be that in the name of re-jecting empiricism or objectivism, everything is consigned to the regime of the signifier. As a result, we critics are left with an untenable choice: either to counterpose nativism with a textualism preoccupied with demonstrating *différance* or to assume that since the "what" is in the realm of indeterminacy, the "who" reigns supreme.

So while the ethico-political imperatives of representation cannot be overemphasized, reckoning with them involves more than donning the raiment of the native informant qua reflexive subject—as if learning to make like a metropolitan intellectual automatically produces, with the additions of irony, rhetorical flourish, and a few mea culpas, what our "naive" anthropological counterparts were unable to produce: namely, indigenous insights. The dangers of assuming the role of what Frantz Fanon pejoratively called an *évolué* are not bypassed by theoretical in-vocations of performativity, hybridity, or deconstructive awareness. Like-wise, the corrections required to overcome witting or unwitting mis-representations can only be approximated in the contestation of concept and reality. The difficulty is precisely to avoid lunging from a relativis-tic constructionism to a rock-kicking pragmatism; such is the agon of contemporary humanistic inquiry.

On my reading, the knowledge that cultures are "constructed" does not obviate examining the actualities of those constructions. One can-not assume that the surprises of a given cultural construction are in-herently mirrored by the structure of analytic propositions posited to explain it. If that were the case—and indeed some forms of postcolo-nial criticism proceed as if a "commitment to theory" (Homi Bhabha's phrase) were equivalent to an engagement with civic or psychic actual-ities—the imponderabilia of social existence would not have to be re-garded as surprises at all but quite simply as "spaces of witholding" or hidden traces.[31] In the context of theorizing a far more resistant object designated as postcolonial experience, dialectical analysis provides what we might regard as an escape hatch out of the tautological notion that the rules of a theoretical game simultaneously provide the abstractions to help explain and the explanations to help abstract concrete realities.

As might be evident from the above line of argument, presuming a willed reflexivity that allows the represer to make canny turns in and out of texts and contexts (here stopping to note what the text cannot or will not say, there commenting on how the native does in fact reinforce the truth of a situation) elides any accounting of a critical method. I do not wish to suggest that shadowboxing with questions of method is peculiar to any particular disciplinary orientation. But displacements with regard to the elusiveness of method have become very charged in disciplines such as cultural anthropology, in which the relations between subject and object, represer and represented, signification and reference are both obvious and difficult. Though much is made of methodological considerations in the thought-provoking revisions and "experiments" in ethnographic inquiry, the kind of epistemological skepticism suggested by a rigorous questioning of categorical imperatives and evidentiary claims (as adumbrated by the Frankfurt school's critique of positivistic rationality, for example) is seldom approximated in practice, either in anthropology or in most other practices of studying lived cultural expressions. In fact, the metatheoretical work of the Frankfurt school has gone largely unnoticed in anthropological circles, except when the critique of "culture industries" is cited to make routine observations about consumerist ideology and capitalist production relations.[32]

I will have occasion later to take up some methodological issues as they relate to ethnography in its dominant, anthropological mode. But this is the moment to suggest that in the enterprise of refinding itself, anthropology has deflected the charge of hiding behind positivistic science by flipping over into hypostatic and sometimes ecstatic celebrations of a textual positivism centered on a descending spiral of hermeneutic preoccupations about "*writing* culture."[33] Even if we rightly dispose of reflection theories of knowledge in order to engage the problem of narrativity or figuration, the prisoner's dilemma of how one knows what one knows is not resolved by repatriating all questions about the value of knowledge to the terrain of subjectivism. For my part, a rigorous consideration of *how* knowledge is produced in the contingent interactions of subject and object, shadow and substance, or affiliation and estrangement begins but cannot end with the thematization of interestedness or inscription.

It is to thematize the political pitfalls of a too-hasty conflation of ontology and the ontic that I invoked Fanon in the first epigraph at the beginning of this chapter. At the end of the day, Fanon forces us back to the vexed methodological terrain of distinguishing between "what is" and "what happens" (indeed, this discontinuity emblematized some of his disagreement with Jean-Paul Sartre). Though Fanon's *Black Skins, White Masks* is an oft-quoted text within postcolonial and minority discourse for its construction of a political anatomy of racism, his more dialectical and polemical enunciations in *The Wretched of the Earth* seem not to provoke as much commentary.[34] I should like to suggest some crucial, if overlooked, aspects of Fanon's elaboration of the "pitfalls of national consciousness" relevant for a critical intervention into the arena of postcolonial experience and representation.[35]

Fanon proposes that the evolution of the "native intellectual" is scored through by an uncertainty that is political and methodological without being ontological. In the context of outlining the activity required to produce a national consciousness (in decolonized spaces) he remarks, "The search for truth in local attitudes is a *collective affair*. Some are richer in experience, and elaborate their thought more rapidly, and in the past have been able to establish a greater number of mental links."[36] Along the same lines, he later says, "We must not voodoo the people, nor dissolve them in emotion or confusion."[37] The context of Fanon's writing or the circumstances of consolidating intellectual activity in the moment of African (or Indian) decolonization are obviously not equivalent to our present interest in postcolonial intellectual production in the metropolis. But the underlying imperative to represent "the people" is ultimately not that dissimilar.[38] Especially if one considers how the figure of Fanon has been appropriated as a synechdoche of postcolonial consciousness, his position on the status of the native intellectual acquires a specific poignancy:

> For [the national middle class] nationalization does not mean governing the state with regard to the new social relations whose growth it has been decided to encourage. To them, nationalization quite simply means the transfer into native hands of those unfair advantages which are a legacy of the colonial period.... *The national middle class discovers its historic mission: that of intermediary.*[39]

If we substitute "postcolonial intellectuals in the metropolis" for "the national middle class," the extreme contradictions of knowledge-production-as-commodity-exchange begin to emerge. What we have is an interlacing of a political betrayal with a methodological or, more accurately, procedural difficulty. How does one assume the enunciative charge of representation without reproducing, however unwittingly, the instrumental function of the intermediary? It is not our location (as postcolonials, feminists, or oppositional intellectuals) that provides sheltering mechanisms against the overdetermined logic of seeing difference precisely *as* identity. To believe this would be to reinscribe faith in a naive individualism in the face of its repudiation within an oppositional cultural politics. Instead, the refusal of instrumental positioning is made possible by a constitutive refusal of the category "human" as given in the procrustean formula of the world according to the West. And such a refusal can only emerge as a condition of doing something other than reflecting back, if only in colored forms, the specular distinctions of knower and known, assimilated subject and segregated native, and finally, human knowledge and inhuman lies.[40]

This point can be clarified by referring again to Fanon's charged characterization of the embeddedness of Western norms of thought in colonialist dogma:

> The Western bourgeoisie has prepared enough fences and railings to have no real fear of the competition of those whom it exploits and holds in contempt. Western bourgeois racial prejudice as regards the nigger and the Arab is a racism of contempt; it is a racism which minimizes what it hates. Bourgeois ideology, however, which is the proclamation of an essential equality between men, manages to appear logical in its own eyes by inviting the sub-men to become human, and to take as their proto-type Western humanity as incarnated in the Western bourgeoisie.[41]

While we may want to rethink the "Manichaeanism" of Fanon's insurgent point of view (given our own inextricably contaminated academic locations and the different strategies of engagement required by the politics of postcoloniality), the epistemological thrust of his critique is still well worth considering. The new humanism Fanon endorses is neither an "overcompensation" (Bhabha's reading) nor naively transcendental (as implied by Christopher Miller).[42] Attention to the passage quoted above reveals Fanon's recommendation that native intellectuals distance themselves from the ideology of equality fundamental to bourgeois humanism. The invitation to "sub-men to become human" is one that can never be accepted because its very terms are tendentious. As Fanon suggests, racism and humanism are the twinned components of a heads-I-win-tails-you-lose logic, one that places the bourgeois Western "human" in perpetual judgment over whether or not the "sub-human" natives will acquire the status of proper subjects.

Thus native intellectuals need to define themselves and their constituency by means other than those available through a conception of humanity allowed in Western normative categories. The "new" humanism that Fanon proleptically conjures is incommensurable with the old, which continues to privilege, surreptitiously, the value codings of ontological and hence colonial discourse. "Leave this Europe," he says in the conclusion to *The Wretched of the Earth*, "where they are never done talking of Man, yet murder men everywhere they find them, at the corner of every one of their own streets, in all the corners of the globe. For centuries they have stifled almost the whole of humanity in the *name of a so-called spiritual experience*."[43]

Let me return this discussion to the point of its contact with the problem of representation as I wish to pose it. If the ontologizing thrust of humanistic knowledge production is to be displaced by a responsibility to represent something other than preprocessed "information" about whether the native is human, we no longer need the native informant, who can only reproduce the terms of imperial sovereignty: Does the postcolonial have an identity or a being? Is there a form of consciousness recognizably human(ist)? Is it all a lie to cover up that there is no such underlying consciousness?

There remains a quite distinct task demanded of those who would take up the struggle to think about the conditions and possibilities of intellectual engagement in a postcolonial cultural milieu. In the vocative sense, the place of the native intellectual still (and urgently) requires filling not by those who would be "authentic" or "organic" in relation to some mystified (proto)human community, but by those who wish to help articulate emergent discourses of the other from within the crosshatchings of power and desire, representation and misrepresentation, totality and localization.[44] The "native," then, need not be an other, since her place or voice is tied not to some originary bond of existence but to that "worldliness" invoked by Said.

Rice Peasant or Tribal Sheikh

At the beginning of this chapter I adduced Geertz on the problem of the native's point of view. Let me do so again, even though his reflections on local knowledge appear to be an unlikely source for sustaining an "insurgent" conversation about native intellectuals. Throughout his long and illustrious career, Geertz has avoided an engagement with anything resembling the relay between power and knowledge (except insofar as such principles were transformed into tropes within his elaborations of ludic and dramaturgical social systems). His intellectual predilections are entirely consistent with a liberal humanist model of anthropological knowledge (something he readily admits), whose legitimacy it seems impertinent to question in the light of all that we have come to learn about cockfights and theater states, not to mention the "works and lives" of anthropology's forefathers.[45] Still, Geertz represents the "document" I would like to revisit, not only to brush him against the grain, so to speak, but also to make use of the archive his work lays out. Perhaps this is a matter of hating tradition properly, as Adorno phrased it, for there is much to be gleaned from old-fashioned, even orientalist scholarship. After all, orientalists took their traditions and objects very seriously, whereas new-fangled dilettantes in otherness often seem to be convinced (in a more surreptitiously disturbing brand of liberalism) that cosmopolitan intellectualism alone can provide the secret combination to the locked doors of cultural incommensurability and native thinking.

On reading Geertz, one encounters a lucidity and sardonic humor about the enterprise of localizing oneself in the field—which, it must be said, recommend themselves more than do many utterances about the presumptuousness of speaking for others. In his 1988 reflections on ethnographic writing, *Works and Lives,* Geertz describes the fieldwork situation as increasingly one in which the representer is between the proverbial rock and hard place: either "mere digging in ('Don't think about ethnography, just do it') or mere flying off ('Don't do ethnography, just think about it')."[46] In part, I use his comment as a heuristic to foreground my own interest in linking the modalities of thought and action, often regarded as mutually exclusive. Additionally, Geertz's interpretive essays illuminate, in a manner akin to Jameson's adumbrations of Marxist theories of literature, what is at stake in formal propositions about culture.

If we read him symptomatically, that is, if we mine Geertz's insights for purposes other than the ones he intended, the problem of perspectival understanding, of *constructing* the native's point of view, can usefully be addressed. Take, for example, his explication in *Local Knowledge* of the distinction between "experience-near" and "experience-distant" concepts (adapted from the work of psychoanalyst Heinz Kohut):

> An experience-near concept is, roughly, one that someone—a patient, a subject, in our case an informant—might himself naturally and effortlessly use to define what he or his fellows see, feel, think, imagine, and so on, and which he would readily understand when similarly applied by others. An experience-distant concept is one that specialists of one sort or another—an analyst, an experimenter, an ethnographer, even a priest or an ideologist—employ to forward their scientific, philosophical, or practical aims. "Love" is an experience-near concept, "object cathexis" is an experience-distant one. . . . Confinement to experience-near concepts leaves an ethnographer awash in immediacies, as well as entangled in the vernacular. Confinement to experience-distant ones leaves him stranded in abstractions and smothered in jargon. The real question [is] . . . how, in each case, ought one to deploy them so as to produce an interpretation of the way a people lives which is neither imprisoned within their mental horizons, an ethnography of witchcraft as written by a witch, nor systematically deaf to the distinctive tonalities of their existence, an ethnography of witchcraft as written by a geometer.[47]

If we are not in the business of producing "an ethnography of witchcraft as written by a witch," but, with Fanon in mind, if we are also not to be swayed by voodoo itself, then Geertz's propositions might commend themselves as food for methodological thought. They fortuitously highlight the tension constituting the encounter of concept and reality. The problem of "vernacular" signification is neither that it exhaustively expresses native experience nor that its meanings are structured exclusively in the slippage of signifiers. Rather, the remainder between felt realities and convictions on the one hand and their broader, "experience-distant" narrativization on the other is what gives the lie to any securely experientialist or "native" account. The remainder, then, is not simply a leftover of linguistic functions. For Geertz, "[p]eople use experience-near concepts spontaneously, unself-consciously, as it were colloquially; they do not, except fleetingly and on occasion, recognize that there are any "concepts" involved at all. That is what experience-near means—that ideas and the realities they inform are naturally and indissolubly bound up together. What else could you call a hippopotamus?"[48]

There are, of course, intractable difficulties of assuming along with Geertz that *calling* a hippopotamus a hippopotamus is equivalent to the cognitive operations required to decipher it *as* a hippopotamus and not, as in Louis Althusser's charge against the ideology of pragmatist knowledge, a poached baby elephant.[49] By somewhat casually conjoining Althusser and Geertz here, I want to interject the question of mediation onto the latter's undialecticized framework. To evoke an Adornian image, what Geertz neglects to see, Althusser reinforces as a splinter in the eye. Whereas for the former, "[i]n the country of the blind, who are not as unobservant as they look, the one-eyed is not king, he is spectator,"[50] for the latter this proposition would beg the question of the necessary symptomatization of sight itself. Adapting Althusser's critique of classical political economy to the present discussion, we might say:

> [W]hat [the anthropologist or native] does not see, is not what [he or she] does not see, it is *what [he or she] sees.* . . . The oversight, then, is not to see what one sees, the oversight no longer concerns the object, but *the sight* itself. The oversight is an oversight that concerns vision: non-vision is therefore inside vision, it is a form of vision and hence has a necessary relationship with vision.[51]

By this light, the perspective of the rice peasant or tribal sheikh is not what constitutes an understanding proper to its production as such. Neither is the task one of producing a descriptive answer to the problem of identity construction as experience-near or experience-distant. Being an immigrant Indian is, for the immigrant Indian, ipso facto experience-near; assuming the subject position of a postcolonial migrant, is, likewise, an effect of the experience-distant tropology characteristic of theoretical language. If, for the moment, we remain with Althusser's interpretation of Marx's method, then the "correct" answer to the problem of perspectivalism is one that is in process, emergent, since it is an answer to a question "that has just one failing: it was never posed."[52]

This dialectical twist, or what Althusser calls the "overdetermined" aspect of the problematic, is at the heart of constituting a field of vision; it is also the principle of contradiction articulating truth and falsity.[53] Among the first tasks required of a would-be dialectician in the field, then, is not to make determinations about true and false statements. By the very nature of their emergence, the narratives of one's interlocutors do not locate themselves according to a true-or-false logic because every visible lie is accompanied by an invisible truth, and the problematic represents their condensation. In his analysis of Marx's conceptualization of capital, Althusser proposed that the singularity of

Marx's "answer" to the problem of labor power rested in his seeing what classical economics did not see *while seeing,* and that this was identical with what it did not see at all. The remainder that emerges from this contradictory "sighting of a non-sight of the seen" is, thus, the effect of dialecticizing the givenness of a particular problem or reality.[54]

Returning to the beginning of this discussion, to the chapter's second epigraph, taken from Marcel Griaule's pronouncements about the "nature" of his Dogon informants, we might see the benefit of a symptomatic reading of his ideas about jest, fear, venality, and dissimulation. As a particular historical dynamic in the ethnographic situation of the native informant facing the master narrator (not to mention the master narrative), "lying" might very well have provided the truth of the Dogon's condition of possibility for being. On this reading, what the native informant may have said, regardless of his motivations, was not a lie but—in the sense of experiencing one's being in the constrained relation with Griaule as the European subject—the strictest possible truth. The exceptional quality to this truth, however, is given in the European's constitutive inability to see its magnification, given that he himself was internal to its production.[55]

"The concept dog cannot bark."[56] Through his wry importation of Spinoza's utterance, Althusser points to the dilemma of all attempts, including my own, at mediation. How does one take the concept of postcolonial identity and make it "speak"? The dialectical road I have chosen (one less traveled for many reasons, including its difficulty) finally forces us onto a crossroads where, as it were, one pitches one's tent and looks out in order to resolve the distances among what is proffered, what is withheld, and what is secreted in the relation to one's interlocutors. A unique reprieve issued by dialectical understanding is that it is irrelevant to ponder whether or not the subaltern speaks because, like the concept dog, subalternity is itself a conceptual relation and does not, if I may put it so facetiously, bark or speak. But this insight is also reinforced more literally if we recall that Gramsci's subaltern (since it is from him that contemporary celebrations of the subaltern derive their influence) was, after all, a petty officer within an institutional army and not, as the traveling theory often suggests, an archaic representative from some outer margin.

If what I have said so far is persuasive as a protocol of interpretive activity, it may be useful to take a second look at some of the claims and crises of authority staked out in various thematizations of "anthro-pology in reverse."[57] Having laid out what I hope is a different way of thematizing the problematic of representation, I should like to draw some of the disparate strands of my theoretical engagement together with the localizations and vocalizations of my ethnographic experi-ence: to square the dialectical circle.

Given the wide-ranging efforts to reflect on questions of the ob-server's authority, I shall restrict myself to a brief consideration of James Clifford's provocations about the new optic of "traveling cultures."[58] Clifford is worthy of attention partly because he has been very influen-tial in taking an anthropological conversation across the barrier of du-biety with which it is met in critical or comparative theory. While I would like to maintain that anthropology has not really wrested itself away from the generalized paradigm of romanticist knowledge pro-duction (which found its apotheosis in Goethe's comparatist model of "world literature"), Clifford's attempt to articulate a hybrid interpre-tive agenda with contemporary cultural politics represents a departure, though I would argue that its possibilities are as yet unrealized.

Traveling cultures—a trope made fashionable because it is seen to originate in the Surrealists' celebration of the twin discourses of mobil-ity and urbanity—represent for Clifford a model for theorizing the connections between theory (particularly given its early etymological links with spectatorship) and practices of modern travel and travelers. As he puts it, Clifford's interest is "to open up the question of how cul-tural analysis constitutes its objects—societies, traditions, communi-ties, identities—in spatial terms and through specific spatial practices of research."[59] He takes his charge from the by now familiar emphasis on spatiality and spatial consciousness derived from Surrealist accounts (such as that of Louis Aragon or Michel Leiris), in which the valoriza-tion of *flânerie,* or a certain spatial decenteredness, was seen as a kind of revolt against the temporally driven, linear values of bourgeois self-consolidation. But early enthusiasts of Surrealism (including members of the Frankfurt school, such as Benjamin) later came to recognize that the movement stalled at the gate of aestheticism, offering little by way of social transformation.[60] So it is unclear why or how the politically impotent European avant-garde movements of the early twentieth cen-tury—with all due regard to the aesthetic experimentality of their pro-ductions—can provide a model for an oppositional representational praxis, as forwarded by Clifford. Even when nomadology (of a surreal-istic sort) is actively disparaged, postmodern experiments in "deterrito-rialized" cultural analysis appear to dress up the old wine of bourgeois aestheticism in new bottles of cosmopolitan homelessness, though Clifford is by no means the worst offender.[61]

The suspect historical premises of his model notwithstanding, Clifford correctly emphasizes that international flows of capital and labor have made cultural dispersal into a transnational structure of feeling—a sit-uation that has produced a certain elasticity in the relations between theorizers and theorized. Consequently, unlike the generatively com-promised nature of Surrealism's politics, in which the anxieties of urban decenteredness could only be played out against intractable, if ignored, imperial realities, the contemporary traffic in knowers and known does accommodate more than a one-way street (to echo one of Benjamin's formulations about the culture of capitalism). Even if exchanges between traveling theorists and traveling cultures remain fleeting and for the most part emblematic of commodity relations—as indicated by discourses of tourism, ethnic careerism, eco-fetishism, and so on—it is apt to say that modernity, with all its appurtenances, is "at large."[62] Keeping in mind the difficulties of an ahistorical adoption of a Surrealist-inspired fla-neurial optic, then, we might still find it valuable to examine Clifford's suggestions for the need to reverse traditional ethnographic authority from the observer to the observed:

> Nowadays when we see these pictures of tents in villages we may find ourselves asking different questions: Who, exactly, is being observed? Who is localized when the ethnographer's tent is permitted in the center of a village? Cultural observers, anthropologists, are often themselves in the fishbowl, under surveillance (for example, by the omnipresent kids who won't leave them alone). Who is being observed when that tent is pitched in the middle of the village? What are the political locations involved?[63]

Here Clifford posits the advantages of blurring the genres and bound-aries of ethnographic knowledge. "Who determines where (and when) a community draws its lines, names its insiders and outsiders?" he asks.[64] In my view, some answers to this question are easier than others; for one thing, the point is not to take either a community's or one's own representations about existential status—insider or outsider—on the terms that they are offered. As for the issue of agency, concessions of hospitality or politeness are always political concessions. Even had we not learned that lesson from Pierre Bourdieu's explication of the logic of social taste and judgment, it would be apparent to anyone—perhaps *especially* a fieldworker—who has outstayed her welcome.

Clifford's more global proposition, to subvert the "constitutive modern opposition [of] traveler/tourist," does indeed contain a translative capacity, although I would suggest an inflection to the problematic of translation that is different from his lament of *"tradittore, traduttore* [*sic*].*"*[65] In the face of waning interest in and support for cultural comparison (within the academy, at least, witnessed by the nationwide decline of national and comparative literature departments), decrying linguistic or institutional complicity is not very helpful. These days it is less a problem that other cultures are *traduced* in translation than that they simply do not matter in the hegemonic construction of culture and **modernity** "at large." Rather, if we presuppose the necessarily distortive **effects** of the commitment to intellectual work, one need no longer **tarry** over whether (to quote Neil Lazarus on the subject) we are "[throwing] out the baby of representation with the bathwater of ideological appropriation."[66] To the extent that postcolonial representation is about the effects of dislocation, it is also parapraxis: *traduttore, traditore* (translator, traitor). Indeed, Clifford's error in deploying this Italian proverb speaks to the problem of the irrelevance of cultural specificity.

The necessity and irreducibility of cultural representation receives perhaps an unlikely support in the later work of Roland Barthes—unlikely, because the disparagement of representation-as-violence is a position that is heavily influenced by his early poststructuralist views on the deformative aspects of writing. In his essay "Change the Object Itself" (1971), Barthes underscored the need for "rectifying" semiology— given that the demystification of language has itself become a "mythological doxa." He argued that the currents of contemporary social alienation necessitate that "the direction this combat [the specific labor of representation] must take is not, is no longer, that of critical decipherment but that of *evaluation.*"[67] This insistence and Barthes's perhaps surprising exhortation that we reengage "Feuerbach to Marx" reposition representational concerns squarely and literally on the terrain of the production of value. What Barthes seems to be suggesting, then, is that the moment to decry the "violence of the letter" is well past. Our preoccupation with the epistemic or philosophical vexations of representation need to give way to a more localized and political struggle over meaning, given that present history exposes the alienations of capitalist modernity far more than it does the mystifications of language.[68]

In Althusser's scheme (which Barthes endorses in his challenge to "change the object itself"), the former proposes that the problematic of representation is rendered especially complex because the terms of its interrogation are ones of evaluating structural absences (as opposed to content). In his characteristic way of posing the problem, Althusser argues that "'*Darstellung*' and its avatars" are the epistemological keys to Marx's theory of value, in which the concept of *Darstellung* turns not on presence (we might replace this with formation or deformation) but on effectivity, or the "designat[ion] of the mode of *presence* of the structure in its *effects*."[69] In other words, Althusser too affirms the historical necessity (following Marx) of reading the problem of representation as a problem of adjudicating its productive capacities, its avatars.

Darstellung and Its Avatars

In Sanskrit the term *avatar* means "incarnation" and, relatedly, "the descended" (as in the god who descends to earth having assumed a new incarnation). Althusser's use of this metaphor to think about the problem of representation is doubly ironic in the context of discussing a predominantly Hindu community's postcolonial reconstruction. First, let us note the obvious linguistic irony in the phrase "*Darstellung* and its avatars"; the phrase seems to be meant to conjure up the image of Vishnu, the protector of the universe in classical Indian mythology, whose embodiments, or avatars, are the human and nonhuman forms he takes to rescue the material world from the domination of *maya* (illusion, excess). In the present context (from entirely outside Althusser's frame of reference), we might say that an avatar metaphorizes productivity itself. Second, the word "avatar" (literally, from the word *avatarana*, "to descend") encapsulates a sense of the plasticity of form as well as the down-to-earthness of representation. By this light, "*Darstellung* and its avatars" evokes "the descent of representation," whereby representation is seen as conjoining form and idea, matter and imagination—a descent, as it were, from an idealized realm of *Darstellung* to the practical re-creations necessitated by the contingencies of the everyday world.

I recount this emphasis on the material, incarnate aspects of self-representation opportunistically, since Althusser's metaphor permits me to connect ideas whose rhetorical provenance is poles apart; to wit, production and incarnation, Continental theory and Hindu mythography. Moreover, with regard to the ways that immigrant selves are remade, the work of representation has very much to do with the representation of work, mine no less than that of my interlocutors. To date, many influential versions of postcolonial analysis have taken their cue from psychoanalytic criticism, centering their explications of identity on terms of the imaginary and surrounding discourses of the libidinal.[70] Though I would not wish to jettison the importance of the unconscious to questions of identity formation (as exemplified by my attempt in chapter 3 to account for some elements of psychic identification), it seems to me that a materialist focus must *also* take itself at face value and do a little digging where the ground is actually visible.

My desire to redirect the discussion of identity from focusing predominantly on unconscious processes of "working through" history, the past, tradition, and so forth is bolstered by Adorno's speculations on "The Meaning of Working Through the Past." In this important if somewhat underconsidered essay, Adorno insists on clarifying that whatever the charge of unconscious processes of retranscription, there remains a concrete burden of the past on the present in the form of the practical, physical tasks that have to be performed to clean up and clear away the cobwebs. For his argument, Adorno relies on the commonplace inflections in German of "working through" *(Aufarbeitung)* in order to signal that managing the past is not entirely about the ineffable pressures of the psyche but is also about the mundane work of the everyday. That is, however modish it may be to render the pressures to assimilate one's past identity in psychoanalytic terms of transference, melancholia, overcoming, and so on, the idea of "working through" very much depends on "work" itself and derives from the common sense of dispatching tasks. "Working through" thus also connotes practical activity, active self-management rather than an "acting out" of self-mastery.[71]

To integrate this observation with my earlier disagreement about easy analogies between Surrealist depictions of *flânerie* and the postcolonial predicament, there is a material point of comparison between the two, one that has not entered, substantively, the theoretical conversation about migrancy and diaspora. Although psychoanalytic readings of the flaneur (and its imputed similarity with today's "traveling subjects") are commonplace, we may want to recall the specific influence of Bergsonian psychology (with all its conscious, behavioral ramifications) on the Surrealists and their inheritors. Perhaps more significantly than an exclusive focus on the unconscious dynamics of subjective fragmentation readily admits, Surrealism attempted to depict the material alteration in sense perception induced by the pervasive influence of modern technology, urbanization, and the privatization of social experience (the work, for instance, of Aragon and André Breton along with the inspiration the Surrealists derived from Charles Baudelaire's nineteenth-century lyric poetry). In this more corporeal vision, the excesses of bourgeois experience result in the loss of the sentient capacity to experience *(Erfahrung)*, accompanied by libidinal disinvestment.

The figure of the distracted observer, the flaneur, allegorizes this inward turn by referring it to the analogy of shock (which is the body's way of parrying disturbances to the nervous system through "checking out," as it were). There is thus a historical, as opposed to a merely formalistic, parallel to be drawn between early twentieth-century experiences of industrialized subjects and the contemporary predicament of immigrants whose encounter with capitalist modernity is belated. This relates to the crucial though paradoxical symptomatization of modern subjectivity proposed by Benjamin. Following Freud's clinical writings on shell-shocked veterans of World War I, Benjamin argues that shock-experience—the absorption of minute but consistent shocks to the neurological system—is the subjective condition of being modern. Modernity is *not* characterized by the individual's perpetual traumatization. On the contrary, the repetitiousness of contemporary experience and the alienated interactions of everyday life act to prevent trauma to the somatic system. That is, modern subjectivity is to be comprehended as a series of epidermal, which is to say surface-level, reactions to the "breakdown" of experience under capitalism.[72] This is Benjamin's classic dialectical reasoning: the determinate contradiction of alienation in and through the alienated mechanisms of everyday life.[73]

What I find intriguing about this rereading of the constitution of modern (bodily) constitutions, so to speak, is that it is quite unlike the theoretical prominence given to Michel Foucault's conceptions of subjection in dispersed writings about postcoloniality (Bhabha is only the most cited in the range of possible examples). In Foucault's version of things, or more precisely, of the *dispositif*, those most subject to the operations of power are, by virtue of a heightened consciousness of their bodies, most able to manipulate (microphysically, of course) the signs of the "apparatus."[74] But as almost every critical commentator has noted, nowhere does Foucault give us the mechanism of such subjective agency. Despite being compromisingly elliptical at times, Benjamin's coupling of alienation/subjection is far more trained on the problem of the value codings that determine how and why modern subjects cope with the perverse suturing of dead labor and deadened consciousness. Perception is *exactly the barrier against* permanent damage; invoking, once more, the trope of sight, it is perception that allows us to see without looking and whereby, as a corollary dynamic, our skins have to ward off the threat to the self. To my mind, such a thesis is profoundly important in the context of diagnosing the management of everyday racism by subjects whose skin color everywhere proclaims their alterity.

The estrangement from prior community; from links with tradition; along with the distracted interactions of everyday life: Such are the peculiarities of modern, reified existence (again most complexly elaborated by Benjamin in his explications of Baudelaire's relation to the emerging bourgeois city space). Such depictions give us a historical similarity between the Surrealists' view of perceptual fragmentation and the present-day conditions faced by the dislocated postcolonial, whose primary mode of being in the world is very much entrapped in capitalist alienation. Although this might lead one to argue with equal justification for a theory of psychic fragmentation that enfolds *all* subjects and not just various constituencies of the marginalized (indeed Gilles Deleuze and Félix Guattari as well as Jean-François Lyotard have done so in their various Eurocentered elaborations of postmodern "schizo" subjectivities), I think my take on the issue is a little different.

For one, I do not wish to offer a paradigm case in which the postcolonial subject merely dissimulates and reverses the centrality of the European or imperial self. For another, my contention is that there is something to be made of the empirical fact that embourgeoisement has such a solidifying appeal for migrant subjects. Though middle-class immigrants are most readily able to adapt to and realize the imperatives of "naturalization," others aspire to it as well; indeed, capitalism depends on the universality of its lures, which are dissimulated as the most stable values. Instead of focusing so much attention on the "deterritorializing" features of the subject's psychic formation, then, we might be well served to interrogate the territorializing aspects—the literal consolidation of identity among subjects who must everyday parry the shocks of cultural alienation, not by recourse to some ineffable mimicking of dominant ways of being in the world but quite simply through deploying the realm of the everyday as a buffer against the routinization of labor and life.

This constitutes one of Benjamin's more radical insights in his writings on modernity (influenced by Freud's investigations of neurasthenia). The realities of labor, the repetitious motions of work in the capitalist system, the serialized and sterilized products of consumer culture—all work to articulate a dialectical response whereby the shocks of daily existence result precisely in an anaesthetized consciousness (a very different image from that of the blasé flaneur traveling through the world with disjointed but cosmopolitan cool). What this conception of modernity stresses is less the processes of deterritorialization and dispersion—which tend to be invoked in terms of distributive force (that is, velocity, speed, spatial movement)—than the *congealment* of affect and energy.[75] The management of psychic anxieties and cultural disruptions proceeds very much by way of smoothing out and scaling down the unpleasantness of an everyday life unhinged from any sense of propriety or continuity with previously established understandings of the self or of one's place in the world. If, therefore, the postcolonial subject mimics the discourse of dominance, it is in the reflex action of a "mimetic shock absorber" rather than in "sly civility."[76] One of my early lessons in practical knowledge was that what you see is not necessarily what you get in currently fashionable theorizations of hybrid or diasporic subjectivity.

The initial stages of setting up an ethnographic study are always the most tenuous in the whole business of demarcating "being there" from "writing here" (which is how Geertz constructs the split process of adjudicating two entirely different fields: that in which one participates versus that in which one is professionally accredited, however nominally). Part of the instability of entering fieldwork relates to the delicate mental negotiation of deciding on the kind of value to place on already established analytic trends (within institutional forms of knowledge production) with respect to what one encounters in practical experience. I am being only partly facetious when I say that some of my early doubts about the viability of my study surfaced because I, like others, was caught up in the discursive afflatus surrounding notions of splin-

tered subjects and sutured selves. I knew that these sorts of propositions would have to be reckoned with, if only because poststructurally
inflected theories of colonial discourse have nowhere to go without
them and consequently insist that thinking can only advance by privileging the decentered sign, the inevitably "in-between," the hybrid, and
so on. But the givenness of cultural theory's diagnoses, whether of mor-
bidity or emergence, cannot be assumed a priori; it is only commensurable in the field of the empirical, as "actualities."

When I first contacted people in the Indian community to see if I
could engage them in an ethnographic exploration of how they represented themselves to themselves, I put it to them that much of the theoretical interest in colonial discourse centered on the recovery of historical narratives of racism and stereotyping. I suggested to people that
they might like to think about the connections between self-understanding and a colonial past (especially given that many members of
the community had come of age, so to speak, in the decades before and
after Indian independence). I hit my first snag right away: My assumptions about the force of such a powerful discourse as colonialism simply did not accord with the perspectives of my would-be interlocutors.

Years later (and from the other side of the pedagogic divide), I try to
tell my students that one cannot go looking for a "discourse" and expect
to find it—although the too-easy importations of Foucault's ideas in
the critical literature might suggest otherwise. Foucault would, however, be the first to remark that the point about a discourse, or an epis-
teme, is precisely that it is taken for granted and thus does not yield itself up all that easily. This difficulty was brought home to me during
the planning of my ethnography when one person who learned of my
interest in linking colonial discourse to postcolonial identity asked, "To
whom is it surprising that the colonizers colonized?"

It was, in other words, an undeniably obvious fact, quite unworthy
of greater consideration. My interlocutor expressed his surprise that there
might be a scholarly enterprise in trying to establish linkages between
European cultural contact and the domination of non-Western people;
this to him represented the *ground zero* of his own understanding, and
consequently he was at a loss as to why it merited any speculation; for
him there was no alternative possibility to explore. What this exchange
suggests is that regardless of whether our theoretical constructs require
annexing the complications of colonial ambivalence (wherein the dis-

courses of both colonizer and colonized are equally "stricken" with an indeterminacy about things like difference and identity), the more active processes of uprooting and rerouting one's subjective trajectory obey a far more banal and mundane logic.[77] According to such a logic, the formation of selfhood may be fraught, but not everything in life is subject to an *askesis*. And so it is that for many of my ethnographic informants, an everyday understanding of a received narrative of colonial experience is managed without difficulty, as well as with a good deal of disavowal.

These days ethnographers face all kinds of induced and intuited *crises de conscience;* mine was about how to realize an analysis of postcolonial subjectivity that at first glance refused to proceed along the course I had sketched out for it. The pressure that a particular culture or history puts on people exists not only invisibly but also visibly in and through the materialities of daily experience. However, this could only become known in the active relay of theory and practice, as a constitutive facet of writing the field. At the threshold of my foray into fieldwork, I could only relate the unsaid aspects, the contradictions of people's self-representations, in terms of prepackaged theoreticisms about difference and heteroglossia. That such terms were "canceled" in their actualization was on the order of an elusive dialectical image not illuminated for me until much later.

At any rate, I did not unburden the weight of my theoretical preoccupations on anyone in the community, but it was with some trepidation that I tried to explain my reasons for wanting to conduct an examination of people's everyday lives. Even if people did not actively resist my ideas, they were by turns disdainful and indulgent about the prospect of any useful knowledge emerging out of what appeared to many as fancy and "unscientific" footwork. Consequently, despite the fact that most people I approached were quite ready to accommodate my requests to visit them with notebook and tape recorder in hand, I was aware that they were skeptical about the utility of intellectualizing matters like marginality, assimilation, or the "colonial mentality."[78]

My project of interrogating the identity of bourgeois postcolonials is troubled because it lacks the exoticism of subalternity but also because despite the historical distinctiveness of patterns of embourgeoisement, an avowed certitude about the propriety of one's beliefs and place in the world seems to cut across all who are thus interpellated. With respect to my ethnographic community, most of whose constituents were middle-class subjects in technical occupations (as engineers and in a few cases as medical doctors), the upshot of a certain professional success, combined with a willed investment in the rectitude of their worldview, made for some dogged assertions about "the way things are," the "obviousness" of this or that, and ultimately claims about "what is natural." This difficulty was, for me, magnified as a result of my own position in the field—which is to say within the community I sought to write about. I was acquainted with many people who later became my informants in part because they knew my parents (who were latecomers to the same community) and also because I was introduced to the social circuit of Indians in southern New Jersey as someone with an "independent mind" who had decided to pursue neither the desirable professional trajectory of becoming a doctor, lawyer, or management executive nor, barring such career goals, the life trajectory of a candidate for an arranged marriage.

So I spent some time during my initial inquiries into people's willingness to participate in the project having to defend the value of humanistic inquiry (such as anthropology or history; knowing it would not signify, I left cultural studies out of the mix). I also had to find ways to avoid being challenged to take a position vis-à-vis what constituted a proper lifestyle for a "young woman" such as myself. The translation of bourgeois normativity takes such strange turns that what appears alien and somewhat shocking to mainstream Americans, the primitivism of arranged marriages with all their connotations of an absence of patriarchal constraint and sexual choice, represents the very emblem of personal honor and female propriety for middle-class Indian immigrants.[79]

Needless to say, questions about personal choice are never entirely settled, and in fact the ambiguity of my position as neither a properly professionalized subject nor a properly domesticated one later allowed many women in the community to voice their doubts about their own situation in ways that perhaps would not have been possible had I walked into the encounter with the discursive machinery and ideological clout of a "scientist" or, contrarily enough, as one of them. For then they might have had to contend with the presumptively authorized force of my evaluative judgment (either as a practitioner of some discipline they privileged as scientific on the one hand or as a peer on the other). As it was, much of what I learned, indeed much of what is valuable in any interpretive act, took the form of storytelling and the education of a misguided but well-intentioned daughter—that is, someone decisively lesser in personal and professional stature, but someone whose "humanistic" whimsy they were quite willing to indulge.

So, referring once more to the second of the two epigraphs at the head of this chapter, we can see that the problem of what one is provided as information in the field is certainly marked by dissimulation (whether it is a "dangerous" lie of the sort Griaule was concerned about or whether it emerges as a byproduct of the belief in so-called science). But as I have tried to establish, the nature of the exchange between representers and informants has a generative life of its own, so it does not make much sense to regard the encounter of subject and object in terms of a hermeneutic of truth and falsehood. While this might be readily accepted within the current state of thinking about problems of representation, it should be recognized as a dynamic that operates as well on the other side—from the observed's point of view, so to speak.

The fact is that the entire project of deciding about motives, premises, and explanations rests on the kind of uncertainty that Bayes's famous theorem in statistics posits as the principle of exchange: *chance*.[80] I do not think this remits all interpretation to the dustbin of a radical relativism (not least because the roll of the dice, as the Bayesians would insist, is always loaded), but it does foreground the chances that knowing interlocutors themselves have to take in the game of *Darstellung*. In my case, it was *my interlocutors'* resistance to being appropriated (albeit their resistance was born of a generalized cultural disregard of anything supposedly unscientific) that provided the determinate conditions for the emergence of the "sighting of a nonsight." If the nongeneralizability of ethnographic narratives stems from their singularity and the chances one takes in hearing or telling a particular story, then it is also the enabling condition of what gets told. My interlocutors' ideological conviction—born of technocratic and utilitarian assumptions about the unscientific status of ethnography—predicated my informants' willingness to entertain me (as I retell in chapter 4, where I discuss the elaborate signifying practices of food).

I am perforce aware that what I say above may sound literally too chancy, though I have been risking this argument all along, with respect to the dialectical necessity of reckoning with the inadequations of conceptuality as well as regarding the constitutive uncertainties of the knowing subject. Just as so much of what counts as good ethnography depends upon the individual reputations of scholars (rather than on the demonstrable veracity of what they assert as the true picture), so it is that the situated nature of the ethnographer's location in the field—her personal stakes and credibility, if you will—determines which description of the elephant will be revealed to the blinkered wise man or woman (to continue with the motif, set up via Geertz and Althusser, of elephants, blindness, and insight). And although such determinations are only discernible with time and effort, their emergence allowed me to let go of my anxieties about being both a bad daughter and a bad ethnographer.

Feeling the weight of the banality of my field's location and the lack of my own authority (both inside and outside the boundaries of disciplinary thinking), I was nonetheless convinced of the need to redeem fetishistic descriptions of anthropological locales. The contemporary turn away from unproblematized holistic descriptions has not gone very far toward displacing the naturalism smuggled underneath the ethnographer's eyewitness accounts seeking to establish the "thereness" of anthropological location. With niggling doubts about whether I could delimit a field for doing fieldwork (given the encroachments of interstate highways and the dispersed conurbations of U.S. cities), I set out to take measured steps to map the field's contours.[81]

One takes Route 295 (north, when approaching from southeastern Pennsylvania; south, if traveling from New York), through what is actually among the least industrial parts of New Jersey. The landscape is dotted with suburban office and residential complexes, and what used to be farmland landscape increasingly features strip malls and sprawling supermarkets (each of whose produce sections appears to stock more than enough to feed an entire town in some other part of the world). One crosses lesser towns like Paulsboro, Clarksboro, and Mickleton and arrives at the very nerve center of southern New Jersey, defined by the existence of and hustle-bustle surrounding the Cherry Hill and Deptford malls.

Most people in my ethnographic community live in various mid-to-upscale residential developments between the townships of Cherry Hill and Deptford; most are members of the India Association of South Jersey (and also have affiliations in "regional" organizations such as the Bengali or Gujarati Association and the Maharashtra Mandal). For the majority of these immigrants from the subcontinent, their membership in the Indian community signifies as a primary marker of social identity, although there are a few exceptions to this rule. I knew of a few people who wanted nothing to do with "ethnicizing" themselves in any manner, but because my purpose was to investigate how postcolonial Indian identity actively signifies, I did not try to seek out those who had gone to some effort to divest themselves of their links with the immigrant community. There are probably some disadvantages to my decision, but for the most part I was satisfied and quite pleasantly taken aback at how many people were willing—if only as a bit of a lark—to take me on board and into their homes.

As it turned out, through the established social networks I was able to interact at close range and for more than two years (intensively during the summers when my graduate school schedule permitted it, but also at other times) with subjects whose self-designation in the immigrant context was first and foremost as Indians or Indian Americans. It is quite possible that the same formation of people are less likely, back in India, to have such a ready attachment to being Indian (since regional affiliations—whether, for instance, one is Tamil, Bihari, Punjabi, or something else—might take precedence). All the same, it should be said that even in immigrant circumstances regionalisms carried over from India make their presence felt with regard to claims about the richest traditions, the most classical languages, truly authentic practices, and so on. How people invest their energies in matters of food (given the great variety in regional Indian cuisines), the arts (the weight attached to musical accomplishment or particular literary traditions, for example), and, to a less visible extent, matters of caste and class formation—all this contributes to the production of an overarching signature of Indian culture and identity in the diaspora. Such intragroup distinctions speak to dynamics internal to the community; because I was interested in the externalized constitution of an expatriate postcolonial consciousness, I chose to disregard regionalistic inflections or the remains of caste consciousness in the process of selecting my informants. I ended up with access to approximately twenty families (originally from the Indian states of Bihar, Gujarat, Karnataka, Uttar Pradesh, and West Bengal) who represented my regular ethnographic contacts; however, my most intensive interactions were with a group of twelve families and, even more particularly, with the women in that group.[82]

In a work focused on the discursive afterlife of colonialism, it is difficult to assess how much attention to pay to representational forces that are inherited from a discontinuous set of sociohistorical problems and whose salience in the postcolonial context has diminished or, at least, been translated into terms comprehensible within the dominant culture's logic of ethnicity.[83] This is integral to the wider problematic of identity in this culture—where, for example, immigrant Sicilians and Neopolitans are all rendered Italian. So it is with immigrant Indians (perhaps even with subcontinentals as a whole). My project specifically sought to interrogate the production of an external, ex post facto ideology of an Indian identity, what the novelist Amitav Ghosh has called "an epic relationship" to India and its articulation as a postcolonial discourse. The only directive approach I took in the entire process of designing the project had to do with the decision to constellate issues of immigrant experience and postcolonial consciousness around more "global" descriptors of Indianness rather than on "locally" demarcated divisions (which of course do fold in on the crease between the supposedly temporary "here" and the imaginarily permanent "back home").

To explore local, internecine clashes of caste and communal ideologies would have required a "microtonal" analysis beyond the scope of my present interests. In fact, I felt it was important not to get tied down by what Freud described as the narcissism of small differences. In any case, the projection of a totalizable narrative of the Indian diaspora (as given by a "representative sample" of castes, classes, or linguistic groupings) would be both unwarranted and untenable, given the historically specific circumstances of this community's consolidation. Marked primarily by the phenomenon of the "brain drain," that is, the extraction of middle-class populations with scientific and technical expertise (during the late 1960s and early 1970s), the pattern of Indian immigration to the United States has been different from earlier exportations of proletarian populations to various parts of the former British Empire. Contrasted with other diasporic Indian subjects, who, as indentured and contract laborers, displaced slaves in providing quotas of cheap labor to the capital markets, these latter-day arrivals clamor to be taken on board with all the contradictions of class, culture, and capitalization.

Among the reasons to interrogate the articulation of a middle-class Indian identity is that it allows us to see more clearly how the appurtenances of diasporic consciousness—memory, myth, belongingness, and tradition—are not sui generis. They are cast in their own shadow of inclusions and exclusions, all of which attempt to introject an image of totality that must be contested even as it is thematized as part of the ideological work of self-consolidation. In the end, I can only hope that my decision—to pick and choose from the wealth and range of information that I was given with generosity and humor and without expectation of any return—is justified. Not all of my informants' concerns about immigrant life found their way into my thematic preoccupations with the postcolonial predicament, though I should like to justify such exclusions on the terms this discussion has tried to secure: What emerges from the fieldwork encounter cannot be the perspective of the rice peasant, the tribal sheikh, or indeed, the Indian doctor.

The subjects whose everyday narratives I solicited for my project were all married and were mostly in their forties (although in a few cases I had dealings with older immigrants who were among the first to leave India and settle in the United States). All of them had children (in high school or at university). As this profile suggests, immigrant Indians are heavily invested in heteronormative familial arrangements, and I never felt able to broach issues of sexual practice or lifestyle choices. The merest hint of an overt interest in sexuality would have been inappropriate and immodest, so although questions of sexuality might underlie everyday concerns about their children or themselves, such topics were never openly discussed by my informants. The dictates of cultural modesty circumscribed what could and could not be said about one's sexual subjectivity; for me this indicated the extent to which norms of bourgeois propriety define what comes to be understood as an "Indian value." What is interesting is less that people are unwilling to admit what they do behind closed doors (which is not all that enigmatic, after all) than that sexual modesty is utterly naturalized as being Indian.

My interactions with the community usually took the form of visits to people's homes, participation in cultural or religious events and the occasional wedding of a younger person in the community, and a few shopping trips with some of my female informants who were not employed outside the home. There were some constraints on the tone of my interactions with men, though I was not unduly troubled by them, in part because patterns of gendered communication were familiar to me (as someone who was herself Indian) and in part because the study was premised on not dissipating the force of gendered self-consciousness in

consolidating forms of identity. I was also not committed to hypostatizing the variable of gender, as if that by itself could illuminate the
complications of everyday life (I speak to such issues at greater length
in chapters 3 and 4). Given the specificity of my interest in the everyday—which, if only by force of women's greater participation in "home
work," is feminized—I was happy to be able to spend more time with
the women (who taught me much about Indian cooking, classic Bom-
bay films, the latest *ghazal* singers, and the trials of characters on *General Hospital*).

A few last words are in order about the limits to intersubjective agreement in the search for meaning. The disjunction of self from other always *tends* toward paranoia (even if it does not actually submit to it) in
that the subject's textualized understandings of issues of appearance
and reality, of discursive fragment and social totality, threaten to take
over the object's destiny. Even the presupposition of the impossibility
of an actualized totality—such as a realized postcolonial Indian identity—is often not a sufficient safeguard against the vicissitudes of reifying the field, the object, one's own hermeneutic operations, or all of the
above.

Paul Smith's observations on the paranoid predicament of ethnography shuttling between, as he puts it, "self-affirmation and self-defense"
(the classic symptoms of paranoid subjectivity) have been very instructive in reminding me to put some breaks between what he calls ethnographic or hermeneutic "bad faith" and dialectical claims about the
singularity, however ideological, of cultural explanations.[84] Whether or
not interpretations of events and encounters of the sort I have tried to
construct escape the kind of "claustro[philia]" that Smith finds objec-
tionable in humanist interpretations, is (alas) not for me to say. As he
rightly points out, despite attempts to import the productive insights of
poststructuralist critiques of representation, narrative interpretations
(especially, perhaps, ethnographic ones) teeter back and forth between
a fundamentally unstable world "out there" and a defensively coerced
coherence "in here."[85]

This much admitted, what any interpretive practice is up against is,
of necessity, the gap between what one feels and what can be said. My
own way out of this impasse and into the practical experiences of looking out of my metaphoric tent—to revisit Clifford's image of the ethnographer's circumstances in the field—was simply to assume that the

lament about representation is still only a lament, perhaps with its own paranoid elements. On the very terms offered by Freud's analyses of the paranoiac's imagined mastery of his world (but without necessarily subscribing to its psychopathological delineation), I thought it might still be useful to lay out the mutually constituting closures that my interlocutors and I effected around each other. In at least one respect, ethnographic fictions have the possibility to "overcome" the limits of enclosed narratological readings. Precisely as the paranoid subject, who must willy-nilly look out of her tent and be localized (or risk falling into a decline within), the fieldworker exposes all the distortions that neurotics keep hidden.[86]

CHAPTER TWO
The Antinomies of Everyday Life

What interests the historian of everyday life is the *invisible*.
—PAUL LEUILLIOT, preface to Guy Thuillier, *Pour une histoire du quotidien au XIXe siècle en Nivernais*, as quoted by Michel de Certeau, Luce Giard, and Pierre Mayol

The extent to which a middle-class community fits the designation "the postcolonial subject" makes an exception out of unexceptional lives. My examination of such a community may well invite the disdain often met by "unexotic" sociological inquiry. "The last sad look at the voluntarily damned" was the description Raymond Williams gave to "high" literary theory's view of sociology's mundane preoccupations.[1] But sociological criticism, particularly of the sort that takes its lead from Williams, from the literary sociology of Lucien Goldmann, or from the sociological studies of the Frankfurt school (now discounted because its aesthetic philosophies have assumed greater currency) continues to offer a lot. For Williams, at any rate, a sociological perspective has much to say about the organizing structures of a community and is better able to distinguish between the *trope* of a worldview (the Greek world-picture or the Elizabethan world-picture, for instance) and the *consciousness* of people in actual circumstances. Committed to what could be written off as the "merely" sociological, Williams developed his notion of "structures of feeling" in order to get at the elusive links articulating an "ordinary history of consciousness." Relying heavily on the genetic structuralism of

Goldmann and, more important, on the work of Georg Lukács, his idea of a structure of feeling stresses the tension between "the actual, with its rich but incoherent multiplicity [and] the possible, with its maximum degree of adequacy and coherence."[2]

In this chapter I want to retrace the conceptual trail that leads *back* from Williams's proposal about structures of feeling (a term that has come to serve as a kind of shorthand for understanding experience) to Lukács's complementary though more rigorously specified insights into the incompatibility of consciousness and self-interest in *History and Class Consciousness.* If thinking about postcolonial experience is to be more than "disseminating" otherness (an echo of Homi Bhabha's influential but obfuscatory casting of postcolonial emergence), we must account for why structures of feeling are associated with forms of consciousness, especially perhaps oppositional consciousness.[3] The association reveals a basic confusion whereby experience (of someone or some group, for example) is ritually invoked as substantive evidence for the "truth" and translated into assumptions about self-consciousness or subjectivity. Indeed, experience may lead us to a clearer picture of the truth, but one is not absolved of the responsibility to demonstrate, also, how self-consciousness is limited and limiting.

My task, then, is to derive a theoretical genealogy of the problem of experience. A dialectical critique of postcolonial identity such as I am attempting here cannot really proceed without considering what makes it possible to connect the generality of everyday life with the particularity of postcolonial expression. And the category of experience is at the core of it all: as a "thing-in-itself," an index of consciousness, a closed circuit of interactions and expressions underlying routines of daily life, and, finally, a privileged mode of organizing what would otherwise just be behavioral responses to external stimuli.

In the discussion where he most clearly elaborates what is at stake in structures of feeling, his essay "The Welsh Industrial Novel," Williams makes a case for taking conceptions of the pastoral out of the ambit of literary representation and considering them within an understanding of the sociological and historical constitution of pastoral elements.[4] It bears keeping in mind that Williams clarified the import of structures of feeling—a term that has traveled so influentially within the circuits of cultural theory, in an essay on national/cultural marginality. The Welsh industrial novel emblematizes a kind of fiction in which there is no getting away from social relations (which are also economic ones):

> [I]ndustrial work, and its characteristic places and communities, are not just a new background: a new "setting" for a story. . . . The working society—actual work, actual relations, an actual and visibly altered place—is in the industrial novel central: not because, or not necessarily because, the writer is "more interested in sociology than in people"— which is what a degraded establishment criticism would have us believe—but because in these working communities it is a trivial fantasy to suppose that these general and pressing conditions are for long or even at all separable from the immediate and the personal.[5]

We see Williams advocating a literary sociology in which questions of labor, work, and struggle are fully presupposed in narratives of experience, particularly where that experience stems not from refined ideas about existential consciousness but from exigencies of labor. What is more, Williams suggests with his typical optimism that the hardship of an industrial existence, even as it reveals "what it is like to live in hell," also expresses a nascently positive movement: "[A]s the disorder becomes an habitual order," he dwells on "what it is like to get used to it, to grow up in it, to see it as home."[6]

Of particular interest to me is the way Williams recasts the place of work and labor from being regarded as the entailments of a vulgar and sociologistic Marxism to the stuff of industrial pastoral, so that it becomes difficult if not impossible (at least for the materialist) to separate private ideals of the personal from the realities of *and* settlements with alienation. Structures of feeling represent movements in and out of the social and the fictional: They not only indicate the collective nature of self-understanding but also complicate relations between fictional and experiential constructions. If industrial novels provide glimpses into an alternative consciousness, it is because this alternative already resides in the rhythms of industrial experience even if it is unrealized. Structures of feeling emblematize the ways that collective experience and fictionalized narratives both express a common vocabulary of concerns, constraints, and hopes. Williams, in other words, contemplates his own fictionalizing—or rather, his casting into the novel form—of a pastoral sentiment that he insists resides immanently in Welsh industrial "experience." For him to speak of a structure of feeling is simultaneously to declare the reality of a labor-sublime and to describe, in retrospect, a concept of aesthetic form that has been, in important ways, de-aestheticized. This peculiar double life he ascribes to what is, by all accounts, his most famous coinage points us to the wavering hold we have on the category of "experience" in attempts at postcolonial understanding, where some of this same inarticulate structuring tends to be misconstrued as a subjective invention of "identity" after the fact.

At this point one might ask how Williams's literary-sociological analysis of the industrial novel in Wales has any bearing on the everyday life of middle-class Indian immigrants. The answer lies in a conceptual refinement embedded in the idea of structures of feeling. To wit, although experience does not guarantee the truth, underground motivations, underlying worldviews, and unstated relations find symptomatic release in it. Novels embody a form of this "expressive causality"; they exemplify one mediation of experience, though for me the point is that other practices do so as well. The misleading simplicity of the concept "structure of feeling" belies the contradictoriness of Williams's argument: he emphasizes reality and possibility at the same time as he posits an investment in experience through the highly antagonistic resonances of structure versus feeling. What I find productive is the way Williams rejoins pastoral themes of landscape, place, and labor to the constitution of experience. That said, it must be added that he compacts, even implodes, the tension—or what is more properly thought of as an antinomy—between subjective consciousness and objective conceptualization of self-interest and social character.

It is on the terrain of antinomy that Williams entirely muddies his Lukácsian inheritance. Contemporary cultural theory has usefully retained the specification of structures of feeling, but it has disregarded and often compromisingly reproduced the problems attached to Williams's conceptual conflation of Lukács's theory of experience. As philosophical propositions go, the one about antinomy is quite difficult to grasp, so it is not too surprising that even as astute a reader as Edward Said, in his highly influential excursus "Traveling Theory," should have read Lukács's "astonishingly brilliant account"[7] of classical and bourgeois philosophy as ending up in a methodological trap. Said defends Williams's culturalist recuperation of social experience, which, he says, "always potentially contains space for alternative acts and alternative intentions."[8] The relay of theoretical modifications among Said, Williams, (Goldmann), and

Lukács is posited on the ground that Lukács was trapped within a contradiction that could not reconcile reification with his own insurrectionary theoretical practice:

> For all the brilliance of his account of reification, for all the care he takes with it, Lukács is unable to see how even under capitalism reification itself cannot be totally dominant—unless, of course, he is prepared to allow something that theoretical totality (his insurrectional instrument for overcoming reification) says is impossible, namely, that totality in the form of totally dominant reification is theoretically possible under capitalism. For if reification is totally dominant, how then can Lukács explain his own work as an alternative form of thought under the sway of reification?[9]

We have become accustomed to hearing either that Lukács saw theory as itself the fight against reification (making of him an Althusser *avant la lettre*) or that his theory was incoherent because it could not explain its utterance from within the system of thought he was criticizing. This is to ascribe (wrongly) a scheme of contradiction to him, when in fact he was proposing an explanation of exactly how the "act of consciousness overthrows the objective form of its object."[10] Lukács, that is, operates in the domain of antinomy, not contradiction, which makes it simultaneously possible for reification to objectify thought *and* for thought to reach the point at which "capitalist rationalism becomes irrational" so that "the immediacy of the given [can be] overcome."[11] No methodological trap here, but a conceptual reckoning with the crisis of thought so that it is disallowed from making claims about its independent existential status or on behalf of a totally administered worldview that, to import Said's words, "causes reality to appear to be only a collection of objects and economic *données.*"[12]

It seems to me that the antinomy of thought and experience is still very much a vexed issue. In the next section I should like to reread Lukács on the conceptualization of this antinomy, less as an exegetical indulgence of my own than as an exercise integral to understanding everyday life as a moment of crisis. To take up the relay between Lukács and Said again on this matter, crisis bespeaks both the essence of life under capitalism as well as its fault lines; indeed, we can think of modern existence as fully subsumed by oscillations between one crisis and another, and the ruling rationality as precisely that of "crisis management." However, it is *in* crisis that, as Lukács says, "the qualitative existence of the 'things' that lead their lives beyond the purview of economics as misunderstood and neglected things-in-themselves, as use-values, suddenly becomes the decisive factor."[13] Said appropriates this point about crisis into his humanist vision of the task of criticism: The "one opportunity" for the "mind to know itself as subject and not as a lifeless object" is in "the very act of looking for process behind what appears to be eternally given and objectified.... Crisis, in short, is converted into criticism of the status quo."[14] I want to stress a somewhat different aspect of Lukács's argument: In crisis the "qualitative existence of 'things'" is also thrown into relief so that both reified reality and reified thought can be examined under the same light. If, that is, crisis permits consciousness to become active and take stock of the *données* surrounding it, then there is also pressure exerted in the opposite direction: *from* the contingencies of lived lives *to* self-understanding.

Experience versus Understanding

In order to address the antinomial relationship of thought and experience, it may be useful to remember that the term "antinomy" is defined as an opposition of two principles or a contradiction between two statements, *both apparently obtained by correct reasoning*.[15] In "Reification and the Consciousness of the Proletariat," the logical problem of antinomy is pressed into service by Lukács for understanding both the possibility and form of bourgeois thought (his own included).[16] The riddle of "commodity-structure" is, as he parses Marx, "the central structural problem of capitalist society in all its aspects."[17] Cast in terms of riddle, hieroglyph, mystery, and enchantment, the problem of commodity-structure is not so much that it produces false consciousness (a theoretical conception from an earlier moment in Marx) but that it reveals and conceals, hides as well as exacerbates the true character of social relationships. Despite their sophisticated commentaries, Said and Williams continue to position Lukács within the problematic of false consciousness even though he had worked his way forward into the hieroglyphic complexities of commodity-structure. For Lukács the problem is specific to the "age of modern capitalism," and the question he asks is: "[H]ow far is commodity exchange together with its structural consequences able to influence the *total* outer and inner life of society?"[18]

The immediacy with which forms of capital present themselves "in the minds of people in bourgeois society" as "pure, authentic, unadulterated forms" speaks to the thoroughgoingness with which reification has quantitatively and qualitatively altered social existence. At the same time, the real success of this "enchanted, topsy-turvy world, in which Monsieur Le Capital and Madame La Terre do their ghost-walking" depends on the "divorce of the phenomena of reification" from their economic bases. The result is that subjective shifts effected upon values, relations, and ideas appear to be both qualitatively different and disarticulated from objective consequences of the "split between the worker's labour-power and his personality."[19]

As I read him, Lukács is interested in etiolating Marx's arguments about the mystified nature of the commodity. He moves Marx's emphasis on dead labor to deadened consciousness in order to relink the question of subjectivity to a particular form of historical emergence, that of the bourgeoisie. The turn from the objective category of labor power to the subjective domain of "personality" introduces a vocabulary and a theorization of the subject (for Lukács this is ultimately the proletarian subject). Such a turn keeps faith with the inspiration Marx himself drew from Ludwig Feuerbach's insight into the inverted and abstracted character of religion in life, while proleptically looking toward what Walter Benjamin would later appropriate under "capitalism as religion."[20] In other words, the "phantom objectivity" characterizing the commodity shades both social existence and social thought. The fundamentally relational and contingent aspects of existence and thought—contingent, that is to say, upon the capitalist system—appear with all the clarity of an inverted image in a camera obscura and are taken up with quasi-religious zeal not only in convictions about the autonomy of matters like experience or identity but (and this is important) in the theorization of such matters.

The cunning of history is thus the cunning of capitalism, allusively captured in Lukács's image of the "ghostwalking" of Le Capital and La Terre. If the regime of bourgeois history is also the regime of capital, this would seem to bring up short any claims about the critical impulses of contemporary historical experience (whether it is filtered through categories of subalternity, hybridity, queerness, femininity, or something else). Or, and this is very much at the heart of Lukács's arguments, such histories would have to take on the burden of self-consciously outwitting the cunning of capital, a task not managed by mere position-takings about the subaltern or about oppositional agency. In Lukács's delineation of the project of consciousness, it is specifically the proletariat for whom

> the way is opened to a complete penetration of the forms of reification. It achieves this by starting with what is dialectically the clearest form (the immediate relation of capital and labour). It then relates this to those forms that are more remote from the production process and so includes and comprehends them, too, in the dialectical totality.[21]

Whether or not Lukács's theoretical faith in the historical emergence of the working class has merit is of course an open question (because our understanding of the working class now has to take into account its fragmented constitution across the international division of labor, the dissipation of manufacturing constituencies within labor, the decline of the Eastern Bloc, and finally, the fact that the working class, at least in the United States, has shown little awareness of its revolutionary destiny). But even if we were to forego necessitarian propositions about the working class, Lukács is still extraordinarily relevant for understanding the conjunctural dynamism of capitalism through which "ideology" is mutated into "worldview." For it is undeniable that the seductions of bourgeois life have not succeeded in sublating the difficulties of a social existence in which the threat of unemployment lurks behind all acts of self-making. And this is a threat that acts as the ground beneath everyone. In this sense, anyway, there is no zone of the "beyond," just as in this rendering, consciousness has become crisis-ridden for more than the nominally working-class subject of history.

So perhaps we can begin to imagine a different end for some vexed constituencies who, in a strictly Lukácsian scheme, would be seen as hopelessly caught in the thrall of a "petrified factuality"—insofar as they were bourgeois or petit bourgeois. It is not so much that the burden of reification equally robs the "spiritual" patrimony of those with money and those without, because that has always been the case. Rather, there are objective limits preventing class interests and group ideology from merging into a "worldview" for subjects whose belated entry into bourgeois lifestyles betokens a certain discomfiture, an out-of-sorts-ness with those very lifestyles. Such "nonsynchronousness" (if we want to call it that) has nothing to do with psychic ambivalence, performances of hybridity, and so on; rather, it is more specific to the experience of middle-class subjects who have wagered on the meaning of happiness while knowing that the deck was stacked against them. By rendering "nonsynchronousness" into a matter of positional perspective based on class realities, I am explicitly distancing myself from the line that finds favor these days; namely, the idea that postcolonial subjectivity signifies, or rather, performs, a "temporal split" or "time-lag."[22]

Whatever the utility of this version of thinking about the problem of *Ungleichzeitigkeit* (nonsynchronism or nonsimultaneity), I should like to remain faithful to its original, dialectical formulation in Ernst Bloch's "Nonsynchronism and the Obligation to Its Dialectics" (written in 1932), where he presents it as a blockage (against social mobilization) and not, contra Bhabha et al., as agency.[23] "One has one's times," Bloch avers, "according to where one stands corporeally, *above all in terms of classes.*"[24] Synchronism, in Bloch's view, is far from being the flattened-out temporality of clock and calendar; rather, he contends that it represents the liberation of "the still *possible future* from the *past* . . . by putting both in the present."[25] Bloch's position is consistent with that of Lukács in that the former as much as the latter regarded nonsynchronous beliefs as "nebulae" and as "mirages and picture-puzzles—treasures of a not quite completed past" that kept immiserated middle classes in the grip of an ascetic contemplation of "the unresolved myth of dark old being or of nature."[26]

Self-understanding is thus the stuff of an objective recognition of impeded futures as opposed to subjective if sublime preoccupations with "the care of the self" (to paraphrase Michel Foucault). Taking up this theme from both Bloch and Lukács, Theodor Adorno laid out in a later discussion how affirmations of existential consciousness are haunted by the "need for residences," a quasi-eschatological faith in the "sheltering of Being," and other such ineffabilities. These felt convictions represent the scandal of capitalist existence, which transmutes anxieties over material needs into fixations about subjection and subjectification. As Adorno puts it in *The Jargon of Authenticity,* "He who has not been given a life ticket could in principle be sent away tomorrow."[27] What I have to say in this book has everything to do with the rather banal consequences of the struggle for the "life ticket," which, as Adorno says, makes of "shelteredness"—that is, faith in the homeliness of the self— an existential value and turns it "from something longed for and denied into a presence which is now and here, and which is independent of what prevents it from being."[28]

Thus, to adapt a phrase from Fredric Jameson, identitarianism is the "logic" of late capitalism. Despite its claims to resistance, the proliferation of identity talk represents another form of closure against social transformation and is part and parcel of the reifying processes Lukács described. Bourgeois thought *symptomatizes* the schism produced by and through reification, so that on the one hand, "values, relations and ideas" appear immediate or natural and on the other, the "correctness of thought" (theory) is assumed to be logically a priori while simultaneously subject to the test of whether it is reflected in reality. In the context of contemporary cultural analysis, we might with justfication say that the idealization of identity through the validation of experience is how reified existence thinks itself—in forms of knowledge no less than in accounts of lived experience.

The charge of thinking against the pure enthusiasm of experience on the one hand and the contemplative purity of reflection on the other is one that Lukács fully confronted (pace Said). In fact, such a charge was central to his critique of Kant's philosophy, and it is worth rehearsing the simplicity of his refutation of doubled (or antinomial) thinking: "[R]eality is not, *it becomes*—and to become the participation of thought is needed."[29] In other words, the separation of reality from thought—in thought—expresses the same process of abstraction and inversion whereby the reified individual is alienated from recognizing the "true reality" of being and consciousness, experience and understanding.[30] The "pernicious chasm" of the present depends on this putative unbridgeability of subject and object—a paradigmatic problem of epistemology that Lukács casts as the problem of commodity fetishism in toto—being reduced, or perhaps more appropriately *exhumed*, in terms of the alleged "correctness" of thought or reality.

I do not think it overly polemical to suggest that the Möbius surface of Lukács's theoretical arguments about the inside/outside of bourgeois philosophy remains largely unreconciled within debates about "post-representationalist" theory or "post-Marxist" cultural analysis. Writing more than seventy-five years ago (in 1922), well before the contemporary transformation of the dialectics of negation into what one might call a poststructuralist (and oxymoronic) "dialectics of supplementarity," Lukács insisted upon the nonidentity of thought and existence *not* on account of the operations of language but because the very question of identity or nonidentity is an abstraction and as such is unable to overcome antinomial thinking. There is no escape hatch to the program that requires thought to correspond to existence while demanding their separability as a conceptual matter. To quote Lukács, "[T]hought and existence are not identical in the sense that they 'correspond' to each other, or 'reflect' each other, that they 'run parallel' to each other or 'coincide' with each other (all expressions that conceal a rigid duality). Their identity is that they are aspects of one and the same real historical and dialectical process."[31]

In a manner more convincing than my contentions here can aspire to be, Jameson has written about the ways that antinomial thinking continues to haunt what he calls the "current hegemony" of nominalist and formalist distinctions between identity and difference. As he puts it,

> Identity and Difference are, rather, the realm and the domain of the antinomy as such: something they readily offer to demonstrate by effortlessly turning into one another at the slightest pretext. . . .
> Paradoxes of this kind are not, however, in postmodern discourse, the telltale scandals of anomalies (the failure of a star to correspond infinitesimally [sic] to its predicted trajectory) that used to incite to the rethinking of the paradigm as a whole. Here, rather they provide the bread-and-butter concepts of all of so-called contemporary theory (or theoretical discourse), and offer training in state-of-the-art mental gymnastics.[32]

If experience of the everyday, of one's subjective being, and of the world appears with all the self-evidence of a force of nature, it does not, however, mean (to give the last words on this matter once more to Lukács) that having "unmasked the fiction of its rigid reification," we are any closer to being able to "annul the 'reality' of this fiction in capitalist society."[33] Any such annulment is the grounds for dialectics—a "practical theory" that would overturn the real world; to reverse, in effect, the reversal that reification engendered in the first place. The possibility of transformative thought, then, is not merely formal, just as experience is not simply reducible either to a hardened factual realm or to an infinitely self-generating subjective "construction."

For the purposes of this study, the question of identity relates to speculating about a different, even extreme, moment in the hierarchy of bourgeois culture. It has to do with the "tendency" latent in the experiences of middle-class postcolonial immigrants consistently threatened by a lapse into proletarianization yet anxious to secure their "rightful" place in the mainstream of U.S. social life. Though obviously not the constituency for a "proletarian dialectics" foreseen by Lukács, these minoritized subjects are belated entrants into the theater of Le Capital and La Terre, and their objective circumstances of living are shot through with contradictions. These contradictions have not occasioned in them an *effectively* oppositional consciousness, although they do bear witness to the quotidian ambiguities preventing consciousness from becoming agency. We are once more reminded that neither as a doxalogical verity nor from any voluntarist affirmation does "difference" produce social agency. The positional tenuousness of this particular community—the fact that its members are middle class in temperament, aspirations, and earnings yet are unassimilated into the dominant culture's sense of the ideological givenness of a way of life understood to be "American"— has, instead, produced a peculiar sensibility (which I referred to in the introduction as a "morbid symptom"). Despite being cognizant of its alienation and perhaps even because of it, the group attempts to anchor itself via narratives of economic redemption while constantly betraying the anxiety of tenure (in more than an academic sense of the word). "Last man in, first man out." So to undertake a consideration of the terrain on which difference is played out in scenarios of the everyday is to theorize the crisis of self-representation as internal to the constitution of materialist critique—a marking of limits.

"What interests the historian of everyday life is the invisible." This statement, which also serves as the epigraph for this chapter, returns us to a specific consideration of how narratives of the everyday function and why, as structures of feeling, they represent the determinate conditions of postcolonial experience. Whether these conditions can provide the terms for a general accounting of *the* postcolonial experience is, frankly, beside the point, since from a dialectical perspective any general theory can only be adequated through concretion. However, to say that the historian of the everyday is interested in "the invisible" is to signal two things: first, that everyday life serves as the largely invisible backdrop against which more reflective acts of narration and poeisis are read. It is therefore often ignored as, literally, a poetic practice on its own. Second, and more pointedly, the quotidian is secretive; not in the sense that its practical rituals or routines have to be ferreted out (though this is true enough) but in that it is the "underground" place where subjective understandings are diverted when they are blocked off from being expressed otherwise.

To take this most literally, let us pause to think about what happens when the old-world subjects of my new-world ethnographic community arrive at the doorstep of their dream locales, the land of opportunity—what we, echoing a phrase from Lukács, might term the theater of capital and the world. From the moment of their physical landing in the United States—in most people's memories, this involved stepping into the high-tech chaos of John F. Kennedy (JFK) Airport in New York City—there is a disorientation that is both literal and figurative. Only somewhat dulled by time, the memory of an eighteen-hour flight from the "homeland," combined with the scheduling vagaries of international air travel (usually involving delays and layovers), is rendered into an aerial rite of passage, a liminal experience of extreme proportions.

At the time I was conducting the ethnography, one of my informants recalled his first flight to this country. After finally arriving, he had fallen into an exhausted sleep during the cab ride from JFK Airport; when he woke up he glimpsed signs for places like New Holland and Berlin flash by as he was carried along the New Jersey Turnpike. Wondering how he could have so thoroughly confused his destination as to end up in what the signposts indicated was Europe, he decided to give himself up to his sense of fatalism and to "the mercy of Lord Rama." He reckoned that he was simply not cut out for the United States, having proved incapable of even getting there, although in prior months he had tackled all obstacles and acquired, against expectation, a green card. Anyone who has withstood the process of getting a green card—fingerprinting, police reports, blood tests, medical screenings, legal affidavits on one's financial status, marriage certification, pledges of allegiance, the Test of English as a Foreign Language, avowals of noninvolvement with communist ideas, proof of employability, and attestations of the lack of intention to overthrow the U.S. government by force or fraud—knows that naturalization is hard won. And for some reason, it is required that the right ear of the newly naturalized subject be visible in the identifying photograph embossed on the green card. In Georges Bataille's ruminations on the meaning of Vincent van Gogh's severed ear, we are told that the very intelligibility of van Gogh's paintings (particularly those known as the Sun paintings) depended upon the excess produced by the signification "Man with the Severed Ear."[34] If van Gogh's missing ear thus circulates as the mark of his artistic genius, then we might well say that the immigrant's ear, readily apparent in every green card photograph, signifies the excesses of the entire process of naturalization—such that the image of an ear comes in to designate the subject's reality and legitimacy.

The delirium of dislocation notwithstanding, there is a seductiveness, even a utopian quality to everyday life's initial offerings to the immigrant. The fantasy is of a new beginning, of a different place, and of possibilities attached to the narrative of self-betterment and personal success. It is the other side of reification, as it were, because the moment of arrival is one in which the "outer" world has not yet collapsed into the "inner," the obviousness of *this* way of life has not yet been secured. Everyday life in the new world is suffused with an aura: the "unique phenomenon of a distance" (to quote Benjamin's description of it) linking past to present and present to the future. So it is that the reified experiences of daily life are where the "fantasy bribe" of an alternative reality or a different future is proffered and accepted.[35] Louis Marin has elsewhere analyzed impoverished imaginations of the future (drawn completely from within the image repertoire of consumerism—to be found, for example, in the production of Disneyland) in terms of "degenerate utopias." Nonetheless, the utopian dimension exists as the spark, to be doused for sure, of a self-knowledge that gives the lie to the deracinating aspects of the everyday.[36]

A degenerate utopia: This is how we might think of the everyday, with all the antinomial force of that utterance. I take my cue here from Marin's coinage and, more particularly, from Jameson's adaptations of it in his "Reification and Utopia in Mass Culture."[37] In that early venue, Jameson argued on behalf of the utopian impulses of mass culture, saying that even degraded mass cultural texts exhibit a certain tension between anxiety and hope, without which they simply would not get the job done of legitimating the existing social order. The fantasy bribe, in other words, must be offered if anxiety about the meaning of life is to be managed in the realm of culture and for capitalist interests. Moreover, the fantasy bribe must be lived out as fantasy rather than as bribe or corrupt currency so that the implacable aspects of a means-ends calculation appear seamless, natural, and, indeed, outside of any calculation. Making his case with reference to works of mass culture, Jameson sought to extend our understanding of reification to show how, under the "universal exchange value of money, . . . the quality of the various forms of human activity, their unique and distinct 'ends' or values, has been effectively bracketted or suspended by the market system, leaving all these activities free to be ruthlesly reorganized in efficiency terms, *as sheer means or instrumentality.*"[38]

If by dint of such instrumentality, we regard everyday life as one such form of human activity (along with other products of culture) now re-organized and commodified, it follows that utopian sentiments, however inchoate and hampered, cut across the reification of everyday experience. Again, this is not to argue for the view that the everyday is irrepressibly oppositional, even for a community whose positioning within the social fabric is at best awkward and at worst alienated. Rather, the point is to follow through on the implications of what Jameson (or, for that matter, Lukács or Marx) has to teach us about a "quasi-materiality" or a "feeling tone" of daily practices caught within instrumental imperatives of identitarianism and self-interest on the one hand and longings for a form of freedom not for sale amid the blandishments of acquisition or consumption on the other. That, at least, has been my intention in considering the antinomy of experience, one that forces us to reckon with a discredited everydayness without canceling the possibility of utopian imaginings of a collectivity somehow closer to and continuous with (if only as a fantasy) a preimmigrant past.

In the concluding section of this chapter, I want to connect my discussion of consciousness and the everyday with a narrative on how the problem of experience has been formulated within a critical history of ideas. Two citations throw into relief the problems in theorizing experience and, by the same token, the necessity of doing so. The first citation is from Henri Lefebvre's *Introduction to Modernity*. In the opening lines he says: "With or without dignity, sumptuous or slovenly, in plush or in tatters, more and more brutal, more rapid, more noisy, the modern world marches on. How very pompous—or whimsical—of anyone to require something precise, such as definitions or theories: concepts."[39] These words seem obvious; nevertheless, the problematic of everyday life invites us to *work through* obviousness. For with obviousness we are firmly on the terrain of the ideological or that which goes in the name of "common sense." The rush to make claims about abstract issues of modernity, subjectivity, or postcoloniality (to name a few of the most fashionable theoretical desires) has sometimes left behind its intended object, with the result that everything on the way to theorizing is taken for granted in the quest for the unacknowledged "end" that is theorizing itself, usually (and paradoxically) accompanied by dismissive rebukes against "teleology."

Lefebvre is, as we know, among the most influential commentators on the everyday, and he belongs to a generation of critics who did not sacrifice conceptual clarity at the altar of signs taken for wonders.[40] His comments here are an acerbic reflection on the ways that the oppositional force of everyday life is asserted and on the ease with which demands for rigor are written off. Contemporary cultural criticism often betrays the assumption that unlike, say, art or aesthetics, the category of the everyday is self-evident; this is particularly true of approaches that see themselves as intervening "from below." As an example of this problematic assumption, let me turn to the second citation, from Paul Willis's study of youth cultures and symbolic creativity:

> [N]ecessary symbolic work is spread across the whole of life. It is a condition of it, and of our daily humanity. Those who stress the separateness, the sublime and quintessential in "art" have actually assumed a mindlessly vulgar materialist view of everyday life. They counterpose this to their view of "the imaginative." They thereby view daily life as a cultural desert. The imagined symbolic deficit of everyday life is then, in its turn, to be repaired by recourse to a free-floating "imaginative realm," to "useless things," to "art for art's sake," to the "socially redundant." But this is not only circular, it's incoherent. It's like trying to make time go faster by speeding up clocks. "Art" is taken as the *only* field of qualitative symbolic activity, the one-per-cent transcendental value that preserves humanity. . . . We insist, against this, that imagination is not extra to daily life, something to be supplied from disembodied "art." It is part of the necessariness of everyday symbolic and communicative work.[41]

While it is certainly true that imaginative or symbolic work cannot be set off from the rest of daily life *except as a category mistake* (such as breaking a thermometer in weather that is too hot or speeding up a clock to make time pass quickly), conceptual distinctions between "art" and "life" are not erased merely through insistence. The elitist idealism of holding up "art" as a category of abstract contemplation is, in Willis's account, supplanted by an equally idealistic voluntarism surrounding the elevation of the "creative symbolic elements of ordinary life."[42] The point is that symbols (whether they are designated as art or otherwise) do not tell us much about the relay between their signification and usage. Consequently, the reified nature of everyday life in the modern world is not addressed simply by declaring, for instance, that "[f]ar from being the passive victim of commercialism's juggernaut, the consumer has progressively been recognized as having substantial and unpredictable decision-making power in the selection and use of cultural commodities."[43] If wishful thinking is not allowed to replace critique, the penetration of what one experiences as choice or decision making in one's lifestyle—by the ideology as opposed to the actuality of freedom—must itself be seen as a chief victory of embourgeoisement. The division of the quotidian into work and leisure, so that the work of consumption appears to be separated from the work of work (the scheme of life implied by Willis), actually permits the projections of modern experience in terms of mutually sustaining illusions about public and private selves. So if we regard ensembles of postcoloniality as being articulated in contests between differences of race, culture, or language on the one hand and demands of material existence on the other, then the illusory coherence of the self papers over the ways that the experience of racial or cultural difference demarcates *not* the truth or reality of one's life but, rather, its mystifications.

To say this is to repeat the substance of much of what I have so far argued. Alienation—whether felt or lived through racial-cultural understandings on the one hand or class constraints on the other—necessarily mystifies issues of class, race, and culture, so that perception of one's "objective" situation is confounded by the age-old inversion of appearance *(Schein)* and reality *(Wirklichkeit)* familiar from the history of materialism. In the self-understandings of the middle-class community at issue, such mystification takes the following form: "Being Indian has prevented me from getting ahead in my company" (whereby a racialized narrative is ushered in to account for the "barriers to entry" on which capitalism depends). We might remember Stuart Hall's apt phrase from the 1970s that "race is the modality in which class is lived"—a phrase that updates Marx's crucial insight into reification and the reversals entailed in the ideological taking up of metaphysical "truths" (of god, man, racial identity, or experience).

An explication of what constitutes everyday experience might at best seem whimsical in the way Lefebvre suggests. At worst, it may appear to be another distraction from "getting down to the business of describing the stuff of real life." But it is also the untranscendable condition of thinking dialectically about reification, since the category "experience" is at once dense and transparent. Every one of us leads a life filled with what we easily recognize as experiences—at times unique, more often routine. Through it all, the *fact* of experience is apparently easy to grasp even if its value is less intelligible. This is where the fact/value dichotomy begins to exert its first, most troublesome pressure. How does one separate the misleadingly obvious signification of experience from the imprint of ideology (with or without a capital I, à la Louis Althusser)? In one of his sustained attacks on postmodern cultural criticism (of which I take the above example from Willis to be an unexceptional variant), Terry Eagleton referred to the ways that the problem of value is erased through a "simple conflation: fact *is* value."[44]

Attempting to avoid such a conflation of my own and in the manner of someone forced to retrace well-worn paths, I turned to Hans-Georg Gadamer's reflections in *Truth and Method* for some conceptual help on the question of experience.[45] Sometimes written off as difficult or old-fashioned, Gadamer is much more accessible and humorous (even in translation) than one might expect. The decline in the disciplinary fortunes of *Lebensphilosophie* (outside Weberian sociology) and a corresponding boom in the post–World War II analytic frameworks of poststructuralism have resulted in the neglect, within critical theory, of Gadamer's work. The following remarks are intended to suggest that his ideas may still be useful for rethinking issues of experience and consciousness.

Gadamer makes clear that the concept of experience *(Erlebnis)* is of relatively recent provenance, although the practical designation of experiencing something—condensed in the verb *erleben*—is of older vintage. Only in the 1870s does the noun form become common, although it first appears in one of Hegel's letters.[46] In a sense, the conceptualization of experience as a modality of existence represents, as does Hegel himself, a watershed mark of the normatively modern in its self-consciousness and (as Lefebvre also asserts in his theses on modernity) in its bid for reflective knowledge. Gadamer glosses the term's secondary derivation from the verb form (extant since Goethe's times) accordingly:

> Erleben means primarily *"to be still alive when something happens."*
> Thus the word suggests the immediacy with which something real is
> grasped—unlike something which one presumes to know but which is

unattested by one's own experience, whether because it is taken over from others or comes from hearsay, or whether it is inferred, surmised, or imagined. What is experienced is always what one has experienced oneself.[47]

The form *"das Erlebte,"* Gadamer avers, is also used to signify "the permanent content of what is experienced." The German coinage *Erlebnis* thus reflects the doubled character of the concept of experience: as the bare necessity of sentience (which is phenomenally transient) and as a more lasting condensation of what happens collectively under its sign. I take from Gadamer's genealogical refinements that, insofar as the history of the concept reflects particular preoccupations of Western phenomenology, the privileging of experience as a category of both sentient knowledge and representational value appears as a belatedly modern concern.

Let me be at pains to stress that by allotting this space to the linguistic development of German ideas about experience I do not wish to attach some epistemological primacy to European conceptual thought or feeling. On the contrary. My purpose is to draw attention to the predicament of theory and, as far as the problematic of experience goes, its historically delimited evolution. To the extent that German linguistic forms reflect the historical concerns of broadly European, specifically Germanic thought, the concepts and constructions we now presuppose to be objectively generated by an interest in the question of subjectivity reveal not only their own situated character but also the limits inevitably imposed on forms of theory that must think through and across "the West."[48] As with Williams, who, we gleaned earlier, was spurred on to a critical consciousness by a felt conviction about his national and cultural marginality, German thinkers from the nineteenth-century onwards wrestled with the issue of their own historical belatedness. So any presumption of the coherence or imputed superiority of European thought is disturbed if we only look past the edifice of the "system"—a looking past that also enables a looking beyond to the circumstances of our own thinking while slaying the dragons of historicism and universalism.

With such retrospection in mind, we can see that situated constraints often serve as spurs to historical and personal emergence. Hannah Arendt makes a similar case in her introduction to Benjamin's *Illuminations*.[49] There, the constitutive problem of presenting a culture and experience in translation—on terms whose force stems from alien domains of thought—is clarified with reference to Franz Kafka and the difficulties of interwar German-Jewish intellectual production. Remarking on the parallel between Kafka and Benjamin (which the latter himself felt very keenly), Arendt suggests that both were caught in a dominant cultural system within Germanized Europe whose anti-Semitism continually undermined the very possibility of their existence. *At the same time,* they were alienated from an assimilated Jewish society that remained antipathetic to any discussion either of its own prejudices or of those against it. Kafka described the situation as characterized by a threefold "impossibility": the "impossibility of not writing; ... the impossibility of writing in German; ... and finally, the impossibility of writing differently." Arendt quotes Kafka as concluding that "[o]ne could almost add a fourth impossibility ... the impossibility of writing."[50] In the introduction to *Illuminations* that serves as a latter-day postscript to this discussion, Arendt proposes that the contingencies of Benjamin's or Kafka's location exemplify the fraughtness suspending their production both as subjective beings and as writers, since under the conditions they inhabited, writing could only be seen as a "moratorium."

Paradoxically, then, the appropriation of a language or a system of thought "not acquired but stolen," as Kafka put it, from one's oppressors was (and remains) the enabling condition of continued thinking and existence. Such are the parables and the predicament of writing in the shadow of "the West," "in German," "against empire," and so on. They are perhaps instructive in bringing together the many incommensurabilities of experience—from its abstract and even alienating conceptual provenance to its myriad unfoldings in the practices of everyday life. Benjamin's or Kafka's case signals the impossibility of avoiding discourses that bear the ideological as well as linguistic baggage of Eurocentric and imperial systems (though one is charged with having to distinguish between the differing resonances and histories of English and German in different places).

We might say that the assimilation-alienation dialectic that provoked Benjamin and Kafka throws light on the formal possibilities and constraints of carrying on in an alienated tongue, be it the German of marginalized Jews or the English of immigrant Indians. Their example also establishes that domains of experience are where provisional resolutions to differences between conceptual alienation and felt convictions are effected every day. Sites of experience help to disarticulate the messy tangle of transience, between what is strictly phenomenal *(Erlebnis)* and that which represents continuity, or *Erfahrung* (which, because it has no adequate equivalent in English, can only be approximated as something akin to the mnemonic traces of past tradition in present experience).[51]

The expressivity of daily life betokens the myriad detours between alienation and critical consciousness. Benjamin and Kafka are historical exemplars of how alienation has the potential to produce transformative thought and engender peculiarly critical sensibilities. But we are inescapably witness to the evidence that we, like most others, cannot transcend the conditions of our own existence—in thought or even in our desires. The very exemplarity of a Benjamin, as well as his ability to look beyond his own phenomenal circumstances, indicate how much of our own alienation is obscured by the seductions of everyday life.[52] This is to say that the imagination is no more exempt from reification than any other process of consciousness. The agonistic sensitivity of Benjamin, whom Arendt called a mind that was sui generis, testifies to the material and discursive blockages preventing the transformation of consciousness in *less* exemplary subjects, whose thinking founders where it encounters the logic of capital.

My point in adducing Benjamin, apart from borrowing his insight into the distinction between experience-as-stimulus *(Erlebnis)* and experience-as-expressive-form *(Erfahrung),* is to underscore the difficulty in making comparisons between a critical consciousness such as his and the self-understanding of ordinary folks. Benjamin's common sense was most uncommon; it instructs by way of revealing its "meta" constitution, a theorized experience already apart from the ideological or from that which happens "while one is still alive" (to echo Gadamer from earlier in this discussion). If Benjamin offers us a "science" of experience through his own example, his is a privileged perspective on ideology *not* accessible to the man on the street caught in its machine.

I want to conclude this discussion by retying the strands separating partial from privileged perspectives and resituating my attempt to theorize the problem of experience within its banal and even deadening location: daily life in the suburbs of New Jersey. What we face is not the panorama of conventional possibilities of pleasure, desire, and happiness but the shock of a landscape constructed entirely out of interior and exterior resettlements, out of rearrangements of inner and outer disorder into placidly familiar places and practices. Out of these displacements from an old world and older habits grow experiential convictions about the ordering of self and home.

The home itself becomes hypostatized as the last refuge of individual and collective fantasies. Narratives of self-enhancement, individual success, and community standing are all mapped onto the space of the home; life is set out on the walls, or *bios* graphed, to use Benjamin's characterization in "A Berlin Childhood," in which he also produces the luminous image of "the prosaic rooms of our...understanding."[53] The consolidation of an identity in and through the annals of home takes on a representative as well as an exceptional function, particularly since both terms ("home" and "identity") are shot through with specifically conjunctural anxieties about belonging and not belonging. The home is where one most emphatically belongs, if only because one's status elsewhere in U.S. society and within mainstream circuits of cultural representation is highly troubled. (One only needs to think of the character Apu in the putatively "alternative" social vision of the television show *The Simpsons* to recognize, again, the problematic coding of ethnic difference whereby a sophisticated critique of corporate America runs into unsophisticated parochialisms about English accents, Indians as petit bourgeois owners of convenience stores, and the cravenness of social customs from "over there.")

In the chapters that follow I will explore the specificities of the desire and the internal tension embodied in claims to identity, here an Indianness, solidified through the comforting, even if by no means convenient, rituals of daily experience. So let me end this discussion by recalling its beginning, which drew attention to Williams's evocative depiction of Welsh experience and the literal and metaphoric ground under it: the realities of industrial life. To avoid overly semanticizing what Williams in that discussion refers to as "accents of fidelity," one must be attentive to what one might call the discursivity of the economic itself.[54] I am thus led by Williams's focus on the interior "landscape" of laboring communities, by his insights into how a "whole way of life" might be construed accurately and even paradigmatically as a way of labor. For if there is anything definitive to be said about the Indian diaspora (middle class or otherwise), it is that diasporic identities are subvented by the relationship to modes of work. In my ethnographic example, who one is, where one lives, how one relates to the world or to the past, and indeed, why one puts up with the intractabilities of an immigrant existence are all played out in the setting of another industrial pastoral, this one cobbled together no less from the chrome and concrete of the southern New Jersey landscape than from the sandalwood and brass of domestic arrangements.

CHAPTER THREE

Personal Memory and the Contradictions of Selfhood

> Language shows clearly that memory is not an instrument for exploring the past but its theater.
>
> —WALTER BENJAMIN, "Berlin Chronicle"

"Would you like to hear *Songs to Remember from Indian Films,* the *Evergreen Hits of Mohammed Rafi,* or *Haunting Melodies by Lata Mangeshkar*"? This was the question with which my hostess greeted me as I entered one of the Indian households participating in my ethnographic arrangements. My arrival was a prearranged affair, and after some initial indecision, we decided that Lata's lilting, female voice would be the least intrusive accompaniment to our proposed conversation. Earlier in the week, I had spent an evening querying the past with my hostess's husband and a few other men from the community. At that time she promised me an afternoon meal if I were to return for her recollections of the past. We both wanted a relaxed opportunity to talk about the matter of memory, and here it was—an event "haunted" by the melodies of popular music from Indian films of the 1950s and '60s. Not that such haunting marked itself as a framing device for what was said that afternoon; rather, my point in commencing this discussion with reference to it is to underscore the sense of belatedness made apparent by our choice of music. Reiterative appearances of forms of lateness in daily life that can only be described as a "nostalgia for the future" shape the sensibilities of the postcolonial immigrants under scrutiny in this book.

My contention is that nostalgia in the form of active investments in, for example, a bygone era of popular music, replayings of old Hindi films on videotape, or reinventions of presumed ideals of the past does not simply embody a reactive and reactionary disposition. That it may do so as well is evident in any search for a lost time or golden age. But such nostalgia also bespeaks a certain futurity and a desire for what is not yet possible.[1]

In this chapter I examine how memories of the past provide a crucial discursive terrain for reconsolidating ideals of selfhood.[2] I take as my point of departure the argument made by Peter Stallybrass and Allon White that divisions and discriminations governing the separation of self/other and us/them are premised on corollary demarcations between high and low, public and private, as well as history and memory.[3] Thus, rethinking the self/other problematic requires paying close attention to these attendant demarcations in the domains of daily life. Stallybrass and White further suggest that discriminations in the symbolic domain are structured and legitimated with reference to four sets of discursive hierarchies: psychic forms, the human body, geographical space, and the social order. According to them, "[c]ultures 'think themselves' in the most immediate and affective ways through the combined symbolisms of these four hierarchies."[4] They also remind us that symbolic categories are never entirely separable and, in fact, are enforced through a logic of transgression.

By the terms of this logic, if the terrain of memory is integral to our understanding of psychic forms and the unconscious dimensions of subjectivity, it also exceeds its own categorization, signaling its slippage into other sites of experience connected to the refiguration of selfhood. So, to say a bit more about the paradoxical construct of a nostalgia directed toward the future, we might think of it as a relay between a private discourse of memory and public discourses of social presence and cultural identity. Whatever is or is not available or imaginable is thematized in the wake of the past, either as a repetition of something lost or as a repetition that throws its own antecedents into doubt. Moreover, what was unavailable in the past or is unrealizable in the present represents the stuff of the future. To adapt Walter Benjamin's unsurpassed insights in "The Image of Proust," memory is a symbolic world like the Christmas stocking, which is a bag and a present at the same time; rolled up, it can spark dreams about the known past as well as the unknown future.[5] Unrolled, it is, as Howard Caygill elaborates Benjamin's theory of experience, just another household item: a sock.[6]

Benjamin also reminds us that "an experienced event is finite—at any rate, confined to one sphere of experience; a remembered event is infinite, because it is only a key to everything that happened before it and after it." The point here is that the infinite exists in memory, and for that reason, memory cannot be the preserve of the particular. Benjamin goes on to describe the moment of personal reflection: "We might almost call it *an everyday hour;* it comes with the night, a lost twittering of birds, or a breath drawn at the sill of an open window."[7] The ground of memory, Benjamin avers, is therefore unexceptional: "[A]ll lives, works, and deeds that matter were never anything but the most undisturbed unfolding of the most banal, most fleeting, most sentimental, weakest hour in the life of the one to whom they pertain."[8] Actually, Benjamin casts the preceding utterance as a question: "Can we say [this]?" I wish to propose an answer in the affirmative—to which the only coda is that, as a matter of the sociology of knowledge, such universality has not been extended to those subjects who, like ritual objects, have remained "auratic" on account of their perceived alterity.

The realization that *le temps perdu* constitutes everyone's consciousness in the present and does not just represent the agon of Western forms of expressivity leads us to a corollary recognition that despite the tremendously varied enterprise of representing experience and subjecthood in the *post* (however conceived), the redrawing of narrative boundaries of subject constitution still manages to position the other in an alteristic relationship to a dominant self. This seems to be true whether the relationship is characterized in terms of colonizer/colonized, West/non-West, global/local, or yet a different construction of spatiotemporally distanced consciousness.[9] Yes, the other exists, but somehow only as a narrative genre or as the endlessly deferred product of signifying processes: a Gibreel Farishta of Salman Rushdie's rendering, an acutely ambivalent figure in a Hanif Kureishi film, or an ethnographic invention of the voice of a !Kung/Kwaio/Kaluli/generic subaltern. It is all too evident that chants of reflexivity notwithstanding, many experimental modes of ethnographic representation continue to locate the other in a distant place and reduce her voice to a metaphoric turn.[10] Instead, I hope to examine the inscription of a contingent form of otherness in the practical aspects of remembering the past and in everyday exigencies of being in the world.

The following discussion attempts to pick up on the unexceptional proposition that recollections of the past serve as an active ideological terrain on which people represent themselves to themselves. But the past's resonance acquires a more marked salience with subjects for whom categories of the present have been made unusually unstable or unpredictable. In the case of my ethnographic informants, the dislocations of postcoloniality have meant that the present produces repeated encounters with uncanny and alienating circumstances. For instance, an inherited ethic of collective well-being runs up against its newly available counterpart of personal happiness; likewise, a firmly embedded consciousness about caste has to reckon with an entirely different value system based on class in its economic determinations; and ideals of social intimacy conflict with the wide belief among community members that in this country one cannot be intimate, except sexually. It appears to them that the very notion of identity is here caught up in contradictions of sexuality (which some of my critically minded interlocutors regarded as the fault of an overinvestment in psychotherapy). As I suggested in the introduction, habits and convictions that derive from a "grammar" of being that is different from mainstream cultural mores seem anomalous. As a result, the process of shoring up the present requires it to be squared with reference to an assimilated if disjointed narrative of the past in which references to official narratives about colonization and a historical memory are tangled up with private acts of rememoration. Such is the state of exception binding *bios* to *cosmos*.

How does biography become history? Or, to put this another way, what is the relationship of everyday memory to a historical sense of the self? The beginnings of some answers can be found in Antonio Gramsci's writings on the quotidian and worldly bases of philosophy. Gramsci saw everyday subjectivity as constructed out of a sediment of understandings about the ways that the past permanently marks the present. He proposed that the "strangely composite" *(mode bizarre)* nature of the personality contains "prejudices from all past phases of history at the local level [as well as] intuitions of a future philosophy."[11] Present experience is illuminated by this "common sense," and thus the task of a philosophy of the quotidian is to unravel this prereflexive narrative that has "deposited . . . an infinity of traces, without leaving an inventory."[12]

Gramsci's ideas have been productively followed up in the work of the Popular Memory Group on oral history and the production of historical knowledge.[13] The group argues that subordinated and private memories can only be amplified in the context of dominant historical representations in the public field. On the question of the construction of common sense, it proposes that

> [p]rivate memories cannot, in concrete studies, be readily unscrambled from the effects of dominant historical discourses. It is often these that supply the very terms by which a private history is thought through. Memories of the past are, like all common-sense forms, strangely composite constructions, resembling a kind of geology, the selective sedimentation of past traces. . . . Similarly the public discourses live off the primary recording of events in the course of everyday transactions and take over the practical knowledges of historical agents.[14]

We might say this line of thought links Gramsci to Benjamin. The two share the premise that the past, an absolutely vital element in the negotiation of identity, is made up of a renovated and selectively appropriated set of memories set against a larger backdrop of public events. The leakiness of the category of individual history and the seepage of public and private, past and present, all attest to the contaminations of temporality, ideology, and selfhood. In the context of this inquiry, understandings about what constitutes Indianness are referred without any real historical basis to ideologies of ethnicity prevalent in the United States, just as narratives of immigrant life are constructed against belated and not altogether consistent notions about the value of individualism. Even as immigrant subjects take on individualistic investments, their interpellation into this most basic of capital's values is pressured by a prior form of social being in which a communally embedded identity made more sense. Immigrant life becomes the ground on which contrapuntal relationships among temporal, cultural, and economic imperatives of identity are worked out even as psychic uncertainties produced by a specific history of colonization are worked through.

The most elementary level of such a parasubjective matrix of "working through" reveals that the authority of the past depends on subjective understandings of the present and vice versa. Consequently, the stories people tell about their pasts have more to do with shoring up an interiorized self-understanding than with historical truths. This relational character of memory revealed itself during my ethnographic encounters. The personal remembrances of my ethnographic subjects reveal a past-present relation that is continually dynamic and at the same time eminently contradictory. If the Indian community's present is heavily laced with the past, it betokens a Freudian generality about retroactive (nachträglich) mechanisms of self-understanding that pressure consciousness tout court. But in addition, for these particular people memories have taken on a special import because they represent the only set of discursive understandings that can be appropriated and fixed. Disambiguating the past permits people to make sense of uncertainties in the present, and the tendency of my informants was to repress at least one set of uncertainties by rendering the past in coherent, unequivocal, and undoubtedly artificial ways.

As I have suggested both above and in my discussion of reification in chapter 2, a self reminted in the United States and within the terms of a Western logic of embourgeoisement is riddled with all the contradictions of reified existence. One specific example is the way that constraints against social mobility and the perceived glass ceiling of corporate management structures are often thematized in terms of a new brand of casteism. An anxiety specifically produced by capitalism is assuaged by being displaced onto received ideas about the inevitability of caste discrimination; here it is the glass ceiling, "back home" it was the accident of birth. But of course glass ceilings and the limits of caste are not fungible values, and their forced translation into one another induces a further displacement within forms of self-management. This latter displacement has to do with disavowing any sense of a civic consciousness, any recognition of what it means—as an issue of public inclusion or exclusion— to live in a racially demarcated society where social privilege ultimately accrues to a white, moneyed elite. So instead of becoming more socially conscious or coalition-minded, immigrant Indian communities tend to live in segregated enclaves. My southern New Jersey example is no exception. Within these enclaves and particularly when money (which my interlocutors have), rather than cultural capital (which they do not), is no cause for concern, an interiorized discourse of self-empowerment and personal improvement can be given free rein.

In Michel de Certeau's terms, "the annals of everyday life" are scripted almost exclusively through the setting of the home because, as he says, it is where one learns and replays the lessons of how to "behave," to be "proper," and to be. "Here one invites one's friends and neighbors and avoids one's enemies or boss, as long as the society's power respects the fragile symbolic barrier between public and private, between an obliged sociality imposed by the authorities and elective conviviality regulated by individuals."[15] Home is the comfort zone of the self, though it must be said that Certeau's emphasis on its protections downplays the complementary disturbances that haunt the private spaces of the home. We might add that home is also the place where expatriate anxieties are vented and where boundaries are drawn up between insider and outsider, between *apna* (one's own) and *pariah* (both stranger and outcast—a word with differentiated roots in Hindi and Tamil now incorporated into the everyday English lexicon).

While the larger cultural canvas portraying the "diversity" of U.S. identities bespeaks a certain discomort with its South Asian minorities on account of their funny accents, weird costumes, and smelly food, expatriate Indians are in return resistant to the idea of assimilation. Of course, now that U.S. palates have learned to recognize Indian cuisine (largely in the form of that phantom known as "curry"), yet another ingredient of difference has melted into the multicultural stew. Still, for the most part, expatriate Indians do not express their deepest cultural insecurities and investments to those whom *they* view as others. Even as the inherent form of the dominant social order takes for granted *its* notion of center and margin, of self and other, this ordering is inverted within the internal calculus of subordinated groups. Stallybrass and White are once more useful for thinking about the limits and possibilities of such strategies of hierarchy inversion:

> When we talk of high discourses—literature, philosophy, statecraft, the languages of the Church and the University—and contrast them to the low discourses of a peasantry, the urban poor, subcultures, marginals, the lumpenproletariat, colonized peoples, we already have two "highs" and two "lows." History seen from above and history seen from below are irreducibly different and they consequently impose radically different perspectives on the question of hierarchy.
>
> Indeed they may and often do possess quite different symbolic hierarchies but because the higher discourses are normally associated with the most powerful socio-economic groups existing at the centre of cultural power, it is they which generally gain the authority to designate what is to be taken as high and low in the society.[16]

Closing the door to outsiders and refusing the dominant culture's attempts to adjudicate the propriety of the present in terms of taste, habits,
social and gender relations, and so on—all the ineffabilities gathered
up under a presumptive sense of Indianness—operate as the ground
for thematizing how one belongs to the past and how the past belongs
to the future.

Given that there are more than a thousand South Asian immigrant
families in southern New Jersey alone, this is not a milieu in which everybody knows everyone else and everyone gets together in the same location.[17] During the two years of my fieldwork, I participated (and I continue to do so, albeit less directly) in a network of a dozen families, all
of whom fit the norm of middle-class Indian immigration to this country. Of this set, two families hailed from Karnataka, and one each came
from Gujarat and Uttar Pradesh. The couples in two other families represent intermarriages—in each case the wife is Bengali, the husbands
are from Karnataka and Banaras (in Uttar Pradesh) respectively. The
remaining six families are all from West Bengal. In addition to these
people, I got to know several other Indian families through the activities
of regional cultural centers, and I took part in various Hindu and Muslim
religious observances in southern New Jersey as well as Philadelphia.

The profile of this particular Indian community can be sketched very
generally: This group emigrated to the United States after the 1965 Immigration Act eliminated prior quotas on the admission of nonwhites
and non-Europeans. These are people from the professional-managerial classes who, since their arrival in the late 1960s and early 1970s, have
been inserted into the nexus of skilled labor and service sector industries. Their educational and technical training were the preconditions
that made migration to the United States possible under the logic of a
brain drain from the Third World. Speaking to the pattern of South
Asian immigration, Jenny Sharpe has provided a very useful catalog of
"transnational diasporas" and the politics of race inscribed in them.[18]
She points out that, having escaped the "historical frame of United
States racism, South Asians are often paraded as examples of American
success."[19] Their socioeconomic status prompts this community of "married with children" types to assert "family values" as if such values sig-
naled some authentic mark of Indianness and even though the dominant ideology of the family bears little resemblance to postcolonial
preoccupations with the "heritage" and "traditions" associated with In-

dia and an Indian past. Divorce, homosexuality, and interracial alliances do not feature in the overtly thematized self-understandings of subjects in this community.

To make a start on my inventory, in Gramsci's terms, of the covert and "composite nature" of the self, I asked people about their pasts: where they were from, the circumstances of their upbringing, class background, educational details, career expectations, and so on.[20] My attention to questions of individual biography stemmed from the belief that I needed to establish the relationship between people's preimmigrant pasts and their diasporic experience. I hope to establish below how the ethnographic process revealed that the past figures importantly in people's self-representations and narratives of identity, but not for the reasons I had posited nor in the continuous ways I had supposed.

Within the community, weekend gatherings featuring meals of ten to fifteen courses are a commonplace. On these occasions, the practice is for men to collect by themselves (usually in the formal living rooms of people's homes) while the women congregate in kitchens or breakfast rooms. Such spatial separation of the sexes inside the home and during social events should be understood as a matter of women's contradictory privileges in the household rather than in terms of a reductive inscription of gender inequality. In volume 2 of *The Practice of Everyday Life* Certeau, Giard, and Mayol provide some extremely suggestive insights into the complications of domestic space and power. According to them,

> [t]his pinpointing of the occupation of a certain place by a certain sex at a certain moment is not sufficient to account for the extreme *practical subtlety* with which the gender difference is experienced in the space of the neighborhood.... One thus overestimates the capacities of the space to account for sexual symbols, and one underestimates the extreme complexity of the symbolics of desire as it is elaborated by always approximate practices, shortcomings, dreams, slips of the tongue, and, as well, by itineraries within urban space.[21]

From this perspective, the kitchen is a place for women only as a result of what Certeau, Giard, and Mayol call "a procedure within the dialectic of the sexual separation of familial roles, [by which] men are *excluded* from it [the kitchen]; there is another relationship here that inscribes negativity (and not absence)."[22] This way of thinking dialectically about spatialization, domesticity, and gender is in keeping with my own sympathies and sheds light on why I, as one who is also an Indian woman, was able to move seamlessly between men's and women's groups in my various encounters. I remained outside the specific functioning of the dialectic of sexual partnership no less because I was positioned as the transitional figure of an ethnographer than because I was a daughter in the community; someone whose place it is to be "free" in her "father's house."[23] Like other sexual dynamics, the ones that crisscrossed my "itineraries" in and out of gendered spaces were perhaps underwritten by an Oedipalized relation that was invisible but exerted its own pressure. Patriarchal traditions not only do not contradict but in fact depend on the availability of openings whereby younger women are regularly accepted into men's conversational circles.

In other words, if what Certeau, Giard, and Mayol refer to as the "symbolics of desire" operates in terms of a spatial-sexual dialectic, it is because some women can be positioned in sexualized roles while others are not. These unconscious dynamics of sexual-spatial separation are not intelligible as such, of course, because they are unconscious. What can be acknowledged is a more legibly historical dialectic in which the greater mobility of younger women both inside and outside the home represents a simultaneous concession to tradition and modernity. The concession signals the very subtlety of spatial and sexual borders upon which things like tradition rest, even as it is understood to be an inevitable though not entirely undesirable consequence of Western educations and lifestyles. Before I undertook the ethnography, I took for granted the specifically gendered sense of propriety that informs spatial arrangements. Once I decided to embark on the project, I had to become more self-conscious about explicitly noting the "semi-learned grammar" (Pierre Bourdieu's term) by means of which men and women traverse their separate spheres of everyday social activity.

Men's Memories: Return of the Repressed

Sometimes the subject of the past came up in conversations without any intervention on my part; at others, I directly questioned people about their memories and life stories. In one exchange, two men, Botuda and Sudhirda, discussed their pasts in the combinatory language postcolonials use among themselves.[24] On this occasion, the mixture was one of English and Bengali. After-dinner tea had just been served by the women, and as he sipped from his cup, Botuda asserted that no matter how fancy or expensive the label, tea in this country just did not taste like the stuff one bought from vendors at railway stations in India—strong, piping hot, served in little clay cups. Sudhirda, who is a man in his late forties and a classmate of Botuda's from their medical school days in Calcutta, scoffed at this: "You are completely bogus," he said, adding that any tea one bought at a public place back in India and actually *drank* was in all probability likely to induce cholera, or at the very least, dysentery, since it was inevitably accompanied by a "dead fly or a strand of someone's hair."

Botuda admitted that he was only "dreaming" the aroma of that tea in those railway stations and that it was strange that he could remember in such pleasant terms a perfectly miserable experience of waiting for a train that was seven hours overdue. The two men then explained to me the difference between everyday experience in this country and the trials and tribulations of daily life in India. For ordinary middle-class people like themselves, traveling had in the past involved a long series of queues, bribes, third-class compartments, and dirty accommodations. In contrast, they said, here they could "drive up to a ticketing window, charge the ticket to their American Express cards, and go wherever they wanted to, *in style*."

Emigration had liberated them. I asked the two: What about the fact that as Indians we have to go to extraordinary lengths to prove our naturalization or citizenship status, proof of residence, reasons for traveling, and so on, every time we crossed a border? Did this not contradict their notion that traveling in this country was uniformly pleasant or trouble-free? One of them replied, "One just has to be resigned to this sort of thing because our skins are not white and we must expect a certain amount of suspicion. However," he added, "we can do it [be resigned to the scrutiny of authorities] better than anyone else because we grew up on it [suspicion and surveillance]."

This anecdote is typical of the men's memories. For them, thinking about the past serves to affirm how much better off they are in the present. All of them referred to their ordinary beginnings. They had aspired to come abroad, obtain advanced degrees, work for foreign companies, and make good on their own. Their stories were those of self-made men who had transcended their "middle-class" origins in India and struggled to achieve professional success in the United States. Given that the idea of a "middle class" signifies very differently in India and would at best correspond to a more objectively lumpen lifestyle in the West, achieving middle-class status in the United States definitely implies an improvement in socioeconomic standing. These efforts, they averred, had led to the realization of their goals not only toward self-improvement but also with regard to gaining "respect." The anecdote reveals another set of submerged meanings. This has to do with the ways that nostalgia becomes the symptomatic locus of repressed fantasies of identity and belongingness. Fragmented and marginalized narratives of past attachments reappear as wishful thinking, sentimentality, and misremembering. As we have learned from Freud's insights into psychic mechanisms of negation, the anterior language of the unconscious is "translated" and represented in terms that the men see as proper and more realistic. In the course of their acculturation into immigrant lifestyles, these men have been hailed by ideologies of pragmatism, rationalism, and bourgeois masculinity. The result is that their sensuous relationship to things left behind can only appear as phobic symptoms. Neither Botuda's rosy recollection nor Sudhirda's jaundiced one contradicts the idea that both men are equally interpellated, since rationalism and romanticism are twinned aspects of a bourgeois problematic of desire: that which cannot be wished for must be wished away, either as remembered pleasure or as remembered repugnance. In either case, rejection carries with it the imprint of now proscribed and negated desires. As Stallybrass and White remind us:

> These low domains, apparently expelled as "Other," return as the object of nostalgia, longing and fascination. The forest, the fair, the theatre, the slum, the circus, the seaside resort, the "savage": all these, placed at the outer limit of civil life, become symbolic contents of bourgeois desire. These contents, or domains, are subject to misrecognition and distortion precisely because idealization and phobic avoidance have *systematically* informed their discursive history.[25]

Botuda's memories of that Indian tea and Sudhirda's rejection of them in medical, rationalistic terms (on the grounds that the tea would have induced cholera and dysentery) reflect an attempt to mediate the sort of "carnivalesque" displacements that Stallybrass and White have been so instrumental in elucidating: "The demonization and the exclusion of the carnivalesque has to be related to the victorious emergence of specifically bourgeois practices and languages which reinflected and incorporated this material within a negative, individualistic framework."[26] In the context of the exchange between Botuda and Sudhirda, references to travel, railway stations, and tea drinking appear to be tied up with sublimated Odyssean fantasies of masculinity and self-authorization—

symptomatically displaying the mobility and motility of identity construction. The men's rejection of the past as "low" and "debased" is completely consistent with their valorization of its opposite term, that is, the present, with all its bourgeois, cosmopolitan, and individualistic trappings.

The men do acknowledge the material hardships they suffered en route to their present self-consolidation. All of them recounted feelings of homesickness at having to leave their families back in India (most men had emigrated before marriage, so missing their spouses and children was usually not an issue). They mentioned how difficult it had been to get used to everything in this country: the tasteless food, the feeling of being cut off from everybody, and the general alienness of the West. Some men had college friends from India living in this country, and the transition was made easier for them because they were able to insert themselves into expatriate social networks. But most often, as with other immigrants to a new country, the early years had been difficult to negotiate.

Even so, immigration had, according to the men, provided the ticket to financial security as well as to a higher social status. The concern with status can be understood if it is placed in the context of the ideologies of class and caste hierarchy operative in India. The backgrounds of the men bespeak educational but not economic or social privilege. For most of them, their class positions in India would have meant fairly severe restrictions on social mobility. One of my informants said that emigration had made it possible for him "to make more than enough bread." He came from a large family in India and was responsible for the upkeep of many people. For him, the only way to attain respectability had been to earn a "dollar income" that took care of his financial obligations back home and secured him a better life here. Stoically he added that having made his bed (that is, having left India), he had to lie on it and put up with whatever inequities came along with the undeniable improvements in his current material situation. Remembering the past helped him realize that he was, indeed, better off now. This particular rationale is a familiar one: Most men downplayed their experiences of marginality and emphasized the fact of their "material freedom" in the present.

Over the course of two years of keeping account of people's representations, I found that men placed single-minded emphasis on the fact that although they were at times nostalgic about the past, their present circumstances were much more favorable. Remembering the past also served to make them realize exactly how rewarding the immigrant experience had been. In one conversation I pressed an informant on this matter:

K: What you're saying is that you have made the kind of life here that you would never be able to have in India and that your position in this country has afforded you a certain amount of respect that is not available there?

R: Absolutely, that is the case. I'm from a small town in South India, and although my family was quite prominent there, my only career options would have been to become an ill-paid professor at the local college, or a middle-level bureaucrat in the government. Here, I am a manager in my company, my wife and I have a comfortable home, the children are all going to good schools, so what is there to complain about? In fact, let me tell you, things are even better for my wife than they are for me. I still have to go to work and deal with all the stuff in the office. Whereas, she? She drives around all day in her car, shopping, meeting friends—doing whatever it is that keeps you women busy. And this is a woman who back in her village had never even ridden a tricycle.

K: So when you visit India, you must be struck by the contrast between your own circumstances and that of your relatives and friends. Do they comment on the way things have turned out for you? Are they surprised at your success? What do they make of your Americanized children?

R: Oh well, I suppose there is a certain amount of envy. That's natural isn't it? Especially given the way we can afford to throw money around—like *sahibs*. On the other hand, some of my friends have done very well for themselves, too. Last time I was back, I went to visit a very good friend at his office. This fellow is now the police commissioner, and there were all sorts of formalities: I had to give my name to the security guard, he then passed the word to my friend's PA [personal assistant], and finally, after sitting in a reception room, I got to see my friend. He sent one of his flunkeys out to get us some tea and *paan* [betel leaf], and I realized that had I stayed back, I too could have lorded it like this. But that doesn't bother me; he has his prestige of course, but I'm happy. I mean, I don't have to worry about political issues, keeping the minister off my back, and so on. Even if I don't get nearly the same kind of respect and attention, I've got what I need. And if the children don't go astray—become hippies or start dating—then I'll be satisfied.

Later on, I thought about the contradictions and inconsistencies in my informant's story. On the one hand he claimed that his life in this country was much better than it would have been in India, and on the other he suggested that had he stayed there he too could have led a "lordly" life. Then again, his avowed reason for emigrating was to gain respect, yet he acknowledged not possessing the same kind of prestige as his friend. He started out by asserting that memories of the past made him appreciate the privileges of the present. In the end, however, he suggested that his *wife* had reaped the most benefits, since he still had to deal with the exigencies of work. Most poignant was his throwaway remark that he would be "satisfied" with—which is to say, vindicated by—his decision to emigrate if his children (brought up in this country) did not "become hippies or start dating."

In one fell swoop, my informant revealed a series of ambivalences about his position. The explicit reason for emigrating had been to make a better life for himself and his family. This man embodies the ideologies of traditional masculinity insofar as he regards it his economic and symbolic duty to provide for the welfare of his wife and children. Yet he now fears a certain failure because his children, despite attending "good schools," may have become alienated from his own worldview. The only way he could represent this gap between himself and his children was by casting it in the most stereotypically othered ways: with reference to dating and hippiedom. The burden of the past weighs heavily on this man's representation of himself and his offspring. For *were* his children to "go astray" in the ways he dreaded, not only would his decision to emigrate be betrayed but so would his very identity as male, father, and Indian.

The ways that narratives of the past inflect the present are varying and disparate. Another male informant, Rishida, who was seen as one of the more erudite people in the community (at least among the Bengali contingent), said to me that discrimination was a "fact of life" and also that he had been *more* oppressed by its structures back in India. His stated reason for emigrating to North America (he had lived in Canada for a few years before moving to the United States) was because he felt that, in India, Bengalis are made to suffer for their avant-garde stand on political issues. According to him, during the Raj people were well aware that "what Bengal thinks today, India thinks tomorrow." However, he argued, Bengalis are resented and silenced in postindependence India. They are actively disparaged, and neither their intellectual dispositions nor their revolutionary historical contributions are recognized or appreciated. To him, such a devaluation of Bengali men replicated the old colonial ideology of the Bengali *bhadralok* ("gentleman") as effeminate and abnormal. Rishida said that he was deeply offended that this stereotype from the past still circulated in India. By coming abroad and leaving behind such colonial hangovers, he had removed himself from regionalistic prejudices and from the constraints they imposed on his sense of personal agency.

The paradox here (which remained obscured because I did not feel able to articulate it to him) was that by leaving the country and withdrawing from the debate about historical agency—instead of engaging it "manfully"—Rishida may have made himself more vulnerable to the critique of intellectualist effeminacy he found so abhorrent. I have since wondered why theorizing the meaning of masculinity preoccupies many Bengali men, especially in the postcolonial context, where even if Indian men are seen as unmanly, such typecasting is certainly not calculated in terms of their regional origins in India. Whatever discrimination people from Bengal are subjected to in this country, it is no different from that which immigrants from other Indian regions also suffer. The specificity of Indian regionalisms hardly matters in the immigrant context because Americans do not care (and would not know) whether an immigrant is Bengali or Tamil. The relevant criterion of otherness here is that Indians are Indians (when that is not mistaken as "Native American"). But as I have tried to show, subjectivity is not just a reactive proposition; it is produced in and by the present no less than by structures of meaning from the past.

Rishida's narrative of difference and discrimination represents a specific example of the continuing effectivity of colonial modes of understanding. Emigration as a search for mastery is one trope (among many) in the text of the recovery of selfhood.[27] Such recovery exacts its own costs, however. Despite the fact that the ideology of effeminacy no longer has to be contested in the same way as before, it continues to be resented while being reproduced in the postcolonial context. I do not wish to propose a definitive interpretation of the postcolonial male's subjectivity (Bengali or otherwise), though it is clear that any account of identity has to deal with such parochial and paranoid differences because they threaten to disrupt the appropriation of identity as a strategic or oppositional tool. Anxiety about power and masculinity signifies how colonial discourses continue to interpellate postcolonial subjects. Gayatri Chakravorty Spivak and Partha Chatterjee have both made passing references to the idea that immigrant selfhood is, in many ways, caught in the same systems of domination and subordination that produced prior colonial forms of subjectivity.[28] Nonetheless, the specificity of this address has remained largely unexamined.

I have suggested that the Bengali male's disavowal of colonial narratives of emasculation produces the very conditions for his contradictory self-identification as a renovated man. I am speaking here of the diasporic postcolonial subject (although this may also be true of the indigenous male in India). My friend Rishida regarded immigration as an escape from older narratives and as a return to mastery. But bygones can never be bygones, and Rishida's present self remains inflected by the need to respond to and refuse the leftovers of a colonial myth of native effeminacy and degeneracy.[29] The impossibility of erasing difference here remains the ultimate irony.

Men's narratives represent variations and contradictions, but they also indicate an overall matrix within which postcolonial identity is solidified. At this overall level, self-understanding involves a complex distancing from the past. The attempt to consolidate respectability in the bourgeois, diasporic context requires constructing the past as the undesirable other. However, the devaluation of the past indicates and itself produces the present identities of immigrant men. To close this section on men's memories, let us take a final look at Stallybrass and White's propositions about the formation of bourgeois subjects and modern communities: "[T]he *exclusion* necessary to the formation of social identity at level one is simultaneously a production at the level of the Imaginary, and a *production,* what is more, of a complex hybrid fantasy emerging out of the very attempt to demarcate boundaries to unite and purify the social collectivity."[30]

Women and the Past: "The Inappropriate/d Other"

I should now like to turn to women's representations of the past. In so doing, I will have constructed them as the counterpoint to men's narratives and therefore as subsumed under them. My intention, though, is quite the opposite. I want to argue that immigrant women are subjected by the double articulation of discourses of cultural difference and patriarchy.[31] This makes their attempts to negotiate their selfhood in daily life more exemplary of the contradictions underwriting forms of subordinated experience. Having heard men relate the difficulties of their past circumstances, it came as a surprise to me to hear women in the community emphasize the comforts and privileges of their preimmigrant pasts. Whereas men romanticized the present, women were unequivocal in recollecting backgrounds replete with material benefits. I was struck by this consistent inconsistency between men's and women's narratives of personal history; more interesting than the actual circumstances of the past (which men and women seemed to remember in somewhat opposing ways) were the reasons for this gendered contradiction.

It must be said that the inconsistency was usually not made explicit at the moment of its expression because constraints of gendered propriety work to prevent public dialogue between men and women. If a man happened to walk in on a kitchen conversation among women, the substance was shifted subtly, but surely, toward banal issues unrelated to what was being discussed right up to the point that the man entered the room. At times like these, I felt like a wayward pupil back in the cloistered space of the convent school of my childhood, hurriedly switching topics when a nun's arrival was imminent. Needless to say, conversations that were regarded as uncontroversial did not need to be hijacked in this manner. Still, the women were happiest talking about their memories and recollections when there was no danger of an intruding male presence; only then were things recounted with great relish and detail.

Of particular interest to me was the tacit assumption among women that the past was, in fact, a sensitive subject not to be aired with abandon in front of men. Even offhand remarks about "how good it was in the old days" or "in my father's house" and so on would sometimes have unforeseen consequences. On one occasion at which I was present, a man scolded his wife for her wishfulness: The past is a "mirage," he said, and he added that she would do well to keep this in mind. To his wife's credit, she did not accede completely to this version of history as illusion. She simply looked at me and said, "Your *dada* [elder brother] doesn't see things this [my] way," and let the matter drop.

In one of the more uncomfortable moments at a social gathering, a woman, Beladi, was telling us about her extremely conservative and protective father who, in her youth, would not countenance her walking unaccompanied to a friend's house. She said he insisted on sending her in a chauffeured car or, when that was unavailable, with servants walking both ahead of and behind her as protection. At this moment, Beladi's husband walked in, caught the tail end of her anecdote, and loudly challenged, "So where was this chauffeured car when we got married? As far as I can remember, your father had to rent a taxi for the ceremony." There was an awkward moment or two while Beladi scrambled for a response until she came up with the explanation that by the time her marriage was arranged, her father, having fallen on hard times, had gotten rid of his chauffeur and car—hence the taxicab to the wedding. The other women in the room leapt to Beladi's defense. "It's marrying their daughters to men like you that made our fathers bankrupt," they admonished her husband. "Just because you can't keep us in the style we were accustomed to, doesn't mean we weren't brought up better." I shall have occasion a little later to comment on the collective and public solidarity among the women by means of which they protect their own fabrications of the past. For now, I want to provide a glimpse into the particular positioning of these women.

The women in the community have acquired a certain cosmopolitanism; all of them have lived in the United States for many years, have traveled here and in Europe, and have enjoyed the benefits of Western lifestyles. At the same time, they regularly complain about their current lives, which they contend are far less comfortable than they were used to in the past, in India. In a general sense, it is true that daily life in India is more relaxed, even for families without a lot of money. Additionally, ways of being that are familiar and regarded as "second nature" are perhaps enacted less self-consciously than the active work that goes into being Americanized and up-to-date. Women seem to (mis)remember the past in sublated terms, confusing the privilege of being secure in one's sense of self with material security. There are some things money cannot buy; women attest to this truism and compensate for their lack of place and voice by remembering a fabricated past.

Inconsistencies between the men's and women's recollections stem less from the fact that individual memories are unreliable or untrue than from the fact that the past is a resource to which different sets of meaning attach. In this case, the differences have to do with what men and women set store by, how they represent themselves, and, above all, what their experiences are like in the present. After all, the supposition underlying my questioning was not that I would find the real truth, but that there is something to the ways that people actively imagine their history and construct themselves in relation to that imagination.

The women may recollect their pasts as a time of better living not because they are out to deceive anybody (which in any case they do not) but because at some level they refuse the ideology that immigration is a rewarding experience. The everyday lives of women in my community give the deceptive impression of security. Underlying all appearances, however, is the experience of a double dislocation "en-gendered," as it were, by the global dilemmas of postcoloniality and by the peculiar, local position of the middle-class Indian woman, who in most instances is primarily a housewife. So the women's refusal of their putative well-being in the immigrant context is deeply fissured. At one level, they enjoy their current affluence. On another level, it is clear that their material comforts are not what they are cracked up to be and cannot replace the losses incurred by leaving home. On yet a different plane of calculation, their fascination with a Western lifestyle is deflated by the tedium of daily housework and domestic labor (which must be undertaken over and above any employment outside the home). All this is made more complicated by the women's firm conviction that there is no going back and that they cannot undermine their husbands' positions by denigrating the present. They manage these competing and disturbing realities by romanticizing the past. There is no other means of settling accounts with the present because the predicament of postcoloniality is an impossible one—for both men and women, in different ways.

Remaking the past, then, serves at least a dual purpose. It is a way of coming to terms with the present without being seen to criticize the status quo; at the same time, it helps to recuperate a sense of the self not dependent on criteria handed down by others. The past is what these women can claim as their own; it is seen as autonomous and possessing an authority not related to privileges acquired through marriage and emigration. Since representing the self is, for these women, so tied up with representing the past, it is no wonder that some of their memories have more to do with how things ought to have been than how they were. Not that there is such a thing as an autonomous and exact history of memory—rather, the traces of the past have been inventoried in fabulated ways for reasons far outweighing the issue of literal truth.

In *The Symbolic Construction of Community,* Anthony Cohen argues that the reconstitution of traditions and cultural boundaries is common to almost any culture and that the process often takes place "by re-rendering structures and forms of behavior which have originated elsewhere in such a way that they are made congruent with the proclivities of indigenous cognition."[32] One of the more "exotic" (to adopt Cohen's phrasing) ways this is done is through deception and lying, which, he says, is "a behavioral strategy...well documented by students of Mediterranean societies."[33] He adduces the Arabic concept of *kizb*, which has the effect of bolstering rather than subverting social relations through the "masking of reality." Cohen refers to the ethnographic work done by Michael Gilsenan in a northern Lebanese village, which showed how the lie *(kizb)* is itself a manifestation of indigenous belief battling against the new and unfamiliar and how it is expressly seen as such. Cohen quotes Gilsenan as saying,

> It is only in fact by *kizb* that social life can go on at all and the group's fragile corporateness be preserved.... *Kizb* bridges the gap between form and substance, ethos and the actualities of the political economy, but at the same time men directly experience and *know* that it is a false "solution" to the problem.[34]

I want to appropriate this particular understanding of fabulation as a social strategy and adapt it to the situation of my ethnographic community, while hastening to add that I am aware of the danger of making sweeping comparisons between the cultural practices of diverse peoples. Quite obviously, Lebanese villagers are significantly different from middle-class Indian immigrants in metropolitan locations. Nonetheless, one can legitimately compare cultural specificities without on the one hand totalizing meanings or on the other being utterly relativistic about cultural differences. Satya Mohanty has persuasively argued that there is a need for today's critics to rethink the latent tendency to reinscribe an ideology of radical alterity in cultural analysis.[35] I proceed with caution, then, to elaborate on some parallels between the Lebanese and Indian instances.

Both men and women reinvent the past and themselves, but they do so in contrasting ways that are specific to the gendering of experience. The men I spoke to asserted their middle-class backgrounds because, in some sense, it is actively in their interest to downplay their preimmigrant circumstances. What this means is not that men's memories are rigorous or that they tell things as they are or were, but that their reconstructions are differently selective. Men appear to be concerned with representing the constraints of their pasts relative to the privileges of the present. Contrasts between preimmigrant lifestyles and the present provide "natural" vindications of their decisions to emigrate. Materially, at least, people are better off here, so recollecting the hardships of the past is one way of justifying immigration as the right avenue to a better life.

Men's narrratives highlight their individuality, their will to succeed and to make good (despite the odds), and their autonomy with respect to traditional ideals of familial duty, filial obligation, and so on. So what if the good is also accompanied by racism, social marginality, and other such forms of negation of the self? In a cognitive sense, even if the decision to emigrate turned out to be a Faustian pact exacting immense costs, there is not much the men can do except to rationalize that choice. This is done by emphasizing the improvements they have wrought in their current domestic fortunes. In any case, there is no alternative: Life would hardly be bearable if they were to carry with them a constant admission of failure. I certainly do not wish to imply that the men *have* failed in any way; I merely suggest that it is consistent with the men's positioning as the main wage earners in the family for them to claim success by contrasting the past to the present—especially since this belief is repeatedly undercut by everyday experience.

The life histories of men in the community represent a pragmatic solution for reconciling the past-present relation. Clifford Geertz's influential arguments on "common sense as a cultural system" may be of some relevance here:

> It is this conviction of the plain man [and, it should be added, woman]
> that he is on top of things, and not only economic things, that makes
> action possible for him at all, and which—here through invoking
> witchcraft to blunt failures, with us by appealing to a long tradition
> of cracker-barrel philosophizing to commemorate successes—must
> therefore be protected at all costs. . . . Men plug the dikes of their most
> needed beliefs with whatever mud they can find.[36]

For the women in the community, in contrast to the men, the stakes in retelling the past are quite different. As with the case of the *kizb,* these women recount the past in ways that bridge the gaps between the ethos they would like to preserve and their lived experiences. At some level, they know that their histories are deceptions and that their recoveries of the past are effective only as cover-ups of present complexities. But like the *kizb,* these fables of the past are symbolically effective in a variety of ways. These women look back to the past as a happier time when their family and kinship ties were still intact. Since they are from middle-class formations in India in which a great deal of emphasis is placed on kinship and communal ties, they expect to be the mainstays of the domestic order and to fulfill their responsibilities as wives and mothers. From the traditional point of view, maintaining social networks and familial bonds is profoundly important for the women and represents a significant locus of their influence both within the home and in the community. In the diaspora, they find themselves isolated and without the traditional systems of support on which they relied for emotional and psychic sustenance. Moreover, even their domestic roles are reduced in influence; previously they could count on the socially acknowledged power of women in the family, but now they find themselves hemmed in by the role of wife and mother. It is necessary to underscore the contingency, the middle-class provenance of these particular traditional values (regarding women's domesticity) because this provides the key to the specificity of my ethnographic community. One cannot extrapolate from the case of these women to other postcolonial Indian formations (in Britain or Southeast Asia, for example), where immigrant populations derive from different demographic groups with differing cultural ideologies about women's roles.

In other words, I am anxious to distinguish between stereotypic understandings of "Eastern values" and their actual, class-related configurations, both in India and within immigrant contexts. For the group of middle-class women in the southern New Jersey community, ideas about themselves are inflected by the articulation of specific class, race, and gender ideologies. In this respect, I am arguing for cultural specificity—for taking theoretical and empirical account of the heterogeneity of cultural practices and formations even *within* cultures. This is especially the case with Indian immigrants because the diverse class character of subcontinental groups does not lend itself to easy assimilation under a particular tradition or within a generalizable analysis of postcoloniality. I want to suggest that for my female informants the past is cast in celebratory terms because the ideological underpinnings of their histories are, for them, naturalized. The security of their taken-for-granted subject positions—as daughters, mothers, and emblems of avowedly matriarchal traditions—is seriously disrupted in the immigrant context, where such self-understandings are entirely thrown into doubt by virtue of what can and cannot be assumed as their due. Consequently, individuals reremember their personal histories as a way of reconciling disjunctions in their commonsense notions of themselves.

This is not to suggest that middle-class Indian women (either here or in India) are comfortable with the experience of patriarchy and are only disturbed by class difficulties; far from it. But traditional kinship systems do provide a certain authority and status, which, along with the old systems of meaning, are displaced and unavailable in immigrant experience. Women's nostalgia for the past brings with it some uncritical ideas about "how good it really was in the old days," "in my father's home," and so on. The loss of old family structures and networks is a prima facie difficulty for the women. Insofar as they are confined to the household domain, they have little purchase on consolidating a public presence. This is true even of women who have paid jobs outside the home; moreover, access to well-paid, satisfying careers is itself restricted by racist norms governing the workplace. The loss of influence is first experienced within the home—even if spouses and children respect "what Mom does for the family"—because the old reference points, the customary and communal ideologies of familial and matriarchal power and attachment, are now erased.

More important is the acute alienation these women experience when they step out of the house. At least within the security of the private domain, women retain the power of being in charge. This responsibility, albeit structured by a patriarchal ideology, is still a very powerful one for immigrants whose only anchor is their home. Outside this arena, women signify their otherness not only by their appearance, dress, and accents but also by their "inappropriate" deployment and use of privileges ideologically reserved for the dominant culture: expensive cars, clothes, jewelry, and so on. The quality of this impropriety resides in the perverse effect by which the women's attempts to adopt the manners of the dominant culture—to don white masks on their black skins, as it were—fails to produce a reversal.

In a conversation about the lack of social exchange between "Americans and Indians," one woman told me that when she first arrived in this country, she had been anxious to make friends with "white people" and to develop some intimacy with people "from this culture." Over the years she has given up on this desire because she says she feels defensive about her own position: her clothes, accent, and manners and her inability to respond "freely" to men. Now she is happy with her Indian friends who understand her; also, she realizes that white people simply "don't open up to outsiders," even if they are neighbors. Another woman told me that she made it a point to wear saris to the school at which she teaches despite knowing people think she is "weird" and even though they ask if she can "comfortably go to the bathroom."

The women are thus positioned in thoroughly uneasy ways. On the one hand, they have to reconcile themselves to diminished familial lives in which there are no external cultural supports or rewards for their efforts and activities; on the other, they are actively invested in patriarchal ideologies placing institutions of marriage and family beyond reproach. Any compromise is merited if it means keeping the domestic front secure. These women are brought up to believe that even the slightest hint of dissatisfaction with their spouses or marriages is unworthy. For most, no alternative mode of life can be contemplated.

The taking up of notions about Indian values regarding cultural modesty and reticence strictly prohibit the public expression of anything that could be construed as a criticism of the menfolk or as reflecting families in a bad light. As a result, the women I spoke to would only very indirectly voice their difficulty with or frustration about intimate relationships. In conversation, women will occasionally make flippant remarks about some (always minor) shortcoming of their husbands; such critiques are closely circumscribed by boundaries that do not permit substantive discussion of problems. Women are actively discouraged from speaking out about their unfulfillment; this is true especially of sexual matters, but also of life in general.

From these marginalized locations and with these interdictions in place, women devise ways of expressing their subject status and their perspectives on immigrant life. The authorized way of making a critique of the present is through indirection and by deferring to the past. The presence of the past offers a way for these women to say what otherwise cannot be said: that emigration has brought with it a betrayal of the promise of equality. This is, at bottom, recognized by most people, men and women. But it is still an oppositional idea and threatens taken-for-granted assumptions about the satisfactions that life in this country is supposed to garner. Besides, prevailing myths of equality and equal opportunity are powerfully effective within the culture at large; as such, these myths have gained the consent not only of mainstream groups but of minority communities as well.

Many Indians reproduce the ideology of materialist egalitarianism and consequently believe that their affluence should guarantee acceptance into mainstream society. The ritual invocation of opportunity and freedom provides the dominant context against which contravening understandings of difference and discrimination have to struggle to be articulated. To some extent, the insistence on identification with "whites" represents a refusal of the status of victim ("we are like them"). But such an insistence also demands the erasure of difference while being implicated in its reproduction. It leads, as well, to a lack of engagement with possibilities for practical or coalitional politics and has troubling implications for the future of the community.

I should like to return to the point at which I started my interpretation of the women's narratives: It is the articulation of the patriarchal family system with discourses of race and migrancy that sets the peculiar conditions of these women's daily lives. A distinction must be maintained between women's "oppression" within patriarchy as it has been theorized by mainstream feminism and the migrant conjuncture in which unequal gender relations are less forceful than racist and discriminatory "structures-in-dominance" (to recall an Althusserian distinction). This point was made at length by Pratibha Parmar.[37] Hence, though I have retained the conceptual categories of feminism to understand the gendering of social discourses within the Indian community, I want to avoid the reductive conclusion that women's experiences of marginality are centered on gender inequality.

Despite the constraints imposed by the patriarchal family system on women, "marginalization" (as well as "self-marginalization") far better describes their lives and everyday resistances. In fact, I would go so far as to argue that the family remains the only cultural support and source of renewal for the women in this community and cannot therefore be dismissed. The situation of women in the community exemplifies exactly those shifting correspondences between a denatured traditionalism, the ambiguities of postcoloniality, and ultimately the contradictions of patriarchal capitalism. In the case under consideration, patriarchy is the vehicle of discriminatory practices that far exceed its imperatives and is thus effective in the *last* instance.

Conclusion: The Boundaries of Identity

I have focused on the dissonance of the past and the attempts by men and women alike to remake it in terms that are both accessible to the present and in keeping with their ideals of Indianness. The ontological boundaries of that Indian identity or their understanding of Indian values are not pregiven, nor are they secure in representation. Immigrant life occasions specific expressions of identity, tenuously inhabited and even more tenuously understood, given the internal and external contradictions of late capitalist existence. A sense of this fragility is somewhat elaborated in Homi Bhabha's concept of "enunciation," which he promotes to describe the subversive authority of writing in a postcolonial world.[38] According to him, enunciation is an abrogative process that challenges dominant modes of authority and exposes this authority as resting on an "archaic" belief in the "mirror of nature," which, he says, often leads to rationalist political arguments for the ascendancy of powerful cultures:

> It is the very authority of culture as a knowledge of referential truth which is at issue in the concept and moment of enunciation. The enunciative process introduces a split in the performative present, of cultural identification; a split between the traditionalist culturalist demand for a model, a tradition, a community, a stable system of reference, and the necessary negation of the certitude in the articulation of new cultural demands, meanings, strategies in the political present, as a practice of domination, or resistance.... [T]he enunciation of cultural difference problematizes the binary division of past and present ... at the level of cultural representation and its authoritative address.[39]

The renovation of the past demonstrates one such "split" in the process of cultural identification, though the distinction between everyday speech and poetic language, between ordinary people and critics, must be restated and reemphasized. Texts of everyday life are not as reflexively critical as the literary narratives Bhabha has in mind when he speaks of dislodging archaic models of cultural understanding. Nonetheless, the "plain man" and woman (to use Geertz's phrasing from earlier in this discussion) devises his or her own methods of contesting dominant meanings and logics of identification. If we are to understand postcoloniality as more than a literary predicament, such methods of everyday contestation are exactly the ones at stake. By this light, it ought to be possible to extend the concept of enunciation and to use it to illuminate the ways that immigrant identities call up, as well as call into question, referential notions of cultural truth—even, and perhaps especially, without the conscious intent of its enunciators. That there is a gendered component to the enterprise of constructing the past is, as I hope to have demonstrated, one of the unforeseen surprises yielded in and amid the actualities of everyday experience.

Immigrant subjects, both men and women, express forms of consciousness that are heavily inflected by a fragmented though forceful understanding of a colonial past and its dispersed effects on their current experience. The contradictions of selfhood, as revealed in the gendered inflections to acts of recalling the past, reveal that postcolonial identity does not exist as a self-fulfilling prophecy either in the concrete experience of some community "out there," in the theoretical constitution of *ethnos*, in the anthropological fetish of cultural difference, or indeed, in the a posteriori privileging of gendered experience. The constitution of selves, as embodied in the discourse of memory, exceeds such categorical designations. For me, one of the signal lessons of attempting to render people's lives into words was the practical discovery that the ordinary is always more surprising than our investments in the literary might lead us to expect. This is less a naive celebration of "self-presence" than it is a reckoning with quotidian distances between chance and deliberation.

Since one of my purposes throughout the book is to demonstrate the multiple inadequations between ideas and their experiential components, the products of memory—as they express the congealed effects of history, the unconscious, and gendered self-understanding—give substance to an antiepistemological impulse. Such an impulse refuses the tactic of explaining away what is fundamentally surprising by strong-arming it into protocols of knowledge that do not comprehend heterogeneity (as I explained in chapter 1). Complexities of everyday memory also reveal the importance of not conceding the ground of representation purely to imaginative literature, as if the truths of our quotidian recollections were not stranger than fiction.

We have become accustomed to reading accounts of otherness that seek to chart a dubious course between fairly unproblematized claims about, on the one hand, the "allegorical" (read "ethnographic") status of Third World literature and, on the other, continuing affirmations of the nontransparency of literary representation. But one cannot have one's representational cake and eat it too—at least, not without some heavy-duty contortions about symbols and semantics. If we take seriously the idea that postcolonial identity is articulated in multiple modalities of representation, then it is time to scrutinize quotidian understandings and common sense for their symptomatic value. They capture, albeit in flashes, what other forms of expressivity barely apprehend. This discussion has attempted to come to terms with the importance of a particular site of everyday understanding, that of personal memory, and the ways that it authorizes versions of immigrant selfhood.

CHAPTER FOUR

Food and the Habitus

Surely the Indian American Dream is a very potent one, and one
rooted in reality. What it boils down to is choices, as the homes
we've lived in, the values we've been exposed to, the lives we've led,
wrestle for our very soul. And like an industrious tailor, the Indian
immigrant painstakingly aligns the Banarasi silk, the mul-mul and
Jaipur tie-dye of memory with the hundred percent machine-made
smooth polyester of American life, stitching a brave new world from
cherished remnants of the old and shiny strips of the new.

—LAVINA MELWANI, "Morning in America"

The sense one often gets in an Indian home is of having been there before. Not that all homes are identical but that, *to the practised eye,* all
homes are familiar. Cues marking the arrangements of space and the
placement of objects in the household are easily read by those for whom
they are intended because they belong to a uniform code of propriety,
obligation, and self-understanding—aspects that are central to the habitus of a social group. The idea of habitus is a formative one for thinking about everyday, taken-for-granted sites of discourse. Habitus, in Norbert Elias's pioneering description, refers to "second nature" or the forms
of "embodied social learning" underwriting all attempts at subjective
self-consciousness.[1] In this chapter, I will be concerned with the hold
that food has in discharging such a self-consciousness in its relation
to real and imagined ideals of Indian culture and heritage inside the
community.

To begin with a generality: If bourgeois living describes attachments
to propriety or obligation on the one hand and conspicuous consump-

tion on the other, then there is something to be made of the interplay between the two. How is propriety informed or even determined by consumption? Equally, how does consumption relate to particular social obligations? As obvious as some of the answers to such questions might appear, there are certain elusive and potent myths that accompany particular taste preferences, as Pierre Bourdieu has explicated with great facility in regard to the French. The real question remains as to what is made conspicuous by patterns of consumption: money or the magic of mythic associations? The magic has to do with what is masked and revealed in consumption practices, as well as with what is hidden and sought through the displacements of spending money. If, as I have argued throughout, the consolidation of identity is a domesticated affair, it receives its greatest charge from the elaborate staging of ideas and ideals in and through household habits. For the immigrant Indian community, forms of expenditure that center on rituals of household consumption are where the stolidity of what it means to be bourgeois in the New World is, as it were, given a "structural adjustment," which reattaches the sacred with the profane aspects of immigrant existence. By this very token, however, these forms allow for the reconfiguration of commodified lives on terms that disavow that commodification.

By way of picking up the discussion of "adjustments" that serve both as secrets and openings of everyday practice, let me reach for a source that might seem somewhat out of place in the context of my overall analysis: Erving Goffman's study of symbolic interaction, *The Presentation of Self in Everyday Life*.[2] In this locus classicus of qualitative U.S. sociology, Goffman proposes the category of the "staging cue" to talk about forms of byplay that occur in situations where distinctions have to be made between insider-outsider and insider-insider:

> [S]ince it is not necessary to retain social distance or be on guard before those who are one's colleagues in occupation, ideology, ethnicity, class, etc., it is common for colleagues to develop secret signs which seem innocuous to non-colleagues while at the same time they convey to the initiate that he is among his own and can relax the pose he maintains toward the public.[3]

The focus here is on the quotidian maneuvers whereby one's lived environment is negotiated, not only by those involved in undercover operations or clandestine behaviors but just as much by people whose daily operations are conducted entirely out in the open, within mainstream surroundings and in the thick of ordinary experience. Goffman emphasizes the tacit assumptions and unspoken clues placed and picked up by every person in order to make sense of his or her own situation within the social order. Such trademarks of particularity and propriety reinforce horizons of inclusion or exclusion for all subjects in their dealings with intimates. The account is sociological, designed to provide an insight into general social psychology and the remarkable yet unremarked strategies that subjects undertake to maintain rule-governed behavior. But whereas the unexceptional lesson is about daily social intercourse, the peculiarity lies in the way Goffman goes about establishing it. For in the very same passage, immediately after his statement quoted above, he makes the following assertion about a very-far-from-general scenario:

> Thus the murderous Thugs of nineteenth-century India, who hid their annual depredations behind a nine-month show of civic-minded actions, possessed a code for recognizing one another.[4]

This piece of evidence is meant to support Goffman's macrosocial analysis, and it continues with an excerpt from an early treatise by a Col. J. L. Sleeman: "When Thugs meet, though strangers, there is something in their manner which soon discovers itself to each other, and to assure the surmise thus excited, one exclaims 'Alee Khan!' which, on being repeated by the other party, a recognition of each other's habit takes place."[5]

The anecdote's complete implausibility notwithstanding—given that, for the so-called Thugs, exclaiming "Alee Khan" by way of a greeting would be on the order of using "John Doe" as a code name—it draws our attention to the fact that secret behaviors or masks of appearance are common features of intragroup symbolic exchange. Despite, or perhaps because of, his fascination with orientalist tidbits and status-obsessed anecdotes culled from courtly and diplomatic commentaries, Goffman is able to slip in an unexceptional point about exceptional behaviors; namely, that they serve as the ruses, as "secret signs" whereby "one's colleagues in occupation, ideology, ethnicity, class, etc.," maintain a certain recognition of the obvious and the not so obvious. In other words, the dynamic is not specific to "exotics," although exotic subjects may well help to underscore it.

It is in the light of the epistemological entanglement of norms and exceptions—as if to say Thuggee practices of social hailing or growing up in Samoa were the value equivalents of, respectively, the secret hand-shakes of fraternity brothers on a Midwestern college campus or adolescence in Levittown—that a dialectical consideration of taste and consumption practices must be conducted. This is because value inheres, or more precisely, is remaindered in, the distance between the two: norm and exception. This distance is not recognizable, let alone commensurable, within the logic of equivalence set up by a Goffmanesque disregard for the relations of force that determine norm and exception in terms of each other. It hardly needs noting that Goffman's interest in Thugs and how they actually communicate with one another is at best minimal. They are mentioned only to spice up otherwise unexciting observations about the ritual behavior of ordinary people in the mainstream. The other exists, predictably enough, within a logic of substitution: brought in from the margins to make a point of general interest or to adorn a sociological datum, ushered out immediately thereafter. Many critics before me have commented that margins maintain the viability and force of the center; what has been less developed is the precise dynamic of such a relation. In this case, we can see that the problem is *not even* that there can be no equivalence between the social interactions of Thugs and Midwestern Americans. Rather, it is that schemas of knowledge (not to mention power) are drawn up with the weight of American values in mind, thus making of equivalence a nonequivalence. In keeping with Walter Benjamin, we might once more say that the state of exception is the rule.

The exception that is the rule gives us the coordinates for examining the chiasmatic structure of what Bourdieu calls the "reality of representation and the representation of reality." As he puts it in his magisterial analysis of French social life, *Distinction: A Social Critique of the Judgement of Taste*:

> [Systematicity] is found in all the properties—and property—with
> which individuals and groups surround themselves, houses, furniture,
> paintings, books, cars, spirits, cigarettes, perfume, clothes, and in
> the practices in which they manifest their distinction, sports, games,
> entertainments, only because it is in the synthetic unity of the habitus,
> the unifying generative principle of all practices. Taste, the propensity

and capacity to appropriate (materially or symbolically) a given class of classified, classifying objects or practices, is the generative formula of life-style, a unitary set of distinctive preferences which express the same expressive intention in the specific logic of each of the symbolic sub-spaces, clothing, language or body hexis. Each dimension of life-style "symbolizes with" the others, in Leibniz's phrase, and symbolizes them.[6]

This passage permits us to read Bourdieu as following Elias into the claim that the habitus is not just a closed circuit of class-demarcated behaviors but also less determined and deterministic than the idea of class demarcation might suggest. In the current climate of privileging discursive ambiguity, semiotic slippage, and so on, it is not unusual to find the charge of reductivism leveled against Bourdieu (and his variety of socioanthropological analysis). To my mind the charge is unjustified, the result of a speed reading which "always already" presumes the vulgarity of class analysis. On the contrary, Bourdieu explains that the material and symbolic appropriation of objects and practices expresses a certain potentiality *and* an already established logic, a deferral *and* a referral, an (incomplete) preference *and* a (tried-and-true) formula—that is to say, the gap between the given and the desired. In his words, "Taste is the *mutual adjustment* of all the features associated with a person."[7]

What connects the notion of the staging cue and secret sign of ritualized social interaction with a system of taste preferences and the habitus is that each designates elements of social belonging. What separates the habitus of the French working class from that of middle-class Indian immigrants has to do with the radically different ways in which the experience of class is felt in the domain of everyday life.

Of the myriad adjustments that in Bourdieu's terms provide "distinction" to class-configured identities, let us take a closer look at the one most central to and paradigmatic of middle-class Indian circumstances in the diaspora: the definitive relationship between food and identity. It is not my intention to suggest that the metaphoric valence attached to food or any other habitual practice of everyday life is exclusive to immigrant Indians or postcolonial subjects. Such a suggestion would be merely particularistic, not to mention unsustainable, since all communities have attachments to food as well as other icons of belongingness. At the risk of belaboring prevailing commitments, my purpose throughout is to interrogate the dialectic of universal and particular, norm and exception; to say something about the "secret signs" of post-colonial self-understanding very much in and through the common-places and generalities of everyday life.

Though bourgeois societies in the West have traditionally been characterized by the disjuncture between realms of public and private or work and leisure, life under late capitalism betrays even those demarcations so that the public is ever more privatized and leisure is insidiously subsumed under work (as captured by the paradox of the "working holiday"). This collapse puts pressure on all possibilities for personal or social authenticity: to borrow a phrase from Theodor Adorno's reflections in *Minima Moralia*, "[t]he whole of life must look like a job." We might then think of immigrant tastes—one's taste in food no less than one's attachment to Indian jewelry—as representing both the cracks and the glue in the edifice of "damaged life" whereby "[s]ecurity is glimpsed in adaptation to the utmost insecurity."[8] The atrophy of personal security is thus accompanied by the hypertrophy of investments in lifestyle. That commodities have a peculiar hold on our lives is, of course, exactly the reason to engage in a critique of commodification—not by a thoroughgoing condemnation of its seductions but through attempts to prise the husk of appearance away from the core of need. As what does the *madeleine* or this or that object, event, or item serve? Is it not less a function than a symbolic assurance? My account of culinary practices proceeds in the light of these entwinements of constraint and conviction, economy and extravagance.

Dietetics/Dialectics

Meals have an altogether special place within immigrant Indian life. This is not just true of my ethnographic community, nor is it exclusively bounded by religious or class distinctions. Even less is it the case that only immigrants exalt the status of food and eating. Well-being, both personal and social, has always been defined in India by referring it to the capacity to eat and to entertain others with food. In everyday Hindu iconography, Lakshmi, the goddess of wealth, is depicted surrounded by her bounty of coin as well as grain and her *bhandar* (storehouse or treasury) is filled with everything precious, including food items. The Sanskrit aphorism *"Atithi devo bhava"* exhorts the "proper" subject to regard "one's guest as god," to grant him or her the last morsel in the household. But even apart from such dominant (albeit secularized)

Hindu imagery of divinity residing in food, examples can be cited from Mughal and Persian sources as well as in the celebrations marking Christian and Muslim festivals—all emphasizing the signal importance of food as a social fact. So, for instance, the Muslim holiday of Id is celebrated with the ceremonial distribution of elaborate sweets to neighbors (including non-Muslim ones), just as Christian calendrical events are marked much more abundantly and communally than the familial emphases of their turkey-and-pie counterparts in the West might lead us to expect. What is noticeable about so-called national holidays in the United States (such as Thanksgiving or Christmas) is that they are driven by the ideology of the family; one has only to be a guest at a "regular" American Thanksgiving meal to recognize how thoroughly out of place a non–family member is amid the glorification of family ties. Community, it seems, is the unthought and unthinkable; at best it represents the family unit writ large.

In contrast, within immigrant Indian circles, the social fact of food is elevated to the status of a properly *communal* fetish, attaching itself to the collective meaning of being Indian (or, in its hyphenated description, "Indian-American"). Whatever the specificities are of living in an alien present, of "America," of discourses of ethnic hyphenation within the overall matrix of expatriate Indian self-understanding, their emergence is simply incomprehensible without its alimentary component: the portable investment in Indian cuisine. It is what joins the haut bourgeois personalities Zubin Mehta or Ismail Merchant (two readily recognizable Indian names in the culture at large) to myself or my ethnographic interlocutors.

Indeed, it is difficult, if not impossible, to think of immigrant Indian existence in the United States without at the same time thinking of Indian food.[9] In saying this, I do not mean to refer to the growing popularity of Indian restaurants both in such major cities as New York or Chicago and in smaller towns like Champaign-Urbana, Illinois, where I attended graduate school and where, solely on account of my identity, I found myself having to vet restaurants and menus for friends and colleagues as if I were some resident gastronomic expert on the cuisines of South Asia. (The same friends did not expect to be called upon to authorize the veal scallopini or the roasted Rock Cornish hen when we ate at non-Indian venues.) Nor am I speaking of the gustatory cachet that these days is associated with possessing an Indian "spice larder" or cooking from Indian recipe books, as if to suggest that mainstream American palates and cooks had always relied on spices like cumin seed and *garam masala* or dishes such as *matar paneer* or *vindaloo*. The latest cookbook is eager to tell the reader/cook that Indian cuisine evokes a "universal" love of food, now given free rein via preparations ranging from Mughal to Malabar. Such multicultural universality aside, my point is about the ways that meals, food, and the culinary in general signify for Indian communities themselves as emblems of a shared knowledge (about the cooking no less than the consuming) and, thereby, a communal identity.

In the rest of this chapter, my interest will be to distinguish a subjective sense of dietary complexity for expatriate Indians from the form of valorization that food matters receive in the West. To do so, I should first like to turn to one of the many insouciant and lasting insights into postwar life in Roland Barthes's early book of essays, *Mythologies*. I am drawn to the essay entitled "Steak and Chips," which is a send-up of French gastronomic pretensions.[10] In this piece, Barthes satirically invokes the particular "nature and morality" associated with eating steak or its complementary side dish, chips. Commenting on the function of the two in the Frenchman's gastric economy, he says, "[T]here is no alimentary constraint which does not make the Frenchman dream of steak. Hardly abroad, he feels nostalgia for it. Steak is here adorned with a supplementary virtue of elegance, for among the apparent complexity of exotic cooking, it is a food which unites, one feels, succulence and simplicity. Being part of the nation, it follows the index of patriotic values." Barthes then alludes to *Match,* the magazine in which it was reported that "after the armistice in Indo-China '*General de Castries, for his first meal, asked for chips.*'"[11]

The mythic import of this otherwise banal bit of information Barthes conveys in a couple of sentences laced with irony: "What we were meant to understand is that the General's request was certainly not a vulgar materialistic reflex, but an episode in the ritual of appropriating the regained French community. The General understood well our national symbolism; he knew that *la frite,* chips, are the alimentary sign of Frenchness."[12] Geographically speaking, Barthes's referent is, to be sure, very far from my interest in immigrant Indian life in the United States. In fact, even on its own terms—that is, in terms of a consideration of French cuisine—Barthes's focus on much-proclaimed simplicity runs contrary to the commonsense idea that French cooking requires complicated exchanges between gourmet and gourmand in the making and eating of *cordon bleu* foods. But such foods (involving sauces like béchamel or hollandaise) are too fussy, even effeminate, and cannot serve the purpose of representing simplicity when it is most needed: as a mandate for the colonial cleanup of the world's disorders, digestive and otherwise. *La frite,* then, is at the heart—or, more literally, the intestines—of the ideology of colonialism. Not only does Barthes's parodic take on alimentary investments expose the patriotic zeal about food matters to be ideological in the same way as are political pamphlets or advertisements; more pointedly, he highlights something singularly "mythological" with respect to the French for which we can find no equivalent within Indian culture, diasporic or otherwise.

Let me clarify: Indians, particularly those who (as with my ethnographic interlocutors) are Hindu, would at least not overtly celebrate the value of steak; some of the more observant may even be revolted at the idea of eating cattle, however prized the cut of meat. So it is not the particular status of steak and chips that is at issue in my comparison. The relevant point is that there is no single preparation or dish or kind of food on which Indians, collectively, could pin their alimentary hopes and desires. If, as Barthes would have it, gastronomic and communal ideals of simplicity accompany steak, and by the same token, chips conjure up the essentiality of the French nation reconsolidated after the war in Indochina, nothing—and everything—Indian is able to function as the "alimentary sign" of Indianness. As symbols, steak and chips function synecdochically with respect to ideals of Frenchness; they are specific conjurings of the myth of the French nation along the lines of the national flag or the Eiffel Tower. If they are parts of an imagined whole—the paradigm of France–fries and steak–simplicity–citizenship–nation—their place in the "index of patriotic values," as Barthes puts it, is singular; their value cannot be exchanged with that of any other food.

The Indian example is all but unique, because, depending on place and time, any number of different items or dishes—distinguished in terms of provenance and preparation—can spark that epic relationship with the motherland. Of course this has everything to do with the vastness and diversity of the subcontinent, which transports its linguistic as well as culinary diversity to its diaspora here and elsewhere. More specifically, the circumstances of middle-class immigrants are privileged enough to allow them to indulge their palates and sensibilities in ways that they perhaps could not in India itself. What is *dosa* to the indigenous subject from Karnataka or Tamil Nadu, fish curry to the Bengali, or *gajar halwa* to the Punjabi is here transformed into soul food for everyone of Indian origin. Indian food functions metonymically in relation to immigrant identity because the whiff of belongingness, nostalgia, or hope is carried along by the taste and aromas of a wide range of dishes. We might then say that the relationship of food to identity follows a syntagmatic chain of associations of the following sort: India–belonging–longing–*bhat* (generic term for rice, anything from plain basmati to *pullao,* lemon rice, *biryani,* and so on) and *roti* (designation for a variety of breads)–*bhaji* (general term for prepared vegetables)–*salan* (sauces)–*mithai* (desserts), and so on. The essential quality of an undoubtedly imagined Indianness resides in the profound fact of Indian cuisine, whose value can be discharged with flourish as well as simplicity, by appetizer or entrée, as vegetarian or nonvegetarian, by elementary or elaborate delights.

A final point of contrast between Barthes's exposition of the alimentary reach of French nationalism and my conjunctural interest in postcolonial variations: As I argued in chapter 3 with regard to issues of memory and their specific charge in shoring up everyday understandings of the self, ideological attachments of dominant social groups are not reducible to their counterparts within the symbolic hierarchies of those who have been dominated historically.[13] The two are irreducible not only because the myths that accompany marginalization are put to different uses than are myths belonging to those at the top of the social hierarchy, but also because the value of what gets labeled as "ideological" or a "special interest" and so on is formed in relation to existing structures of power. Dominant ideologies and preferences have institutional sanction; marginalized positions do not. In this connection, it bears remarking that General Castries' elemental desire to eat chips after the armistice in Indochina is, as Barthes notes, an index of "the regained French community," an "appropriation" signaling French imperial sovereignty. Chips are part of this imagery and affect of colonial desire—basic, muscular, efficient. Moreover, unlike effete "exotic cooking," steak or chips connotes something of a work ethic; like their imperial counterparts elsewhere, the French know how to get down to the business of ruling over those who spend too much time being distracted by culinary matters. Whereas the commonplace about food is that one eats to live, it appears that the Frenchman eats to rule.

Separated from the Gallic instance by history and disposition, the inventory of food items in the Indian symbolic order is able to mark civilizational complexity without possessing any of the self-assurance of the imperium. Consequently, avowing a preference for Indian foods in the name of a lost or regained Indian community is to be distinguished from that subjective sense of historical smugness that Barthes satirizes. Though assuredly mythic—in Barthes's sense of an "ex-nominated" system of meanings, of the "language-robbery" whereby bourgeois ideology is naturalized as nameless or obvious—a taste for *pakora* or *rossogolla* can only betoken the magic of tautology: It tastes good because it is Indian; it is Indian because it tastes good.[14] But what such magic cannot produce is the sort of peremptory supremacy available to the so-called winners of history: "Anyone civilized would agree . . ." On the contrary, one often finds oneself having to explain to outsiders that "spicy food isn't bad for the digestion." Even today, when multicultural tastes are asserted with great élan, haute cuisine may call up French food; Italian food; perhaps even variants of *nouvelle* cooking with mild combinations of Thai, Chinese, or Indian spices; but hardly ever subcontinental offerings alone. The last belong in the lower echelon of "ethnic" (that is, non-Western or non-European) selections (the French or Italian having long since passed from being worshipped as ethnic within mainstream taste culture). European culture has become, to use Barthes's term again, "ex-nominated"; that is to say, it represents the taken-for-granted norm against which cultural values are determined. The status of immigrant investment in Indian food is thus implicitly measured against such a mainstream calculus of value. Given Bourdieu's contention that taste classifies, and it classifies the classifier,[15] culinary preferences may be said to express a social logic, an *art de faire,* and a historical line of force whose invisibility is guaranteed by the very liberalism of the dictum *De gustibus non est disputandum.*

Liberal tastes indicate cultural capital. And a dietary liberalism is expansively, if tellingly, engaged by my ethnographic interlocutors in the southern New Jersey community. Hypostatizing the home as the fabric and fabrication of identity leads to a corollary set of investments in "the good life," in which good eating is the most privileged practice. Of course this entails a great deal of labor and money spent on food. Not surprisingly, the former provides a de facto justification of women's work in the home, while the latter becomes one of the major reasons for men to work long hours and direct a certain calculated energy toward their middle-management jobs (seldom rewarded in terms of access to the upper echelons of professional-managerial existence). So the measure of one's success is given in predictable material ways, although the valence of food expresses a specific combination of myth and rationalization.

It is not out of the ordinary to be served a fourteen- or fifteen-course meal at a weekend gathering in an immigrant household. These events are quite common despite the fact that a birthday, an anniversary, a graduation, or a religious festival is always found on the calendar to signify their exceptionality. Meals eaten at religious get-togethers are invariably vegetarian in Hindu homes because of the proscription against eating flesh during such celebrations. At other times, the household cook can satisfy the appetite of both her vegetarian and her carnivorous guests with a menu that includes two or three appetizers (*samosas, dahivada, kebabs, chops,* and *pakoras* represent a fairly common selection of vegetable and meat starters); chicken, lamb, and fish curry (each prepared in a mode that is distinct from the others and also from anything one might find in standard Indian restaurants); *pullao* or *biryani,* sometimes both; *dal; roti;* two or three different vegetable dishes (generically termed *tarkari* or *bhaji*); home-made chutney; and, finally, a range of desserts (*kheer, gulab jamuns, sandesh, kulfi,* and the like), made at home or bought from local Indian grocers and sweet vendors. In a humorous inversion of the commonplace adduced earlier, that one eats to live, it is often said that Indians live to eat. If, as Thorstein Veblen held, the hallmark of bourgeois life is conspicuous consumption, nothing is more conspicuously or passionately consumed than these weekend meals.

"What is your recipe for ————?" is a question often heard in people's homes. It belongs to the class of question usually though not invariably asked of and by women. My own repertoire as a cook has been enhanced greatly by all the recipes I have collected over the years from women in the community. With respect to the exchange of recipes, a procedural difference remains between me and other women in the community: Unlike me, they do not require exact measurements of amounts and ingredients; the barest detail suffices to convey a wealth of subtlety. Between the recipe giver and the receiver, there is a universe of unspoken steps that are assumed and implemented: "A little *methi* added to the *garam masala* will give the oil a more rounded flavor" (how much is a little?); or "once you've got the *sheera* made, you can prepare the dough for the *malpua*" (with no indication of how to make the *sheera* [syrup] for this particular type of dessert). In such situations I have always insisted on a methodical if vulgar belaboring of quantities and measurements, thereby revealing my gaucheness. For the expert cook, however, these details detract from one's competence as a cook (and as an Indian). Part of the legibility of one's own culinary stamp resides in interpreting the missing detail, in leaving intact the mystery of the transformation from raw to cooked.

Cookbooks are, therefore, largely inessential; they represent the refuge of the untrained, just as *tandoori* chicken appeals most to the taste buds of the uninitiated. Instead, women in the community are more likely to have their own stock of recipes—gathered from family and friends (both in India and in the United States), innovated from existing recipes (how to improve upon Mrs. *Balbir Singh's Cookbook,* for instance), or invented wholesale using hybrid ingredients and improvised methods. So it is that I have partaken of *samosa*s made with eggroll skins, chicken curry spiced with tomato ketchup, and *alu paneer* made with ricotta cheese and canned potatoes. The premium here is on the shortcut, particularly given the communal emphasis on quantity and variety, although it should be said that the labor-intensive character of Indian cooking is only moderately relieved through such measures. On the other side of things, everybody recognizes that, as the saying goes, real value can only be earned the old-fashioned way and that no substitute exists for the authentic preparation. Authenticity is about distinction and distinctiveness within Bourdieu's conception of the habitus, as well as in the parasubjective sense of a structure of feeling. Of course, the very idea of authentically making an Indian dish in an American kitchen, using materials bought at supermarkets and ingredients that have complied with FDA regulations, may appear misguided to those who take authenticity to be an unsupportable matter of supportable origins. But were one to not discount the investment in authenticity as irredeemably archaic or bound up in a Heideggerian quest for a thingness of things, it might become possible to think of the category of the authentic as a problem of materiality itself.

I realize that my interest in reviving the value of authenticity immediately comes up against Derridean and Foucauldian critical fashions that almost reflexively assert that the idea of authenticity is metaphysical or naive or both: Who could possibly have any intellectual faith in something that smacks of ontology, without at the same time being hopelessly prey to a pre-poststructuralist illusion about the "real"? Begging the question of why an antimetaphysical stance is more radical than are the emphases of a phenomenological Marxism or, closer to home, the Frankfurt school's dialectical conceptualization of the relations between *physis* and metaphysics, contemporary "theory's" privileging of ideals of repetition, supplementarity, and discursivity has led to a correlative undermining of any talk of reconciling consciousness with nature.[16] However, if we were not to lend ipso facto legitimacy to the poststructuralist overvaluation of language games (as if all historical questions could be reconciled theoretically and, moreover, in protocols of reading), we might come up with more insightful negotiations of the apparent impasse between truth and knowing. The issue of authenticity, tied to a critique of origins and to the entire conceptual machinery of Nietzschean thought (for example, "Truth is the kind of error without which a certain species of life cannot live"),[17] is highly, almost ecstatically, abstract.

To take just one example: In a book that garnered much acclaim in literary-critical circles, Susan Stewart regards all narratives of authenticity as *narrative* and therefore as "symptoms" of the prelapsarian desire for a reality that denies "the crisis of the sign."[18] Lest I be accused of paraphrasing too much, let me call on the words with which she expresses some ideas on longing for the authentic:

> The second meaning of *longing* [the first having to do with a pre–eighteenth century notion of "yearning desire"], "the fanciful cravings incident to women during pregnancy," takes us closer to an imagined location of origin, be it the transcendent with its seeming proximity to the immortal or the rural/agrarian with its seeming proximity to the earth; for it is in pregnancy that we see the articulation of the threshold between nature and culture, the place of margin between the biological "reality" of splitting cells and the cultural "reality" of the beginning of the symbolic. Out of this dividing—this process of differentiation and relation—the subject is generated, both created and separated from what it is not; and that initial separation/joining has a reproductive capacity that is the reproductive capacity of all signifiers.[19]

Heady stuff to be sure, particularly given the way Stewart trucks with "language and materialism" (to echo the title of an early book on the subject).[20] The materiality of the maternal body and the indubitable so-lidity of a reference to the earth, to rural/agrarian concerns, and to cellu-lar biology are juxtaposed to make the case that the "generative metaphor of writing" incorporates symbolization in general. From the moment beginning the subject's famous entry into the symbolic, all narrative will retrace and repeat the initial generation and loss of the momentous event of birth seen as a literal and, therefore, semiotic event. The "reproduc-tive capacity of all signifiers" is, as it were, primordially defined from this "initial separation/joining" of reproduction itself, and from such a de-termination (not to mention determinism) is born the narrative of au-thenticity—which is itself doomed to repeat the longing for a rejoin-ing with the maternal body/earthy agrarianism/unsplit cell and so on.

If my gloss sounds ungenerous, perhaps I may be forgiven because my point is to emphasize the degree to which this kind of narratologi-cal explication depends upon dissimulating a materialist interest in the world of objects and of reality (however qualified). In actuality, the ar-gument is entirely analogical, even more than it is metaphorical. It is predicated on a presumed though not necessarily established resem-blance among elements of the series posited (cell, body, enclosure, birth, separation, loss, signifier, meaning, and so on). Such a hyperbolic faith in the ability of narrative to incorporate both subjective and objective realities leads Stewart to exaggerate "the capacity of narrative to generate significant objects and hence to both generate and engender a signifi-cant other."[21] In the process, she blurs the very line between truths and their representation. Once the defining fact of birth has been allowed, no other material fact can be entertained; all facts and all material ap-pear as "fanciful cravings," ideologies *not* of "the transcendent" (al-though that is how Stewart mistakenly phrases it above) but of the transcendental.[22]

Other ways exist to represent the alleged misbegottenness of the idea of authenticity, ones that avoid the excesses of an argument based, as is Stewart's, on Julia Kristeva's semiotic theories. Nonetheless, if they take a poststructuralist lead, the fear of totality (read as totalization, the tran-scendental, the phallus) is not far behind.[23] Authenticity can once more be written off as degraded ideologism. But paths not on the poststruc-turalist road map are also there for the taking, and I shall follow one that allows me to reconnect, albeit circuitously, the issue of authentic-ity with the sociality of food, Indian-style.

In a discussion that has provided much more serious food for thought than made possible by my dietetic considerations here, Adorno uses the term "exact imagination" *(exakte Phantasie)* to propose the conjunction of knowledge, experience, and aesthetic form.[24] (I take the term's translation as "exact imagination," rather than "precise fantasy," from Shierry Weber Nicholsen's impeccable arguments in *Exact Imagination, Late Work: On Adorno's Aesthetics.*)[25] An "exact imagination" designates a nondiscursive form of truth; that is to say, the primacy of the object over language. I would not wish to diminish the importance of recognizing that Adorno's proposition emerges within the context of his writings on aesthetic experience, whose modernist rarefaction put them at a great distance from everyday life in an administered society. And yet, as Nicholsen argues, "the aesthetic dimension of Adorno's work holds out, and is indeed premised on, the possibility of a valid, that is 'adequate' or 'authentic' subjective experience."[26] The ideal of genuine subjective experience, not the "jargon" of *Eigentlichkeit* (the "in-itself" of Heideggerian existentialism), refers to the truth content *(Wahrheitsgehalt)* of material, sensuous reality, which it is our task to decipher.

When Adorno derides the idealism of an "in-itself," he does not do away with authenticity as a concept. Rather, his purpose is consistent with the method of immanent critique, and as Trent Schroyer points out in the foreword to the English translation of *Jargon der Eigentlichkeit,* Adorno's intent is to "include in the perspective of critical reason the *truth of the existentialist concern for the fundamentalness of human subjectivity.*"[27] Adorno, then, saw the rescue of truth residing in the negation of the "pathos of archaic primalness"[28] hidden in the "philosophy of As-If"[29] (the "as-if" of existential subjectivism, the "as-if" of ideology as language, and, we might add, the "as-if" of Lacan's notion of the unconscious structured like a language).

So the authentic for Adorno does not disappear merely because language is incapable of grasping it (in this, as in much else, his thinking differs from that of the French Heideggerians). In fact, he referred to the overburdened readings of the power of meaning alone as "linguistic mendacity."[30] However much one wants to indict Adorno for contradictions in his thinking, the range of his works reveals a conviction about the content of truth pressuring what exists (as art or nature) through its preponderance, without itself becoming identical with truth. Totality, by no means a suspect category in his constellation of ideas, can be conceived as he says, "only in the absence of images."[31] By this light, the authentic is part of the content of materialism, of thinking totality in the present. Indeed, Fredric Jameson reminds us that "Adorno's materialism . . . wishes above all to elude the representational; in it fulfillment and the somatic realization of the object world must somehow exclude the intermediation of the image."[32] In other words, it is the representation of truth that contributes to inauthenticity, not truth itself; moreover, there must be some way, beyond the mediation of the image, to actualize the authentic—not through any simplistic ascription of what Adorno calls a "positive vision of Utopia"[33] but from within the experience of history and as its critical cancellation. What Jameson calls the "necessary dilemma of the representation of 'totality'"[34] is thus at the heart of Adorno's dialectical and materialist relationship to the conceptual instrument of totality and to the negative content of the category of the authentic.

Though a great deal of Adorno's thinking about authenticity, truth, nondiscursive rationality, and subjective experience is conducted at a dense level of philosophical conceptuality, what I take from it is his recognition that it is necessary to return our philosophical or theoretical assumptions about the world to the world itself. Therein lies a secular "resurrection of the flesh."[35]

One would be correct to hear Benjamin echoed in the idea of resurrecting the flesh. Important commentators on the work of Adorno and Benjamin (such as Jameson and Rolf Wiggershaus) have pointed out that much of what Adorno had to say early on in *The Jargon of Authenticity* and later in *Negative Dialectics* were elaborations of Benjamin's critique of Kantian conceptions of the relationship between knowledge and truth. Benjamin's insistence on holding fast to a notion of objectivity (for instance, in his enumeration of the "dialectical image" or of "true" experience [*Erfahrung*]) had occasioned Adorno's early charge (in the Adorno-Benjamin correspondence of 1935) that Benjamin's "dialectics lacked mediation." Adorno retracted this criticism twenty years later in the intellectual portrait of his dead friend in *Prisms* (1981), having incorporated many of Benjamin's insights into the contents of a negative dialectic. There is both subjective irony and objective consequence to the fact that Adorno's later positions vis-à-vis the problematic of cultural truth are very much in tune with Benjamin's emphasis (sometimes muted by Adorno, his institutionally better-established younger colleague) on the necessity to reckon with the "human element in objects which is *not* the result of labor." This human or authentic element, variably cited as a nonsensuous correspondence between the animate and inanimate world, the transmissible and enduring aspects of a work of art, the affirmation of the monad, or the essential translatability even of a life forgotten, traverses the course of Benjamin's own writings from the *Trauerspiel* book, *The Origin of German Tragic Drama,* onward.[36]

Throughout, Benjamin's concern is to retain theoretical and material contact in his "philosophical anthropology" with issues of the flesh or corporeal truth. The world of objects, bound up in processes of reification under capitalism, is subject to the mystifications of the commodity form and *as such* conveys something about reified consciousness that is not altogether caught up within language (since, against idealist philosophies of language, subjective determination is not seen as exhausted within and by operations of the sign). Such a view is simply irreconcilable with the readings to which it has been subjected within poststructuralist conceptions of the role of language in generating the subject (and its others).[37] Benjamin does rely on formalisms between language or signification in general and other "ideogrammic" methods of adequating reality. But for him the proximity of representation to the real takes its definition from "techniques of nearness" (for example, the anecdote, fragment, film, and photography), which share the formal property with contemporary reality of having been structured by the objective social and historical conditions of capitalism. In other words, the relationship of resemblance is very far from metaphorical; rather, it is almost a palpable sense of copresence among the anecdote (or in the case of cinema, the frame), the lived detail, the administered life, and its "click" of authenticity. In Benjamin's constellative system, the flash of the photograph or the click of the camera produces not just a likeness with the fleetingness of truth but its actualization. According to him, "[t]he true method of making things present is: to imagine them in our own space (and not to imagine ourselves in their space)."[38]

In this reading, the question of authenticity has more to do with the phenomenal click of the presence of the past, of some ideal of truth occluded (but not merely fantasized), than it does with the retroactive click of a deferred action in which experience becomes the remembrance of something that was never true in the first place. It is not entirely surprising that such a reading departs from Freud—or, more to the point,

from contemporary Freudian criticism—given that Benjamin (as opposed to Adorno) relied on Freud's writings only occasionally and regarded as exorbitant many of his claims about the constitutive force of
latency or retroactivity in the practical actions of everyday life.[39] Nonetheless, the overall line of argument developed here with help from both
Adorno and Benjamin suggests that tarrying with the authentic is a matter of "making things present," an *exact imagination* of past things in
present spaces.

Food and Value

Let me switch analytic gears and return our attention to the detail that
earlier caught it: immigrant investments in authentic Indian cooking
and eating. It would be flippant but true to say that the food habits of
my ethnographic interlocutors resurrect the flesh in more ways than
one. Not only is there a clear emphasis on a form of sense perception
devalued elsewhere in the economy of bourgeois means and tastes, but
there is also a form of sociability associated with meals that has everything to do with making present a collective—as opposed to individualistic—sense of identity. The hypertrophy of the senses of sight and
sound at the expense of what, in a McLuhanesque mode, may be called
the "hot" media of taste and touch emblematizes a bourgeois hierarchy of
the senses, one in which the interiority of the individual reigns supreme.[40]
Within such a hierarchy, ocular and aural values are privileged in ways
that are not shared by those of touch, taste, or smell, on account of the
latter's association with baser instincts and bodily attractions. None of
this is unexpected as a description of a bourgeois regime of senses, just
as it is by now a commonplace that the bourgeois subject's emergence
is predicated on the *bildungs* projects of reading and listening (books
and music or painting and drama) as contrasted with eating, drinking,
and other carnivalesque practices.

So it is quite appropriate and not all that extraordinary to find extravagant rituals of food consumption acting as local exhibitions of an
ideal of propriety inherited from traditional, preimmigrant, and even
premodern forms of value. Within such an ideal, to touch the feet of an
elder or to eat sumptuously at weddings emblematizes a sensibility and
a respect for the senses of touch and taste quite out of kilter with the
high regard that modern Western etiquette places on visual decorum
and aural civility. To be polite in the West is to listen to one's interlocu-

tor, to not talk all at once, to maintain established boundaries of space between persons, and so on. To be polite Indian-style is to accept and offer food and hospitality. The two practices of social nicety are at odds, almost as if we were talking about very different kinds of things. But the parataxic, maladjusted quality of these culturally divergent virtues of politeness belies the homology underlying them. Each is a social discourse defined in relation to the bodily apparatus of sense perception. One celebrates the individual's self-consolidation within spatiotemporal coordinates and obeys the dictates of the senses of vision or hearing; the other understands the self only in relation to an ethic of collectivity that privileges gustative and tactile modes of comprehension. A resolution to this disparity between the premium on sight and the premium on taste or touch is found by combining them in the display of the communal feast within immigrant life. Food, eaten Indian-style with one's fingers, is inescapably about the synesthetic charge of touch and taste; consumed collectively and conspicuously within everyone's vision, it also becomes an expression of a mode of being in the (new) world, a visual presentation of the self in everyday life.

Weekend meals thus hint at the open secrets of belonging and longing. Culinary activity functions as a sort of "technique of nearness," gathering up into present space the magic of the past and permitting the imagination of ideas, objects, and events that are no longer available or repeatable except in a relay through food matters. Eating well and in the company of others, then, is about not paradise lost but paradise regained. It offers a sense of well-being that has less to do with things as they are now, or with personal comfort and individual success, than with repossessing commitments to oneself. And since the immigrant Indian's sense of self is always jostled by a collective imperative, satisfaction can only be garnered around others. The very taken-for-grantedness of alimentary customs—seeing the elaborate meal as a representation of an unquestioned Indianness—allows people to come to terms with their emergent and upwardly mobile investments in bourgeois individualism. The point is not that Indian traditions exalt the status of food—as indeed they do (as I discuss in the early parts of this chapter)—but that current expectations of "the good life in America" embody a material condensation of those traditions, these lives.

Cuisine, cooking, and eating habits represent particular understandings of the world, its systematic prohibitions and allowances. These discourses have received considerable attention, most notably in the work of Bourdieu, Certeau, Claude Lévi-Strauss, and, earlier, Georg Simmel. I have found this body of work tremendously helpful in organizing my own ideas about that which Lévi-Strauss calls "food that is good to think." But I should like to contend that the anthropologisms (of Lévi-Strauss and Certeau) and, by contrast, the sociologisms (of Bourdieu and Simmel) are escaped or at least sublated in what I have had to say so far. To wrap up my discussion of food matters, let me attempt to distill a few important features from two of these paradigmatic accounts of living and cooking because they reinforce my arguments about Indian food and immigrant conceptions.

"Living and cooking," as readers will no doubt recognize, is the phrase Certeau and his collaborators use (in volume two of *The Practice of Everyday Life*) to capture the gamut of practices surrounding the French concept of *terroir*—everything having to do with attachments to the earth, land, and food and with the borrowing of regional cuisines in the remaking of identities.[41] Since the French have already provided a major foil for my reading of the alimentary customs of immigrant Indians, Certeau's insights allow the comparison to continue. We learn, for instance, the translative fact that "*terroir* is rooted in the popular Latin *terratorium*, referring to earth, land, or soil, which is an alternation of *territorium*, referring more specifically to territory. *Terroir* is often employed in the context of food products that come from or have a flavor unique to a particular region."[42] The connection, we might even say conflation, of territorial and dietary matters underlines the intimacy among what we eat, how we belong, and who we are. However, the connection is not merely metaphorical or synecdochic (as in the saying "We are what we eat"); it is substantive insofar as the materiality of social identities are given their most solid value in food.

In a chapter titled "Plat du Jour," Certeau observes that "[e]ating, in fact, serves not only to maintain the biological machinery of the body, but to make concrete one of the specific modes of relation between a person and the world, thus forming one of the fundamental landmarks in space-time."[43] The alimentary is immensely practical, according to Certeau, although that by no means indicates lack of complexity: "What does one eat? It seems obvious that one eats what one can 'get' or what one likes—a proposition full of false clarity and loaded with erroneous simplicity."[44] The right answer has to do with the interweavings of memory and matter, ritual and calculation that give form to the taste for something definite: the *masala chai* served in the southern New Jersey household no less than olive oil served in Provence. Facts of food also remain the most durable and authentic point of reference in exile or for other brands of "life abroad," away from the genitive and generative locus of origins. These facts are, in Certeau's words, "a way of inscribing in the withdrawal of the self a sense of belonging to a former land [*terroir*]."[45] The interiorized self of the immigrant Indian—the emphasis on domestic discourses and privatized self-fashioning I have elaborated—can be aligned right alongside such an understanding of food as the last refuge of hope for those whose settlements with embourgeoisement have produced both psychic and class anxieties.

The class-configured lineaments of taste preferences including (but not limited to) food practices receive elaborate attention in Bourdieu's *Distinction*. His systematic analysis of the habitus in terms of a social class or class fraction and its ways of expressing a uniform logic across various aspects of lifestyle is a useful corrective to explanations about alimentary prescriptions that teeter between binarisms and voluntarisms. Whereas the binaristic propensity is to regard food, cooking, or eating in terms of theorems about purity and pollution, about the raw and the cooked—that is, as reductively structured—voluntaristic propositions allow for no structuration at all.[46] At this end, the idea is that, like other signifying practices, rituals of food exhibit a semiotic plenitude that resists any reduction or thematization. I would say that both the reductive and the archly semioticized views on dietetics run the risk of mere anthropologisms about cultural alterity. They exemplify alimentary equivalents of the Balinese cockfight: useful in specifying the "function" of ritual acts or in providing descriptive accounts of the plenitude of consumption, but less so for the purposes of theorizing the expressive systematicity of culture.

More reflexive in its approach, Bourdieu's modeling of the habitus and the intersecting coherences of food, clothing, furniture, music, and so on tells us some important things about the subjective choices people make, relative to their objective conditions defined by class position and social status. Suspended between practice and structure, or between preference and determination, Bourdieu's is an exercise in dialectical sociology. The following passage is instructive by way of the contrast it poses between the "working-class meal" and my own focus on middle-class Indian food habits:

> Plain speaking, plain eating: the working-class meal is characterized by plenty (which does not exclude restrictions and limits) and above all by freedom. "Elastic" and "abundant" dishes are brought to the table— soups or sauces, pasta or potatoes (almost always included among the vegetables)—and served with a ladle or spoon, to avoid too much measuring and counting, in contrast to everything that has to be cut and divided, such as roasts.[47]

In opposition to the ease of the working-class meal, the "bourgeoisie is concerned to eat with all due form." Such preoccupation with form, Bourdieu avers, is as much "a matter of rhythm, which implies expectations, pauses, restraints," as of sequencing fish, meat, cheese, and dessert. According to him, the forms and formalisms that the bourgeoisie impose on the appetite inculcate an air of correctness and a disposition defined by restraint and censorship, however gentle and discreet. (One example Bourdieu gives is of the bourgeois male who shaves and dresses first thing in the morning, "refusing the division between home and the exterior"—presumably because he is always and everywhere at home).[48]

The import of much of what Bourdieu has to say about the form and manner of oppositions between working-class and bourgeois practices of consumption among the French is of direct interest to our own case because, among other things, it reveals the combinatory aspects of the middle-class Indian meal. For one thing, the generalized Indian passion for food is akin to the "free and easy" manner of the working-class meal, as Bourdieu presents it. Likewise, abundance is valued and signified by both vegetarian and nonvegetarian dishes (such as chicken curry, *dum alu,* or *biryani*—all of which are served heaped on plates, defying measurement in the same way as do the pasta or sauces of working-class meals). Yet a calculus of restraint and correct eating also obtains in the middle-class Indian case, as with its bourgeois counterpart in France. Though the constraint against eating noisily or carelessly is removed (contary to the manners of the French bourgeoisie), Indians are extremely particular about the proper ways to serve oneself. These range from using the correct utensils specified for each dish to not "contaminating" the general offerings. For example, no cook would ever taste a preparation with a serving spoon and then return the spoon to the pot without washing it first, since it would be both vulgar and dirty to do so. Similarly, no guest would touch the food laid out at a party with a spoon, fork, or fingers that had already been raised to one's mouth. There are other proscriptions and prescriptions in the manner of eating and serving that very much guarantee the propriety of a meal. So though Indians may undervalue judgments about the "vulgarity" of indulging in the immediate satisfactions of food and drink, they greatly overvalue the ceremonial status of food and make pointed distinctions regarding the "correctness" of color, convention, and aesthetic aspects of dietary refinement.

Middle-class Indian tastes thus represent both a midpoint in the opposition between freedom and restraint as well as a reformulation of bourgeois expectations themselves. Moreover, they confound the opposition between (bourgeois) form and (working-class) substance precisely to the degree that the homology between taste culture and class culture expresses, as well as *fails* to express, the specificities of postcolonial articulation. Of such culturally relative confusions is class anxiety made.

CHAPTER FIVE

The Dialectics of Ethnic Spectatorship

It is Indian but it is universal. It is past but it is present. It is personal, immediate, full of high drama and tense story, but it is ceremonial. It is simple, recognizable, but it has another dimension.

—Cover blurb from *The Mahabharata* by
JEAN-CLAUDE CARRIÈRE

[I]n the house of the hangman one should not speak of the noose, otherwise one might seem to harbor resentment.

—THEODOR ADORNO,
"The Meaning of Working Through the Past"

Estrangement

In the 1998 translated collection of Ernst Bloch's *Literary Essays* there is a highly suggestive discursus on the distinction in German between alienation *(Entfremdung)* and estrangement *(Verfremdung)*.[1] The former, Bloch avers, has a peculiarly economic tint to it, "having been applied from earliest times in the context of commercial activity." In the Hegelian tradition and particularly for Feuerbach, the word *"entfremden"* takes on the negative connotation of becoming alienated from oneself. Bloch tells us that only with Marx does *entfremden* get the final gloss of a "system of exploitation wherein nothing remains of the human being who is forced to sell himself except the form of the disempowered worker."[2] By comparison, the word *verfremden* ("to estrange") takes its meaning from the 1842 German novel *New Life*, which depicts the estrangement and deep hurt of parents whose children only speak French in their presence. The parents "feel estranged to the point of being invisible, or reduced to the status of servants who are not supposed to overhear the masters' conversation."[3] Bloch observes that

> [i]t is quite a leap from here to [Bertolt] Brecht's use of the word 'estrangement' [*Verfremdung*] (although the distancing effect of the strange word—the foreign word—may be a point in common). The 'estrangement effect' then becomes one of pulling back, displacing characters or occurrences away from the habitual in order that they can be made to seem less self-evident.[4]

A sense of strangeness overlaps both words, which Bloch sums up accordingly: "'*Entfremdung*' and '*Verfremdung*' are linked by strangeness [*Fremdes*] and externality and yet separated, each in its own specially discernible way, by a *bad contrast and a helpful one*."[5] The "bad contrast" Bloch refers to here is not that between "*Entfremdung*" and "*Verfremdung*" but that between the homely *(heimlich)* and the strange; it has to do with "the unfriendly, unhappy, and unwanted state of that which lies outside, which cannot in any way contain us."[6] It is the kind of alienation that, above all in the selling of one's labor power, reduces and quantifies—whereby, in Bloch's terms, one is "partly transformed into a mass, partly into pieces of apparatus, and partly both."[7] The corollary formulation of a "helpful" contrast is one that is "not unfriendly" because the attempt here is to shed light on an object by holding it aloft, at a distance, in order to make the scales fall from one's eyes, rendering the familiar strange and the strange familiar (the logic behind Brecht's famous *V-effekt*). Bloch's intimations of the commonalities between "*Ent-*" and "*Verfremdung*," that is, of the mutual recruitments of the economic and the linguistic/familial give us an opportunity to pull back from the modernist privileging of estrangement as an aesthetic value and to rejoin strangeness to the sense of disempowering alienation (connoted by "*Entfremdung*").

Having reinserted some of the early force of both a material and a mental calculation into the problematic of self-consciousness, we can now rethink the question of linguistic and commercial currency in mutual terms. Just as the parents who were left out of a conversation in a language they did not understand felt themselves to be discounted and reduced, the language of culture (even when it promotes enlightenment through a detour of otherness) can have debilitating effects on those providing the grounds for such incursions into the heart of darkness.

The problem of ressentiment, which Theodor Adorno, in the second epigraph above, casts in terms of the sense of guilt one must feel at speaking of the noose in the hangman's house,[8] faces those of us who must reckon with our stereotyped reception in the West—*not* because we are outside it but precisely because our speech is enabled by the very conditions that enforce stereotyping, silencing, and reduction. To say that Western anti-ethnocentrism is suspect and that it is a coin whose reverse is a post-imperial self-authorization reflects bad form and unseemly resentment in the face of the intentions of those promoting the cause of multiculturalism, diversity, cosmopolitanism, a non-Western canon, and so on.

The implications of such bad form—the "bad contrast," as Bloch puts it, to be found in that exteriority "wherein one is made strange even to oneself"—will be explored in this final chapter. I will advance my case by using a specific example of media representation, that of internationally acclaimed director Peter Brook's production of the Hindu epic, *The Mahabharata,* to consider how the process of remaking the self proceeds under the glare of the media. For it seems to me that the tension between self-representation and dominant cultural imagery, the distances separating immigrant conceptions of selfhood and Western understandings about (in this case) Indian literature, religion, and mythology, are at the crux of the problematic both of cultural authenticity (in the light of my contentions in chapter 4) and of cultural translation in a world that is simultaneously familiar and foreign. Here, a further curiosity attached to the old meaning of *die Fremde* ("foreign land") may be noted: Bloch tells us that "it once meant 'suffering,' and also 'going astray.'" For him the point is that "these things [suffering, straying] are experienced anew, not as far-removed exterior states, but as conditions of the homeland, in the world of our externalized, commodified, and reified lives."[9] If there is a resonance to the personal pronoun "our" in the context of discussing "the world," the variation yet to be worked out and the one that interests me has to do with the point of view *of* the strange: the outsider inside, or she who suffers as the foil of strangeness so that the unhomely *(unheimlich)* can be assimilated to reassure those who are at home in the world.[10] What is the state of exception when strangeness is experienced as homeliness (where the latter bears the tint of the coarse and unbecoming but relates literally to feeling at home)?

At the very heart of issues of representation, this question has been at stake in one form or another through the entire inquiry into the everyday life of Indian immigrants. Let us now refer the terms of the question to the ground of spectatorship and the consumption of images. Given a media-saturated culture, it is inescapably the case that the "detailing" of selfhood takes place against the backdrop of the mass media.[11] But even if immigrant postcolonials, like everybody else, are socialized by the media into being American (or at least Americanized), watching television, going to the movies, or reading newspapers also produces in them a recognition of the myriad ways that they are out of joint with the mainstream culture. Learning to be socialized thus involves coming to terms with how media narratives work to enforce a sense of strangeness in minority subjects who are, as I said at the beginning of this book, "not quite not right." And as I have tried to demonstrate, this sense of alienation in the promised land is managed through the displacements of the domestic and the everyday, with larger questions about social or political identity transposed onto private expressions of daily life. The turn toward interiority, then, far from being the stuff of a radical impulse, is the last resort of subjects who have been made to hide in the light of their desire for "representation."

For immigrant subjects who witness their own projection as ethnic stereotypes, the imperative of a specifically postcolonial consciousness results from having to pit a *lived* sense of tradition or history against its devaluation in and by the media. Needless to say, the point is not that one expects historically accurate and complexly elaborated representations in the venues of the culture industry, which subjects everything and everybody to the rationality of equivalence and the commodity. In terms of a commodity logic, the Taj Mahal is as likely to be the name of a recognizable historical monument as of a casino in Atlantic City. Nonetheless, it makes all the difference within circuits of cultural capital whether visiting the Taj Mahal or seeing it on television refers to the genuine article or its simulacrum and, by a similar token, whether it appears on the History Channel or in a James Bond film. At stake for immigrant Indians is the issue of what is to pass for authorized knowledge, informed history, and adequate representation, rather than the pabulum of mass entertainment or media stereotyping (which they know to be suffused with the residues of a colonial hangover about India). By the light of this desire to have Indian culture taken seriously, it is hardly surprising that the universalizing impulse behind all that is supposedly good drama, high culture, or literary refinement appeals to immigrant subjects no less than to others invested in the question of cultural value.

Accordingly, the ethnic subject, having entered the machinery of embourgeoisement, has to reckon with the tensions and contradictions between value systems, between what is valorized within the dominant social order and what is prized in any other. In the nature of such vexations, one is made to feel the weight of the bad contrast that makes it seem reasonable to ask if Kalidasa wrote as great an epic poem as Dante or, to take a more recent example, if Satyajit Ray's films match up to those of his Western modernist counterparts. However much one may wish to scoff at the reductivism of such questions, the fact is that not only do they have to be answered or at least faced, Indians (and they are by no means alone) are very much interpellated by the terms of the questions themselves. Thus, they want things Indian to be measured by the same yardstick and accorded the same value as matters that have transcended all contention: for example, the work of Beethoven, Shakespeare, Proust; or if not those, at least the same value as the work of Faulkner, and in a pinch maybe Whitman, and so on (a slippery slope if ever there was one).

The ironies of separating value from history and, equally, history from value may betoken the entire predicament of culture in the postcolonial moment, a moment that is characterized by both openings and blockages, to the point where it is sometimes difficult to tell them apart. In order, however, to have some grasp on what separates a good contrast from a bad one, one is obliged to think concretely about value and prevent it from dissipating into the kind of abstraction that has for so long legitimated particular ideological constructions of beauty, aesthetics, culture, philosophy, and so on as universal—in the last instance, if not earlier. In a world in which horizons of value are as dispersed as geographical or historical ones, alienation itself takes on new meaning and makes it all the more difficult to distinguish economic from cultural estrangement, contaminated as the categories are of culture and economy. Given that their legibility is not automatic and requires factoring in the specific histories informing contrasts between self and other, inside and outside, familiar and strange, the Brook rendition of the *Mahabharata* may be a useful document for examining the complicities as well as incommensurabilities of aesthetic, economic, or cultural experience.

If the self-consolidation of a community located outside the mainstream of American life is subject to the dominant culture's habit of rendering its own particularity transparent and passing it off as universal, Indians (like other marginalized constituencies) have to sustain a twofold struggle: first, with respect to contesting pregiven separations between a "real West" versus an "imaginary non-West," and second, with respect to reimagining the "vitality of tradition" (Adorno's phrase) whereby India and things Indian are made to resonate with immigrant realities.[12] In this enterprise of reimagining tradition, the specificity of spectatorship, that is, the interplay between subject positions and interpretive processes, is crucial to what Stuart Hall calls a "homeward journey" from displacement to the shores of an imagined arrival within narratives of "cultural identity and diaspora."[13] Discerning the materiality of spectatorship is, however, a tricky matter because, unlike critics who depend upon psychoanalytic theory, I am persuaded that the multiplicity of forces acting on self-determination makes such discernment more than a matter of "suturing" an ideological hail in the act of reading or spectating. But the situatedness of one's material circumstances, against and in terms of which all acts of recognizing oneself or one's world on the screen are given a form and an affect, has been the nub of a certain disciplinary (as well as political) problem, one that Jameson has wryly characterized as the problem of "Freud versus Marx."[14] That Freud has "won out," albeit quite unsustainably, is exorbitantly revealed in the critical literature.[15]

My own interest in exploring the question of readership and spectatorship continues to be troubled by a sense of analytic dissatisfaction about the adequacy of a model of psychic processes (made problematic not least because of its historical relationship to notions of the primitive and the anthropological) to explain complex social realities, not to speak of the constitutive mediations of the psychic and the social. So, as in the rest of the book, I "resist" reading conjunctures, that is to say, social and historical contradictions, in terms of specular understandings about formless "subject positions." In this connection, we may want to note that the idea of a conjuncture itself obviates such a reading, since, above all, the conception of a conjunction rests on the sense of a temporal discontinuity that renders moot any notion of an "essential" moment (which psychoanalysis *must* have recourse to in order for its analytic themes to claim validity as historical explanations).[16] No doubt, for true believers such resistance can be subsumed under the psychoanalytic teleology of regarding all resistances as "symptoms" of its own efficacy, but that is not my concern. Instead, what occupies me is the following contradiction: If the repertoire of images defining ethnicity or racialized difference becomes effective only through a dominant vision of history and historical processes, it also makes effective the ethnic spectator's refusal of the presumptive value and validity of such history. Moreover, the simultaneity of seeing and being seen—as ethnic—has something to tell us about the complications of strangeness, since the very means by which ethnic difference becomes visible to the eye of the mainstream beholder reveal the ethnic spectator's distance from the production of that difference. In other words, the relay between the cultural power of hegemonic representations and the contestatory force of everyday narratives is not already settled in favor of the dominant reading even if (and perhaps especially because) the "cunning" of history has favored the master and not the slave or, one might say, the analytic reading over the analysand. In what follows, I engage the standoff between dominant representations and subordinated understandings by breaking it down into some epistemological and experiential components. I look at Brook's extravagant representation of the Indian epic as a problem of failed mimesis, and I read it in the light of my ethnographic informants' reception of such a presumptively "highbrow" and hence desirable depiction of their own civilizational claims. As I hope to demonstrate, Brook's production works to estrange rather than illuminate my informants' sense of their world and themselves. Through a turn of the dialectic, this becomes the occasion for an emergent critical consciousness of the self.

Spectacle

In the spring of 1991, Peter Brook's six-hour filmic adaptation of the classical Hindu epic the *Mahabharata* was serially shown on public television in the United States. Preceded by much fanfare in the mainstream media, the telecast followed on the heels of a nine-hour version that had been performed on stage (receiving enthusiastic reviews from theater critics).[17] The *New York Times* provided "A Viewers' Guide to an Epic Telecast of an Indian Epic," telling prospective viewers that "they should be forewarned that they have precious little time left to prepare for this event. The saga presents nothing less ambitious than the Hindu story of mankind; its plot has the degree of difficulty of Shakespeare's history plays, and it shines with a spiritual significance akin to that of the Bible."[18] The critic for the *Times*, Glenn Collins, cast his preview as a "Cliffs Notes Version of the Epic" and much in the manner of CliffsNotes, Collins prepared his readers with information on the epic's title, source, director (Brook is called a "superdirector," whose impressive credentials include having directed "The Tragedy of Carmen," "King Lear," and "The Cherry Orchard"), text, characters, philosophy, and, finally, an "academic disclaimer" stating that "[t]hese notes are not a substitute for the work itself."

The first installment of the television serial opened with its own preview of the narrative and action. A voice-over narrative of the epic's themes conveyed the essential plot details, which were said to concern "the fate of the world itself,"[19] war, power, revenge, and the unifying love of a woman. Audiences were told that the story dealt with magic and the supernatural (while a monstrous grinning face loomed on the television screen) and that it was about India, whose "pageantry, legends, and beliefs" represented the "source and subject" of the text. Immediately following the voice-over introduction, Brook, the director, appeared on screen to say that he was "very lucky" to have had "an old Sanskrit scholar" first narrate the *Mahabharata* to him, and he claimed that his experience of the story was the same as that of most Indians, who have been hearing it for "over two thousand years" from parents and storytellers, in bazaars and temples, and so on.

According to Brook, the *Mahabharata* is "real historical fact transformed into myth." "It is the story of India, the story of the world, and our story as well," because it portrays a struggle "that tears a family apart," a struggle in which "every one of our notions about right and wrong, good and evil are turned upside down." In a final contextualizing thrust, intended, one presumes, to impress an audience literate in the Western canon, Brook proclaimed that the *Mahabharata* was "longer than the Bible and far longer than Homer"; to render it faithfully, he said, would "take a year." Having thus authorized himself and the production, audiences were sent on their way to experience the show itself. PBS's *Great Performances* series (which included this production) is based on a format wherein a dramatic prolegomenon is followed by announcements of the program's sponsors. Like others in this series, *The Mahabharata* was underwritten by the Texaco and Martin Marietta corporations. The latter, we are told, is in the business of "information management" and of "masterminding tomorrow's technologies"; the former, a readily recognizable petroleum conglomerate, was simply announced by name. Finally, in what is by now a familiar gesture of televisual interpellation, audiences were informed that the "finest in performing arts" is made possible "by the support of viewers like you."

The details of the program's sponsorship, placement in a particular series, and so on not only constitute what Raymond Williams referred to as "flow" (the ways that television instaurates a certain uniformity of message content through the production of a de facto lack of differentiation between advertisements and programming), they also make visible the apparatus underwriting the intelligibility of any message in the first place. The corporate sponsorship of culture is not simply an issue for those who would be detained by a "vulgar" belaboring of the conditions under which images are produced and circulated; it also provides the enunciative frame for all texts and their reception, if they are to be disseminated within mainstream circuits of the media. The question behind any consideration of global cultural representation is therefore always at least partly constrained by the terms of entry of the non-West into the West. And these days it seems to be the case that non-Western art and culture have to negotiate the same economies of scale as do other, more narrowly economic aspects of transnational capital. With regard to the case in point, *The Mahabharata* was brought to American audiences by "tomorrow's technological masterminds": Martin Marietta, the corporation that became more of a household name from having manufactured the ill-fated space shuttle *Challenger*'s O-rings than from its long-standing position as a major defense contractor. The show's cosponsor, Texaco, is of course the company that has for years underwritten the military regime in Nigeria to protect its monopolistic oil interests in that part of the world. Since the capitalization of global art and culture proceeds very much in accordance with the governing logic of transnational capital itself, the traces of this logic are accordingly apparent in the forms and milieux enabling the dissemination of culture as information, to adopt Walter Benjamin's way of describing the instrumentalization of culture. If, after Althusser, we have learned to be mindful of the "relative autonomy" of superstructural elements, the predicament of late-twentieth-century capitalism should leave us wondering how "relative" this autonomy is and how far the distances are between local culture and global economies.

At stake behind such considerations of the auspices under which *The Mahabharata* was hosted on public television are the ways that the logic of equivalence underlying the production of commodities also enforces a logic of uniformity on cultures, practices, and traditions. The result is that completely dissimilar cultural texts are somehow made to fit into a universalizing rubric of "the arts," if only as "ethnic" diversions. Their very unfamiliarity or strangeness becomes the measure of their value, just as their entry into the global cultural scene simultaneously dissimulates the barriers to entry put up by capital in its efforts to capture world markets. One does not have to draw any direct connections between base and superstructure to make the banal observation that there would be no *The Mahabharata* without Texaco and no Texaco without Nigeria; sometimes, as Brecht said in his *Life of Galileo,* the shortest line between two points may well be a crooked line. The complicity of latter-day gestures of "defamiliarization"—now no longer attached to a transformative politics but merely to a consumerist one—with an imperializing vision is belied by the inappositeness of a logic of equivalence within which all cultures are rendered in terms of a collection of unthematized "artifacts" (whose only common ground is their substitutability). Difference is rendered indifferent less as a result of any linguistic capacity of the signifier than from processes of reification accompanying life under capitalist exchange in which the prime imperative is uniformity and standardization. So it is that PBS's recommended diet of cultural fare includes things syncretically assembled, from *Brideshead Revisited* and *I, Claudius* to *The Mahabharata.* The implicit if not explicit assumption of such syncretizing efforts is that cultural forms are digestible in units whose codes of construction are the same regardless of their provenance, history, or modes of signification. Any evidence of recalcitrance or difficulty in assimilating them has only to be subjected to a protocol of instrumentality so that the culture consumer can approach unfamiliar cultures and texts much in the manner of the mediocre test-taking student whose anxiety is alleviated by resorting to CliffsNotes.

The appetite for cultural otherness, satisfied by this sort of wild and woolly syncretism, bespeaks the fetishization of sheer artifactuality satirized in Jorge Luis Borges's description of the apocryphal Chinese dictionary (itself largely made famous to North American consumers of theory by Michel Foucault's reference to it in *The Order of Things*). It may be recalled that in this mythical dictionary, animals are defined in a random series of disconnected items: "belonging to the Emperor," "having just broken the water pitcher," "sucking pigs," and so on.[20] The problem Borges exposes has to do with a certain rationalist faith in the objectivity of objects by which an "exteriority" or a "reification" (to continue with Bloch's note on bad contrasts) enforces meaning on that which is otherwise incomprehensible or strange. Borges's example allows us to draw an unrelated conclusion about the entanglement between objectivism and imperialism and to recognize that the imperium is efficient precisely to the extent that it continues to produce an infinity of images that replay the history of the same. Imperialist discourse demands absolute sovereignty, and in the reconfigured context of postcoloniality (rather than colonialism), this demand is set up to be catered to by cultural products as much as anything else.

So if the logic of contiguity, displacement, and replacement now works to an end other than that required by the precise economics of colonialism, the postcolonial context reveals the efficiency with which promiscuous readings of culture themselves acquire the status of multicultural masterpieces. By "promiscuity" I mean to indicate the ways that eclectic arrangements of texts and practices under the rubric of an expansive cultural horizon whet the cannibalistic desires of today's consumer-tourist for the world's products, be they ethnic jewelry, Shona masks, the Dalai Lama, or chicken *tikka masala*. The expansiveness of cultural tastes does not (and cannot) contend with the structural effects of enforcing availability on narratives that resist assimilation within the symbolic order of the West. This is not to argue for a nativist enclave of cultural authenticity available only to those who remain outside Western contexts (as if that were at all possible). Rather, it is to call attention to the cynical indifference about the world produced by situating cultural forms as if they were merely variants from elsewhere of the West's own well-worn attitudes and habits of psychologizing the uncanny and the strange in order to render them into the other within the self, the other of the self, and other such putative reversals of self-valuation. With *The Mahabharata*, what audiences were given was in most ways conceptually contained within a lopsided production of narrative, fantasy, and self-consolidation—all aspects, as Freud would remind us, of a pleasure principle renounced and recovered in the name of a worldly and cosmopolitan attitude toward "civilization." I shall comment a little later on the local effects of such gestures of cosmopolitanism as they relate to my ethnographic community's reception of *The Mahabharata*.

For now, though, I want to return to some of the fantastical apects of Brook's appearance in the prologue to the telecast.

One cannot but be struck by Brook's self-authorizing gestures. What is at stake, one wonders, in his claiming "equal access" to the *Mahabharata* (as most Indians are presumed to possess)? The issue is certainly not one of verisimilitude or experiential equality, since the acquisition of specific cultural understandings about the *Mahabharata* is a complex matter for Indians, determined by relationships of class, access to indigenous texts and traditions, education, religious affiliation, and perhaps other factors as well. To cast, as Brook does, the dissemination of an oral tradition (such as that embodied by the *Mahabharata*) as instrumentally transmitted—*from* parents and storytellers, *in* bazaars and temples, and so on—is to entirely miss the incommensurabilities of subjective aesthetic experience. One might note that even as a matter of speaking colloquially, it is absurd to imagine that any Indian dashes off to the bazaar for a small dose of the *Mahabharata*. The value of the word "bazaar" in this context has to do with its connotations for the Westerner, who envisions snake charmers and rickshaws and has a generalized association with the exotic much more than he imagines a setting for storytelling. My contention is not that the experience of historical traditions is an ineffable or mystical affair; quite the contrary, since the experience of "most Indians" (should we want to accept such a broad designation) is not commensurable through a naming of places and practices that can then be asserted to guarantee the authenticity of an experience.

What I want to argue, instead, is consistent with my overall understanding of the place of the everyday in consolidating a sense of tradition for its intended receivers. Tradition, that is to say, has less to do with rarefied, mystery-laden entailments of existence than it does with the particularities of a lived reality in which aspects of the past are inhabited as, to rely on Williams's coinage once more, a structure of feeling. Consequently, the receivers of a historical tradition engage its experience and retelling in terms of a quite different configuration of temporal and epistemological relations. These relations have to do with the myriad ways that myth, memory, and an elusive sense of tradition "erupt" into the otherwise inertia-laden aspects of conscious existence—the details, as I discussed in chapter 4, of an "exact imagination" *(exakte Phantasie)* of past things in present spaces. But since such imagination has very little to do with instrumentalizing culture or history, any attempt to marshal it for the presentist purposes of retrieving the contents of a "great tradition" (by Brook or, in a different context, by Hindu fundamentalists, or "saffron nationalists," as they are sometimes dubbed) can at best strike a false note.[21]

This may also be a moment to recall the distinctions Benjamin sought to develop in thinking about community and its erasure in modernity by agents of "progress." For him, the idea of tradition and its continuity (or loss) is inextricably tied to the experience, or more precisely, to the *atrophy* of experience, associated with the shock of being modern. Consequently, reconsolidating the "chain of tradition" requires a temporality no longer easily available in the repetitive and monotonous contemporary predicament. In "On Some Motifs on Baudelaire," the difference is specified between forms of relaxation in a world where storytelling is still possible and the impossibility of the kinds of remembrance proper to tradition that attends the unraveling of community under capitalist alienation.[22] According to Benjamin, the continuity of tradition demands a community of listeners whose collective memory contains sediments of both remembrance and reminiscence. The fragmentation of experience in modernity, however, produces only maculated subjects who can no longer access that "alert forgetfulness" characteristic of a traditional existence (in which a story's significance was marked by the reciprocities between teller and listener rather than by the content of what was told). By contrast, the function of storytelling within an instrumental framework of "who said what to whom" takes on a reified form in which the attempt is continually to evoke "the experience of that which can no longer be experienced," not least because the emphasis on individuality— of the story, the teller, and the self-aware listener—militates against collectivity and collectivization. Moreover, since the ability to exchange experiences between storyteller and listener is overridden by the cognitive constraints of modern life, a quantitative impulse takes over for the qualitative sharing of values, assumptions, and possibilities—not all of them entirely imagined, and few of them calculable through objectivist criteria.

To bring these points to bear on the production of *The Mahabharata*, we may want to mark the importance of such "epistemo-critical" considerations mentioned by Vijay Mishra as that the *Mahabharata* belongs to a tradition of *smrti* texts, an entire heritage of "remembered" texts, whose authority in the ancient Sanskrit canon depended not on its originary status (beginning somewhere around the sixth or seventh centuries B.C.) but on the transformations wrought upon it through time and experience.[23] Unlike its Homeric counterparts, the *Mahabharata* has little to do with an individual's self-knowledge, quest for identity, test of strength, or love of a woman (although all these are epiphenomenally present in its anecdotes as well). Rather, it is constitutively about discordant life; as Mishra tells us, it is "about power and politics, about national disintegration and schisms."[24] If such a description of the epic's themes sounds a bit too modern, perhaps that is because unlike, say, *Beowulf* or the *Iliad*, it is a text whose contemporaneity has to do with the authenticity of its themes, not with its outdated classicism. But, again, these are issues beyond Brook's ken, given his preoccupation with good and evil and love and liberty, issues that seem to exhaust the "subjectivist" parameters of Western narrative and that thus, willy-nilly become the test of the *Mahabharata*'s own validity. As a result, the end product of Brook's ruminations about the meaning of life appears, as another Indian critic, Rustom Bharucha, noted,

> like a rather contrived and overblown fairytale, not unlike their [Brook's and Carrière's] trite adaptation of a twelfth-century Sufi poem by Farid-ud-din Attar in *The Conference of Birds*. The significant difference in the adaptations is one of scale: if *Conference* resembled an oriental version of *Jonathan Livingston Seagull* in its hour-long summary of 5,000 philosophical verses, The *Mahabharata* is nothing less than *The Ten Commandments* of contemporary western theatre.[25]

A compensatory piling on of detail, as if from Borges's imaginary dictionary; a Panglossian faith in the multiplicity of tongues (which in actuality dissimulates its faith in the capacity of a single language, English, to capture not only other linguistic expressions but other cultural experiences); and a self-serving appropriation of a disjunct set of concerns into a Shakespearean tale of love and war—such mutations are ineluctably the result of a miscalculation and perhaps even disregard of the historical and communal specificities of the *Mahabharata*, which Brook makes subservient to the liberal dictates of a pallid universalism. In his extremely pointed critique of Brook, Bharucha implies that in the postimperial context, cultural appropriations of the sort that *The Mahabharata* embodies are part and parcel of a "colonial residue" dressed up to look more appealing to would-be champions of the new "interculturalism." But he says,

> [I]t is odd how closely the text resembles the screenplay of Attenborough's *Gandhi* in its organized, steadily paced linearity, all the actions thudding along with predictable clarity. Both works are reductive encapsulations of epic material, big-budget enterprises that are part of the dominant productive systems in the west. Both represent images of India that are essentially removed from our historical reality, though Brook's orientalism is more apparent in colour and spectacle than Attenborough's more muted representation of the Raj.[26]

Brook's opening remarks suggest the difficulties of attempting to navigate cultural incommensurabilities in the name of an aesthetic of inclusion. By now we have learned to recognize that behind well-meaning gestures toward the "Great Family of Man" (an idea now long since demystified by Roland Barthes) lies the erasure of the agency of those in whose name inclusivity is mobilized. But given that it is seen as bad form to decry inclusiveness in a political and cultural milieu where it has become the watchword of a certain cosmopolitanism, Indian commentators can only sound resentful when they point out, as Bharucha does, that Brook fails to confront the context or community that serves as the basis for undertaking a representation of Indian tradition. "Can a story be separated from the ways in which it is told to its own people?" queries Bharucha.[27] If the ready answer is "no," the question also invites us to think about the reasons for such separations between story and situation, and cleavages between this telling of the *Mahabharata* and its innumerable retellings within Indian communities, past and present. Were we to go along with a certain poststructuralist framing of the problem of representation, it would have to be conceded that since all representations are misrepresentations, Brook's rendition may be as legitimate as any other attempt to capture a necessarily imagined Indian tradition. However, the rub here is that historical and experiential issues are seldom resolved through a logic of the signifier, and questions of affect, belief, or sensibility cannot be reconciled by a linguistic conception of meaning alone. If, as I contend, Brook's *The Mahabharata* is flawed on account of its noncomprehension of experiential truths, it has less to do with his "mistakes" in rendering the text than with his misunderstanding of the very different status and category of the aes-

thetic within everyday Indian structures of intelligibility. Gautam Dasgupta makes a related point when he observes that "[t]he dramatic truth
of this epic resides not in the aesthetic or narrative pull of the story but
in a very human exchange of beliefs that grounds, for the average Indian,
even the most elementary reading of the many tales woven throughout
The Mahabharata."[28]

It is perhaps worth repeating that I am not interested in advancing
an essentialist argument about belongingness by pointing to the force
of a subjective aesthetic sensibility. On the contrary, I contend that a
viable reading of tradition, any tradition, must take into account the
specificity of experiences—*not* essences—that make for an understanding of time, place, and story, particularly since, as Benjamin helped to
clarify, we need no longer think of the "aura" of tradition in terms of
singularity. This point is reinforced by Howard Caygill's reading of Benjamin's theory of experience, in which he emphasizes that "[a]ura is
not the predicate of a work of art but a *condition, now surpassed, of its
transmission.*"[29] Such a condition refers to the way (as Benjamin emphasized with regard to Hölderlin's poetry) that works of art change with
respect to their as-yet incomplete futures, a condition of their transmis-
sibility. This is to say that if texts (such as the *Mahabharata*) are to be
transmitted so that their substance is not violated, the limits and possibilities of what counts as the aesthetic must be faced squarely rather
than imputed to some narrow consideration of "the text." But if capitalist modernity has made it difficult if not impossible for us to conceive of such an expansive sense of the aesthetic—as would, for example, be required under the Indian regime of *rasa* (taste, in the broadest
sense)—it has also truncated our comprehension of experience itself;
to echo Benjamin, "narrative" has been "removed from the realm of living speech."[30] Caygill reminds us that "the often overlooked point [is]
that for Benjamin 'the fate of art' is *symptomatic* of a fundamental change
in the structure of experience which may be traced back to broader political and technical developments."[31]

If Brook (or the reader accustomed to getting his quick cultural fix
by watching television or consulting CliffsNotes) is at a disadvantage
when confronted with the *Mahabharata*'s strangeness, it is not only because the text belongs to a tradition and a history that has little to do
with Western schemas of knowledge and representation. It is also because
the West, in its imperialist sense of entitlement, in the historical imbri-

cations of knowledge and power, has insisted on subjecting that which is incommensurable, hidden, unsaid, and unsayable to its own calculus of experiential transparency—what Benjamin in "The Storyteller" distinguished as "verifiability."[32] At work in Benjamin's view of the constraints on reckoning with traditional modes and mores of experience is the fundamental dissimilitude between *Erfahrung* and *Erlebnis*. The latter involves the experience of the disconnected present: secular, fragmented, unique, "shockingly" modern, ultimately calculated.

By contrast, the former *(Erfahrung)* adumbrates a re-aestheticized— as opposed to *anaesthetic*—everyday experience based on a particular sublation of past and present.[33] A reconnected sense of the continuity between tradition and the present relies on neither a primary access to historical truth nor a consciousness of the primordial origins of traditional narrative. Rather, the conditions for grasping the materiality of the past in the present are given in the traces, or, to use the term Benjamin himself borrows from Baudelaire, the *"correspondances,"* subtending remembrance and experience. The discontinuities and disjunctions that together suspend time, text, and telling in a fragile network can neither be wished away nor simply flattened out for the instrumental purpose of "getting the story right." For they *are* the story, or at least they regulate the story's meaningfulness. In the case of the *Mahabharata,* the centrality of a time-bound consciousness (not the modern time of clock and calendar but a sense of the synchronic as an opportunity to do one's duty, live one's life, and so on) represents a certain aesthetic as well as an ethic of everyday life. This is hardly to propose that modern Indians fully grasp or live out the imperatives of such an ethics or aesthetics. But however difficult to realize in life, the ordinary Indian (diasporic or otherwise) has a very concrete and unexceptional sense of the importance of such ideals—retold in a myriad ways and in any number of situations and betokening the continuities between aesthetics, ethics, and the everyday. That these ideals are out of place within the rationality of modern existence is the reason for at least some of the contradictions of Indian identity, caught as it is between aestheticized investments in duty and obligation on the one hand and bourgeois ethics of self-improvement and independence on the other.

This is to suggest that, very much in the manner of the *madeleine* memory described by Benjamin as interjecting itself into an otherwise reified existence, a text like the *Mahabharata* resonates with its listeners if it can trigger the kinds of "counsel" that are now out of place. It instructs not by virtue of telling an unheard story but by repeating some now discarded and perhaps forgotten lessons about the cycle of life, death, and action. Encountering it now, in the present, thus involves reckoning with the distance between the trials of contemporary experience and the contents of a past wisdom. But such a reckoning is less the stuff of some utterly uncanny fable than it is the reactivation of a sense of lost collectivity. The key distinction may have to do with the kind of "pulling back from the habitual order" that, at the beginning of this chapter, I adduced Bloch as proposing, an estrangement that disrupts the predictability of everyday life through its heterogeneous evocation of other times and situations. If the fabric of daily life is rent by the weight of alienation, a "redeemed" understanding of tradition only proceeds in terms of what Benjamin would call a "profane illumination" based on the permeability of aesthetic estrangement *(Verfremdung)* and anaesthetic existence *(Entfremdung)*. It is crucial to keep in mind that the stakes in such illumination have to do not at all with modernist "technique"—directing estrangement against estrangement—but with a thoroughgoing reckoning of the experiential contingencies pressuring both senses of estrangement.

This, however, is not the sort of understanding or perspective Brook brings to his representation of the epic, which he turns into the monumental "story of India, the story of the world, and our story as well." The sense of "timelessness" implied by this formulation disguises the locatedness of a progressive humanism such that we are once more subject to an equivalence made out of nonequivalence: In Brook's categorical terms given in my first epigraph, "It [*The Mahabharata*] is Indian *but* it is universal" (emphasis added).[34] Brook's muscular assertion of equivalence in fact betrays the marks of a compensatory discourse seeking to make up or make over an authorial mastery of an expansive oral tradition inaccessible to him, on terms that are acceptably within a framework of strangeness rendered into sameness.

To this reductive move, Brook adds a dose of relativizing comparison. His audience is presumably to be impressed with the information that the *Mahabharata* outdistances both Homer and the Bible, the ultimate standards by which all and especially "multicultural" issues are to be measured. If it is too flippant a Freudianism to comment on anxieties about length, let it suffice to say that gestures of inclusiveness teeter on the brink of patronizing political concessions. As political concessions, they signify the power relations obtaining between a dominant viewership comprised of self-assured and self-authorizing cosmopolites and their ethnicized counterparts. For both constituencies, *The Mahabharata* as envisioned by Brook puts into place an irreducibly disconnected series of mythicized markers of the past, of otherness, and of an anthropologically fetishized strangeness unrelieved by any familiarity with or connection to its referents.[35]

This discussion has so far been conducted on terms that have to do with the distortions of appropriating tradition without regard for the constitutive ways that context determines intelligibility. We may also want to pause before aspects of the text itself and look at the details of Brook's representation. As one set of instances, let us consider the early moments of the production, moments that, even if we choose not to be detained by the contents of the entire narrative, make it possible to think about formal problems attending the production.

In the opening scene, the mise-en-scène depicts the recessed chambers of a cave temple, illuminated by scores of tiny oil lamps. Onto this stage appear, in order, an unnamed preadolescent youth who turns out to be a youthful Everyman, or, as I refer to him, Everyboy; the imposing personage of the sage Vyasa, the legend's narrator; and the mysterious figure of the elephant-headed god, Ganesha. Ganesha offers to be the scribe for the "Poetical History of Mankind," and after some initial astonishment on Everyboy's part that the elephant-head might be Lord Ganesha, all three sit down cross-legged to begin the task of narrating the history of the world. Inaugurating the story, though, proves to be a difficult task for Vyasa, who states: "There's something secret about a beginning. I don't know how to start."

To which Ganesha suggests, "As you claim to be the author of the poem, how about beginning with yourself?"

Vyasa agrees and proceeds with

A king hunting in a forest fell asleep. He dreamed of his wife and there was a joyful explosion of sperm.

GANESHA: Very good start.

VYASA: When the king awoke and saw the sperm on a leaf, he called a falcon and said, "Take my sperm quickly to the queen."

Mysteriously, the precious sperm, instead of reaching the queen, ends up in the belly of a fish, resulting (equally mysteriously) in the birth of Princess Satyavati, one of the *ur* maternal figures in the narrative. Vyasa, the storyteller, is then revealed to be the son of Satyavati, and a little later he is revealed as the unwitting progenitor of the entire clan of Pandavas and Kauravas, whose epic struggle he now is in the process of narrating. The misprisions of these early moments require explication in terms beyond the standard question "What doesn't belong in the picture?" because, in terms of a factual, or, rather, factitious logic of presence, Brook's rendering is literally correct. The point, however, is that the requisite criteria of adjudication have little to do with metaphysical notions of linear placement and positive portrayal. The metaphorical suggestiveness of linking the beginning of life and the beginnings of stories is conflated into a titillating adolescent banality about spontaneous emission, and, equally banally, the story devolves into a personalizing quest that has little to do with the text's evocation of the inscrutability of life. In his critique of Brook's (and Carrière's) adaptation of the epic, Bharucha comments on the familial resemblance to Homer's texts that has been forced onto the *Mahabharata*: "This Homeric compaction is felt most poignantly in the characterization of Krishna, who comes across more as a Ulysses than as a personification of the god Vishnu."[36]

Apart from such distortions, which persistently confuse the emphasis on genealogy with a pedestrian preoccupation with character and actor, what is missing in Brook's narrative is the capacious and yet obtuse negativity of the detail. By "negativity" I mean the kinds of anecdotal, ornamental, and everyday networks of semiosis evoked in Naomi Schor's reading of the detail.[37] The history and expansiveness of an aesthetic and imaginative past captured in the in-between spaces of the anecdotal and the unsaid completely elude the grasp of a representation committed to a rather Hamlet-like focus on the consequences of action (or inaction) and to fixing the legibility of "what actually happened." Among such missing ornamental and "negative" detail is any contextual explanation of the uncanny appearance of Ganesha in his elephant-headed form. Recent politically recidivist appropriations of this deity in the reconsolidated pantheon of Hindu gods aside, there exist everyday understandings of the "worldly" meanings attached to Ganesha. The most common is as *siddhidata*, emblematizing beginnings and auguring future success (from the Sanskrit *siddhi*, indicating fruition, completion). At the level of ordinary life, which nonetheless requires its own thematization, Ganesha signifies the absolute contingency (rather than originary status) of beginnings. He marks, as it were, the momentary (as opposed to momentous) place of starting out on a task or, equally, setting off the chain of signification within a narrative act. Reading the expressiveness surrounding the figure of this deity in this way is more than mere scholasticism on my part; on the contrary, it is consistent with the lived nature of a secularized tradition uncoupled from its alternative existence in a rarefied religiosity. It is precisely such an everyday sense of the links between the sacred and the secular that Brook misses with his rationalist embrace of the irrationality of the other. Ironically, the secular Western director seeks and finds religious ineffability in the East's mystical and poetical traditions, despite *The Mahabharata's* own philosophical but secular orientation toward problems of profane existence.

Similar objections about the incompatibility of meaning systems also emerge vis-à-vis the deployment of the character of the preadolescent youth, whom I referred to as Everyboy. In Brook's tale, Everyboy stands as a somewhat mystified and mystifying audience member at the scene of inscription. His presence during the narration of the "Poetical History of Mankind" is akin to that of the chorus in the conventions of Greek theater; he stands apart from the narrative even though it is, we are told, about him: "How [his] ancestors were born, how they grew up, how a vast war arose." And his minor interjections throughout the course of the performance serve more as Brechtian interruptions between actor and character than as mechanisms for linking the story and situation, teller and listener. Again, the point is not whether the use of such modernist aesthetic conventions is literally faithful to the performative tradition of the *Mahabharata* because, strictly speaking, that tradition is wholly improvisational, not to mention dissipated over time. Rather, the weight of such narrative devices rests on the peculiar complicities between aesthetic impulses and their afterlife in the field of power relations. In the current case, for example, the effect of displacing the provisionality of the exchange between teller and told, knower and known, onto a linear story of one family, one race, enacts a teleology of means and ends that has little to do with the text's own interweavings of life, history, and story—even though such displacements are common within a privileged Western framework of allegory.

Just as Everyboy becomes the singular, reductive hinge for narration and knowing, the storyteller himself is transmogrified into the individualized figure of the bard. The complexity of Vyasa's position, to be taken as the *occasion* for and not the bearer of meaning, is collapsed into a matter of authorship and origination. In the highly mediated context of the oral tradition to which the *Mahabharata* belongs, Vyasa's relationship to the epic clan is to be understood as marking a contingency of value, one in which scribes are like artisans, shaping the text through instantiating a known history. To take another example, in the parallel Hindu epic, the *Ramayana,* the figure of Valmiki functions to highlight generic ties between representation and self-representation; he is cast as the teller of the tale but only by virtue of a happenstance, not through any privileged relationship to the essence of the story (in the same way as identities may be thought of as accidental rather than ontological). The relation between teller and telling, or, from another angle, being and meaning, is, then, to be read as symptomatic rather than autobiographical, accretive rather than authorial. Vyasa signals the *mise-en-abîme* that is the experiential nexus of storytelling, with its recursions into and out of selfhood and sociality. Given its dominant construction as a text of otherness, Brook's *The Mahabharata* cannot actually take up this "bilingualism of the other" (to rephrase Jacques Derrida on the "monolingualism of the other") since, from the cloaked perspective of a liberal humanism, all "Third World" texts necessarily display the monolingualism, as it were, of alterity, which can then be embraced in the name of progressive causes.

Dis-Identification

The same spring (1991) that Brook's *The Mahabharata* was scheduled to be televised as the "cultural event of the year" by PBS, I returned to New Jersey to visit my parents and to conduct some follow-up interviews with children from families who had participated in the original ethnographic project.[38] At the conclusion of my official fieldwork, I was beset by misgivings about the fact that my ethnographic venture had not dealt directly with the community's media consumption. As a result, I did not feel able to comment with any authority on people's video habits or television-viewing patterns, aspects of social life that have acquired a certain salience for scholarship on media and identity. Though expatriate Indians consume a great deal of media (especially Hindi films on videotape), my interest had been directed rather more toward the realm of the taken-for-granted or the unliteralized, and had therefore been taken up with the unquestioned aspects of everyday life. From this standpoint, to address media practices as if they existed independently in some ontological category of their own seemed to reproduce the problem reifying "objects of analysis." Though in standard approaches to cultural study, the text continues to have a de facto if not de jure primacy, my own investments made it untenable to reinscribe the metaphysical value attached to such categories as "literature," or equally, "mass media," or indeed, "identity." Nonetheless, I was mindful of the impact of media representations on people's daily lives and had decided that some sort of engagement with the question of the media might enhance my own investigation.

In the course of a meeting with one of my informants, I was told that a few women in the community had arranged to gather and view the PBS broadcast of *The Mahabharata*. I should mention that the arrangements had involved no small reshuffling of their household schedules, given that the episodes were each three hours long and required that alternative arrangements be made about dinners, caretaking for the children, grocery shopping, and other routines at the end of the working day. Three full evenings had to be rearranged, and families had to be persuaded that all of it was worthwhile as an occasion for a get-together. Many women had insisted to themselves and to their families that this opportunity to experience "high quality" Indian culture was not to be missed, given how seldom such celebratory depictions were to be found in the mainstream media. I asked to be included in the collective viewing because, having already made the decision to watch the episodes, I thought the event would also give me a chance to renew my acquaintance with many of the women organizing it. On the evening of the telecast's first episode, I showed up at the appointed hour in the home that had been designated as "viewing central," albeit I had not counted on the ethnographic uses that were later to derive from the experience. I was accompanied by my mother, who, as one of the older women in the community, prided herself on keeping up with the classics and the cultural traditions of India and, moreover, on being familiar with various adaptations of the *Mahabharata* (from Rabindranath Tagore's *Karna-Kunti Sangbad* to C. Rajagopalachari's translation and Irawati Karvé's *Yuganta*).

We gathered around the large-screen television in the family room of our hosts' home. Apart from my mother and myself, there were five other women and our hostess's husband and teenage daughter (the last two were going to watch the show for a while before they decided if they were interested enough to view the rest of the production). As was to be expected in any social situation within the community, our hostess had gone to some trouble to make arrangements for the occasion, having prepared enormous quantities of elaborate Indian savories and sweets, all kept on hot plates in the kitchen at just the right temperature throughout the evening. Our hosts' home had been chosen for the viewing session because, among other considerations, it was set up for a sight and sound extravaganza—surround-sound television, high-end speaker system, comfortable seating for the entire party, the works. Prior to the broadcast, we were told by a friend who had gone to see the stage performance in New York that the production's sound effects were truly impressive and that we should not be able to capture the total quality of the show were we to discount that aspect of things. So armed with knowledge about the appropriate ambience and attitude required of an avant-garde theatrical experience, we sat with the volume on the television set turned up quite high, in postures of attentive and hushed expectation.

Our anticipation was rewarded soon enough with the prefatory sounds of conch shells, drums, cymbals and what can only be described as formulaic aural conventions for representing battle—horses neighing in the background, offscreen cries and grunts of warriors, and so on. Our eagerness to partake in the "spirit" of the performance notwithstanding, the sound was far too loud for people unaccustomed to listening to contemporary Western music, such as that of Philip Glass or Steve Reich, or to encountering the decibel levels at which, say, rock music is blasted out in clubs and discos. So despite everyone's desire to be faithful to the totality of the experience, we had to turn down the sound. Otherwise the whole production would have been not only incomprehensible but literally unbearable. After the atonal discordance of the introductory music died down Everyboy entered the stage in the first sequence, with credits rolling to the musical accompaniment of a traditional Bengali song composed by Tagore: "*Antara karo bikasitha mamo, antara taro he*" [Illuminate the depths of my soul, O lord of interiority]. The song initially elicited some approbation on the grounds that the producers of such an "international" show were so attuned to the internal valences of contemporary Indian music as to select *Rabindra-sangeet* (Tagore's music) for its opening music. This was particularly pleasing to my companions, most of whom that evening were Bengalis (as in the majority of my ethnographic encounters, and perhaps as a testament to the difficulties of making unproblematic claims about a totalizable "Indian" culture or identity).[39]

Nonetheless, as the song progressed, its oddness became apparent even to these enthusiasts. One woman commented on the lack of fit between the lyrics and the context of the epic. The song presented an exhortation for a cleansed and gladdened soul, unburdened from the cares of the world, whereas the story, as we all knew, was about a worldly genealogy; it is the story of the Pandavas and Kauravas and about birth, power, and obligation. So it appeared quite strange that such a song would be used as the preamble to a narrative putatively geared toward depicting the messiness of *maya* (the universe of material responsibilities and illusion commonly associated with the major themes of the *Mahabharata*). The worldliness of the tale and the oddly monastic song did not seem at all to cohere. By the time this disconnection had hit home, the song had drawn to a close and everyone agreed that it had probably been selected for the tune and not for its lyrics. "They probably didn't know Bengali and chose the song for its melodiousness," was the consensus among my interlocutors. Still, since much of the appeal of Tagore's music relies on the apposition of tune and lyric, form and content, the placement and character of the song departed from the ways that his music is understood and performed. Tagore was, if nothing else, heavily invested in exploring the legacy of Romanticism and the capacities of symbolic expression to bring together form and meaning. Such a sense of how the music works within its traditional parameters, its own "colonial" inheritances, or any other consideration of its aesthetic principles was of course missed in the way it was deployed in the opening sequence to signify a generalized mournfulness.

As the story unfolded, we were treated to Vyasa's narration of the *Mahabharata*'s moment of origin with, it will be recalled, a certain prince's wet dream in the forest. Soon after Brook's motley crew of actors appeared on-screen, with their hodgepodge of accents and unrecognizable costumes, our host announced that he had had enough. For him, the "inappropriate casting" of *The Mahabharata*'s major characters boded ill for the rest of the production, and he announced that he was not going to waste any more time on the event. Brook's decision to use a multicultural cast of actors drawn from his international troupe of performers, was not going down very well with our viewing group. If Brook's intention was to draw on Surrealist strategies of disordering and disorienting the eye and the ear, he succeeded only too well, having emptied out the content of personalities from their appearance. As a result, what we saw was *only* difference: a diversity of accents—some muffled, others garbled—and a hyperbolic attention to the color of the actors' skins. It is not that the *Mahabharata* disallows a questioning of difference; in many senses, the entire epic centers on the problem of belongingness and the impossibility of purity (which is why, for example, so much of the text's focus is on the undecidability of lineage). Within its compass, however, difference is not understood reductively to be about skin color and physiognomy alone; as a cultural preoccupation, this one is imposed from the outside but made to appear politically correct. It is perhaps predictable that Brook's preoccupation with the phylogenetic aspects of race have been viewed rather differently—and approvingly—by Western critics. Michael Kustow, for instance, commenting on Jean-Claude Carrière's French adaptation of the text (which provided the basis for Brook's English translation), expounds as follows:

> The *Mahabharata* was written in Sanskrit, but the words you hear are French, spoken with a piquant diversity of accents matching each actor's distinctive shape, skin and race. A diminutive North African Jew as elephant-headed Ganesha, then as Krishna. Vyasa, the bard of the poem, a ginger-haired Gascon. Tiny, tightbound Japanese, long-limbed loping Senegalese, pale-skinned Germans and Poles, a wide-lipped Lebanese, a princess with streaming black hair and etched eyes—the one Indian in this constellation of colours and silhouettes.[40]

Brook's well-meaning concern may have been to depict a multilingual, multidimensional saga of Sturm und Drang, complete with superhuman feats and human failings, but the value system that informs such meditativeness is relentlessly European, although it claims universality on behalf of "the imagination." Brook unwittingly revealed this prejudice when he proclaimed in an interview that "[W]e are telling a story which, on the one hand is universal, but, on the other, would never have existed without India. To tell this story, we had *to avoid allowing the suggestion of India to be so strong as to inhibit human identification* to too great an extent."[41] "Human identification," it seems, only follows if the terms of what constitutes the human are dictated by the creaky machinery of an orientalist vision of an "Indianness" drained of India. By the same token, though Brook's privileging of such a placeless globalism was lauded by epigones of multiculturalism—to take just one example, Richard Schechner endorsed it as "the finest example of something genuinely syncretic"[42]—it missed its mark with my community of Indian viewers. Much had been made in the media about how the director had promoted the cause of respecting other cultures while forging a vision "which carries echoes for all mankind."[43] Nonetheless, the director's claims to these universalizing ideals rang false to my interlocutors, who, as the evening wore on, began quite actively to resist such an assimilationist vision. This resistance first took the form of restlessness, which then turned into disbelief at particular representations of events and people. Finally, no longer able to go along with the absurdities of Brook's presentation, we were reduced to outright laughter. Our collective responses were most clearly highlighted following the narrative's peculiar rendering of the Kauravas' birth. In Brook's version, the clan of the Kurus—the major antagonists in the tale of the battle between order and disorder, good and evil—is depicted as being most horribly and unnaturally born: they literally have to be thrashed from the pregnant queen Gandhari's swollen belly. The *Mahabharata*'s arch-patriarch, Bhishma, is depicted as beating the queen's womb, out of which rolls a huge leaden ball enclosing her progeny of a hundred sons. The metaphor of a difficult birth and the thematization of a mother's nascent horror at the prospect of worldly ills affecting and being affected by her offspring is here transformed into a grotesque literalism. My fellow spectators reacted negatively not only to the symbolic inappropriateness of portraying a male presence at the gendered scene of birthing, but also to the trope of the monstrous feminine stitched into the fetishistic topos of the exotic and the strange.

In retrospect, it was this moment of distaste and dis-identification that made me think of the problematic uses of otherness in the name of an aesthetic of estrangement. Soon after the event, I described the group's rejection-reaction to a colleague whose immediate response was,

> Of course it's entirely predictable that the women in your community would not like the presentation. They're all racists and not likely to approve of black and Asian actors playing "classical" Hindu roles;

moreover, the show's self-consciously minimalist style would obviously not suit their formulaic ideas about ancient splendor and Indian greatness.

While I do not doubt that some of the group's collective abreaction stemmed from conventional expectations based on a stolidly metaphysical sense of an unchanging tradition, it seemed to me that their resistance was more complicated and deserved to be taken seriously (rather than disregarded as narrow-minded). In this connection, it is worth noting that the women in the viewing group did not react any more positively to characters portrayed by Caucasian actors (which would seem to satisfy a purely "chromatic" logic if the problem were merely their racism). On the contrary, what everyone objected to was the gamut of misappropriations involving mispronounced Indian names (indeed, almost all the characters' names were mangled both in the voice-over commentary and by the characters themselves), the inaccurate literalization of metaphoric meanings and associations (as adduced in the example of the wet dream and the grotesque birthing scene, but also as trivialized in the unmotivated speeches and actions of the epic's most important personality, Krishna), and the paradoxical misrenderings of linguistic niceties.

This last detail underscored amusingly and emblematically why acts of cultural translation fail when the emphasis is exclusively on the literal fact of translation as opposed to the figurative contingencies governing translatability. For the entire narrative of the *Mahabharata* turns on and around the figure of Bhishma, the grand and powerful patriarch, who simultaneously symbolizes mortality and the superhuman capacity of renunciation. In Brook's version, the presiding figure of Bhishma is portrayed by a frail-looking actor with a fairly pronounced speech impediment that muffled his delivery and at times made his utterances incomprehensible. The complications of the epic require Bhishma to renounce all material pleasures, especially the love of a woman, in return for being able to choose the time and manner of his own death. Such renunciation encapsulates an entire world of understandings about the antinomies of life and death, commitment and pleasure. This pivotal moment of the drama was all but undermined by the actor's locution, which made him sound as if he were proclaiming, "I *abhor* all women," where the text prompted him to say, "I *abjure* all women." His mumbling occasioned some discussion about the distinction between "abhorrence" and "renunciation" (and whether it made any difference to renounce something if one already abhorred it).

Indeed, what the women recognized as a felt conviction, not only on account of their familiarity with the stories of the *Mahabharata* but also given the contradictions of their own lives, was that happiness and honor may be estranged attributes, that pursuing the goals of personal satisfaction and individual betterment may be inimical to collective ideals of solidarity and self-consolidation. Bhishma is the embodiment of such profound contradictions of existence, larger-than-life and yet expressing the predicament of living itself. This combination of moral complexity and ethical simplicity conjoined in the epic's treatment of the character of Bhishma is illegible in the ways that Brook directs the logic of the text.

Following this particular set of confusions about what the motivations could possibly be for the show's depiction of an unspectacular Bhishma further trivialized by the phatic and staccato quality of the utterances of the actor playing him, there emerged a growing conviction among us: The production was completely inadequate to the representational demands placed on it both by the epic and by the goals of a culturally sensitive aesthetic practice. As it turned out, the cumulative effect of the many misfirings of plot and performance led this group of female spectators to an almost wholesale disavowal of the program's intentions and ethical stance. My participation in the event had its own consequences in that, as someone presumed to have expertise on cultural matters, I was asked to explain how such an ill-conceived production might be regarded by mainstream critics and reviewers as "the cultural event of the year" or as an adequate dramatization of the Indian epic tradition. To my ethnographic interlocutors I offered a less elaborated version of my discussion here on the vexed links between aesthetic and political representation. If the politics of postcoloniality turn on reckoning with the ways that a global commodity logic makes it impossible to separate the category of the aesthetic from other economies of value, it becomes necessary to reinsert the problematic of alienation into our proposals about aesthetic experience itself. To return to Bloch's ideas about *Verfremdung,* we might be cautioned to recall that, in a historical sense, the term reflects not only the "good contrast" of aesthetic distancing but also the "bad contrast" of existential alienation. The predicament of being made to appear strange even to oneself may be salutary if the desired effect is to dislodge the taken-for-grantedness of a certain vision of reality or representation. On the other hand, one is made strange, uncanny, unhomely through linguistic and cultural manipulation as well. The destiny of non-Western or postcolonial cultural ensembles in the West has been an alienated one—by virtue of their deployment within the commodified space of "multiculturalism" no less than through an aestheticist distaste for the contaminations of banal experience. And yet cultural complexity is not merely a matter of textual complication or figural exoticism, for it often involves a continuity between everyday and elevated concerns, between a quotidian aesthetic and a literary or performative tradition. That such continuities have been disrupted within the contrary regimes of differentiation and innervation characterizing modern experience represents the most compelling imperative for a politicized art to confront alienation as a cultural fact. So if aesthetic concerns are not outside quotidian signification, they must be regarded from a perspective that disavows Archimedean critiques of judgment as well as disembodied convictions about the meaning of art—convictions whose effect is only to give us a flattened-out repertoire of images and spectacles Benjamin parodied as "cultural treasures" in his concepts on history. Let me end, then, by marking the importance of an everyday but insistently critical understanding—exemplified by my interlocutors' reception of *The Mahabharata*—of the distance between a subjective sense of a past tradition and its vitiating hybridization in the name of a universal modernity.

Afterword

The sun never sets on the British Empire because the British Empire
is in the East and the sun sets in the West.
                              —Student blooper as collected by Richard Lederer

What are the possibilities for dialectical thinking? At the risk of sound-
ing hoary or pedantic, each of the discussions in this book has attempted
to come to terms with this question—by no means to provide satisfying or complete answers but at least to square off against resistance to
the very idea of dialectics. Even if the sun never set on the British Empire, there are those who prefer it do so for forms of inquiry that take
their lead from the interrogation of value rather than the interrogation
of the sign. Value—understood in materialist terms as the dissimulation of labor and the laborer's identity—is of little interest in a theoretical milieu that prizes textual or subjective but not historical or objective crises. But were one to not go along with the story told about
the crisis of subjectivity as a speculative problem of meaning, to take it
on, instead, as the problem of alienation, one might reach a different resolution of the apparent impasse between consciousness and understanding. Such a resolution may well find that consciousness has its practical
dimensions, making understanding a less dubious and more concrete
matter.

In searching for the concrete, I have not been drawn to any positivist,
falsifiable notion of truth or evidence. Nor am I persuaded that truth is
merely discursive, constitutively subject to the necessity of error. If the

discussions throughout the book reveal anything, it is the conviction that truth proceeds through negation but is not in itself a negative quantity. This has been the epistemological basis for my attempt to write an account of everyday life in an immigrant Indian community. Such an attempt to think concretely about the everyday makes the risk of hoariness unavoidable and, as Althusserians would say, overdetermined— given the glibness with which cautionary notes are struck these days about Marxism's exhaustion, "Left conservativism,"[1] and so on. But the history of Marxism's failures within "actually existing" social experiments no more attests to its political or philosophical inadequacy than, say, deconstructive readings demonstrate their success in overturning the system of value-coding through their efforts at sniffing out contradictions, totalizations, foundationalisms, and so forth. I would submit that deconstructive vigilance against the alleged errors of all forms of structural thinking has shaded into vigilantism, so much so that wherever one looks one runs into rescue operations: meaning rescued from intention, ideas from the system, nations from the state, women from the straitjacket of rights, consuming subjects from the logic of capitalist production, and a lot besides.

Closer to my own interest in theorizing issues of postcoloniality, let me take an example that can serve as a point of departure for some last thoughts on the need to reengage a materialist critique of value; that is, on terms given by Marxist analysis—which, far from being surpassed, have only been caricatured in renditions of this sort. I have in mind Patrick McGee's book *Telling the Other: The Question of Value in Modern and Postcolonial Writing*, less because of its exemplarity than its symptomatic excesses.[2] McGee contends that metaphysical ideas about "what constitutes the human" pervade the labor theory of value (on the grounds, presumably, that the category of labor necessitates understanding it in humanist terms). The critique of Marx along these lines is borrowed from Jean Baudrillard's conception of "symbolic exchange" and Jacques Derrida's of "supplementarity." The stakes for McGee have to do with valorizing the play of difference, which, in turn, supposedly makes it possible to undercut the regime of value production itself, and which he claims is inaccessible to Marxism. In his words,

> There is no place in such a restricted economy for the thought of the incommensurate as a transgression of value, as a disruption of the frame

that mediates the perception of words and things. This is not to say that such a disruption will bring about a "pure" unmediated perception but that the process of perception can be disordered from within, decentered or reversed.[3]

If Marx's formulation of a labor theory of value betrays a "humanist" propensity, it is not on account of some ontological faith in the humanness of humanity (although even were this the case, it is not clear how the limits of thinking *as* humans can be transgressed). Rather, capitalist alienation makes it impossible to reckon with human social relations outside of their atrophied and objectified givenness as things, and Marxism's dialectical emphasis on reification is intended as an immanent critique of an impossible humanism or existentialism. The grounds of this critique is precisely that (human) thought and existence cannot be understood without presupposing that the transformation of quality into quantity—the very basis of commodity fetishism—now obviates any idealist faith in an essential substrate of consciousness stripped from its historical derangement within capitalism. To the extent that capitalist social organization fixes our historical coordinates for thinking about value, it is something of a fantasy (however powerful) to posit a "general economy," no longer restricted by material determinations or social contradictions.[4] Or, I should say, as idealist philosophy goes, this position may be sustainable as more than a fantasy. As cultural criticism professing an ethical dimension, it is rather short of the mark of "worldliness," if by that term we mean to signal an interest in the actualities of historical experience rather than a covertly Heideggerian faith in the ambiguities of meaning and language gathered under a professed interest in the world and in the "splendor of the simple."[5]

McGee, moreover, goes farther than wagging a finger in the direction of value reduced to "purely" human terms, in order to recuperate an encounter with otherness in the abyss of the incommensurate:

> The thought of the incommensurate derives from the recognition that the construction of value necessarily produces an alterity or otherness. Any reading that would reverse fixed value must foreground this alterity and then destroy its binary opposition to value through a deconstructive strategy, not only overturning value to show its dependence on the excluded other but displacing the other toward a more general economy, an economy that is not really an economy since it is no longer reducible to a system of predetermined meanings.[6]

Ushered in as the new call of the wild, incommensurability provides a sort of litmus test for proving the destruction of value within acts of textual reading; this is a considerably problematic rendering of a concept whose purpose is not to mark the transformation or unraveling of value but its resistances to being subsumed under any "political economy of the sign" (to borrow a phrase from Baudrillard). Yet in what has become a fairly standard gesture of theoretical eclecticism, McGee is not content with merely a Baudrillardian or Derridean poetics. Marx, he says, "need not be rejected."[7] Apparently, only the fundamental Marxian idea that, as McGee quotes Baudrillard, "the revolution must be distilled in history"[8] needs to be jettisoned so that one can now revel in the sun of semiotic play and the order of symbolic exchange. Contending that historical materialism is irrevocably prey to the illusions of productivism (given its "idealist" reliance on the distance between reification and the real), McGee's readings advance the optic of a general economy that, in its foregrounding of a radical alterity, allegedly gets beyond the telos of both meaning and production. He sees such alterity, unmoored from a productivist bias, proposed not only in the poststructuralist theories of Baudrillard, Derrida, or Jacques Lacan but indeed in Walter Benjamin's theory of language and his critique of historicism. Making unlikely bedfellows out of Baudrillard and Benjamin—to wit, "Benjamin criticizes historicism in a language that resembles Baudrillard's"[9]—allows McGee to claim that postcolonial criticism can gain a lot from Benjamin's thoughts on the explosiveness of meaning and its opposition to the dialectic:

> Benjamin describes the process by which language is emptied out of "natural" meaning, abstracted from its ideological framework, and reduced to radical alterity: the substance of history as the support of any conceivable, socially determined meaning.... The signifier, in ceasing to be natural, becomes the field of historical intervention, the place from which radical meaning-effects can emerge in opposition to the hegemonic authority of some master-slave dialectic. Unlike the Hegelian other, which is only a detour from the subject, the big Other is radical, irreducible alterity, underpinning every position insofar as it is historical. Such alterity dissolves even the distinction between first and third worlds.[10]

While I agree with McGee that Benjamin's work has much to offer postcolonial studies, asserting the dissolution of the distinction between First and Third Worlds evacuates the ground of history itself. That this view bears very little resemblance to Benjamin's own thinking must be asserted not in the name of Marxist orthodoxy but, rather, in the spirit of drawing attention to the pitfalls of an all-too-quick embrace of the signifying turn. In this context, we might be advised to recall Guy Debord's warning that readings of culture exist "within a historical society divided into classes; what this amounts to is that culture is the power to generalize, existing *apart,* as an intellectual division of labor and as the intellectual labor of division."[11] If we agree with Debord's assessment, it can be said that avowals of the destruction of value in the name of a decentered criticism are at best apologetic in their assumptions and method.

McGee also settles on Raymond Williams as an exemplary Marxist critic who goes some distance, albeit not far enough for him, in rupturing the schema of value and production. Accordingly, Williams is cited as enabling the following link between signification and materiality:

> A sign (or what Williams . . . prefers to call "a signifying element of a language") can always be drawn away from fixed meaning and back into the social process where meanings are made. Any linguistic act that ruptures a fixed meaning makes the reader aware of signification as such a "practical material activity." Williams calls it "a means of production." If language is thought of as a "means," however, it must be subordinated to the end or value of production.[12]

In point of fact, what Williams has in mind with his homological use of language as a means of production is to draw attention to the process of mediation itself. Far from "subordinating" language to the "end or value of production," Williams's intent is to redraw that line, however crooked, between a *means* of production and the *mode* of production. As McGee himself acknowledges, there is no getting around the productivist emphasis in Williams by gesturing to his passing embrace of the sign. For Williams, unlike Baudrillard (and his adherent McGee), the illusion is hardly that of production; it is the degree to which a conception of totality is out of the reach of practical consciousness while remaining the horizon of all possibility.[13] Williams himself is amply clear on the matter in his most definitive statement, the essay "Base and Superstructure in Marxist Cultural Theory":

> I would first say that in any society, in any particular period, there is a central system of practices, meanings, and values, which we can properly call dominant and effective. This implies no presumption about its

value. All I am saying is that it is central. . . . In any case, what I have in mind is the central, effective and dominant system of meanings and values, *which are not merely abstract but which are organized and lived.* . . . [W]e can only understand an effective and dominant culture if we understand the real social process on which it depends.[14]

As my arguments in chapter 2 have attempted to establish, there is a tension, to be sure, in Williams's navigation of the actual and the possible, but his argument never veers off into quite the exercise in virtuality that characterizes McGee's (and not only his) avowal of "the real" as a plastic, discursive event. An economy that is not really an economy, the real that is nothing other than a social construction, an other that is "totally other," all this semanticizes the question of value in ways that are simply unrecognizable within Williams's perspectives on "the selective tradition," "expressive causality," "structures of feeling," and so on. The point is not that Williams falls prey to a productivist emphasis (as if the real thrust of his cultural-materialist convictions ought to have led him elsewhere). Rather, his attempts, like Benjamin's, to deal with the signifying elements of language or the unconscious structurations of meaning were deliberate efforts to produce a "theory of the superstructure" that could account for production per se. If Williams and Benjamin critique the base-superstructure model or the teleology of historicism, the "resemblance" to Baudrillard's language is, contra McGee, very faint at best. This is not an attempt to fix for all time the place of Williams or Benjamin within a "correct" intellectual lineage (although it may well be time to pay closer attention to questions of intellectual history and the sociology of knowledge). In the end, the difference has very much to do with the identity of a historical materialism revised from within the terms of value devised by Marx: the sheer equivalence of money as the paradigmatic value-form of capitalist modernity. Williams's or Benjamin's involvement in discussions of value were family matters, so to speak: efforts to make up for lapses in Marx's account of language or aesthetic production and to resituate the problematic of history within Marx's own inheritance from the tradition of German idealism. As I see it, no handmaiden of alterity is seduced here; no Baudrillardian scheme hatched.[15]

Though considerations of value may appear somewhat abstract in the context of what has been an account of the everyday, I have asserted throughout the necessity of considering abstraction together with the localisms of identity, ethnicity, or cultural practice—not least because we are still constrained by the totality of capitalist globalization in its abstract and concrete forms. The notion that we escape the grip of "master narratives" by just insisting on nondeterministic articulations of diasporic (and hence disruptive) forms of culture is, I think, easily recognized as blind and banal. And yet the presumption that what is really at issue in cultural work today represents the standoff between a textualism that is "theoretical" and a positivism that is not, itself seems to be the kind of light that shines on blindness *as* insight. But given the prevailing view that our lot must be to choose from this way of constituting the intellectual horizon, I am keenly aware that the reader who comes to the book expecting "thick descriptions" of the lifeways and customs of postcolonial subjects is bound to be disappointed. If all the wrestling with the politics and poetics of ethnography or the talk about theory in anthropology has yielded something, it has been to relocate the practice of fieldwork on a different part of the familiar ground of subject and object: the ethnographer continuing as subject (armed with narrative means and reflexive intent) and culture or identity remaining in place as the object.

By contrast, I have made the subject of ethnography my object. The ambiguities of the phrase "subject of ethnography" perhaps lend themselves to the inference that I was the focus of my own study. But this is far from my meaning, since I have tried to suggest, instead, that the question of "what is being studied" can no more be settled by fixing on "who" is doing the studying than by pointing to this or that entity in the world—the self, immigrants, rituals, personalities, and so on. Posing the question of subject and object (as I contend in chapter 1) is itself part of the problematic. My ethnographic experience, no more or less intensive than that of conventionally minded ethnographers, provided the occasion and reason to think critically about issues of postcoloniality. These days, to speak of the postcolonial is to produce an aura of historical ineffability and the *jouissance* of in-betweenness; such is the result of disciplinary scrambles for the object now known as postcolonialism. This has made it difficult to think seriously about the consolidating aspects of capitalist existence, the territorializing moves of the logic of capital, and the ways that experiences and ideologies of living in the wake of a colonial past are centered on banal and solid routines of work, habit, and conviction.

To speak of the book as a critical reflection on such problems is to presuppose fully that what is required is both a meditation on method and, at the same time, an elucidation by example. Such a dual requirement gives the analysis a neither-fish-nor-fowl character, but it is a hybridism I can live with, particularly because my intent was never to rest at the gates of a fetishized "high" theory or an equally fetishized documentation of ethnicity-as-practice. I have tried to grapple with the desire of materialist analysis to cast its stakes in terms of a purported unity of theory and practice. Particularly within cultural studies, this desire has manifested itself in the claim that theory is a material intervention on its own. The conflation of theory and practice also permits a secondary conflation with regard to method; as a result, questions of method are seldom addressed directly, even though they are completely integral to the project of theorizing. So on the one hand we find in forms of contemporary theory an idealist preoccupation with "thought," with the "concept" as such, and with abstract ideas about subjectivity, modernity, reason, and so on. In the revamped language of interdisciplinary cultural analysis, on the other, the focus continues to be putatively practice oriented—on "objects," "instances," or "case studies" of "lived reality." Both theoretical and empirical paradigms leave the question of the mutual constitution—indeed the shared intelligibility—of subject and object, theory and practice, untouched. The end point of such a lurching between "doing theory" and "doing something else" (ethnography, readings of literary texts," and so on) is, as I see it, a disavowal of the challenge of dialectical thought.

This book faces the challenge, however inadequately, of redirecting conceptual thinking toward an analysis of concrete experience. It is a challenge in the tradition of Marx's *Grundrisse* or Theodor Adorno's *Negative Dialectics,* and it involves *thinking with* the paradox of theorizing the abstract concretely and the concrete abstractly. From this perspective, *all* attempts to produce a theoretical analysis are at the same time deliberations on method, just as any attempt to study facts (such as those discovered in ethnographic fieldwork) is a meditation on the conditions of possibility of those facts.

If the philosophical density of *Negative Dialectics* or the *Grundrisse* seem too remote from the purview of culture criticism, Roland Barthes's *Camera Lucida* gives us an illustration that is closer to the descriptively conceptual mode of analysis I am speaking of here.[16] *Camera Lucida* is ostensibly a set of reflections on photography, though it is also a record of Barthes mourning the death of his mother. From the point of view of genre, it is quite confounded. One would expect either meditations on grief or elaborations of photography as a medium, but not the two together, since they seem discontinuous, parataxic. But the book is neither an analysis of a technical form nor a reflection on the ritual of mourning. All expectations about content or descriptive accounting are subsumed under a preoccupation with the conceptual interpenetrability of death and narrative. As a result, one is hard pressed to find in the book the very photograph of Barthes's mother that occasions the greatest and most profound meditation—just as it is difficult to think of the book as a formal study of photography, given its epigrammatic and allusive structure. Instead, we are given an attempt to construct the *object* of photography in terms of the *concept* of mourning: neither one nor the other, but both. Essay and method, case study and conceptual take.

My allusion to Barthes in the midst of a defense of dialectical thinking may appear as out of place as perhaps do references to *Negative Dialectics* within the arena of ethnographic inquiry. But this is not just a matter of taste or appropriation. Though it has become customary to regard Barthes as the foremost guardian of the portals of poststructuralism, it is difficult to agree fully with Martin Jay that "Barthes the sober structuralist decoder transformed himself into the hedonist 'professor of desire', . . . [and that] the militant Marxist with his 'euphoric dream of scientificity' became the self-conscious expert on the nuances of love."[17] In fact, as Fredric Jameson suggests, "[w]hat Barthes was, and what he became, is a complicated and interesting subject,"[18] and the unpredictability of his investment in the quiddity of the local and the everyday in what was to be his last book, *Camera Lucida*, stands in marked contradiction to any facile reading not only of Barthes himself but also an entire series of self-perpetuating "critiques" of the desire for truth.

It is of course not my purpose to develop a full-fledged reclamation of Barthes for any continuing project of historical materialism. Nonetheless, it is only historically accurate, in terms of his own career and the career of his ideas, to state that an emphasis on the real, on aspects of concretion, as well as on the status of the empirical (and not just the signifying process), makes, as Naomi Schor put it, "a spectacular comeback,"[19] culminating in the text I have adduced above, *Camera Lucida*.

And Schor goes on to say, what returns in Barthes "is not a *new real,* not that which *resists* meaning, rather that which *remains* after meaning has been evacuated or, in Barthes's idiolect, 'exempted.'"[20] It is this Barthes, however contradictory, that I have chosen to propose as a model for negative thinking, and if for him the new real can only be understood if we step outside the antinomies of mimetic and non-mimetic value prevalent in the West,[21] then so much the better for a different horizon of postcolonial analysis, a horizon that keeps the reality of the object still in view.

I cannot claim that *States of Exception* is a book on the order of Barthes's luminous one. Far from it, since my goals were much more modest and my means less capacious. But if the conjunction of thought and image, of form and detail, represents the "actuality" of a dialectical inquiry cast between the content of damaged lives and the form of a rarefied identitarianism, *Camera Lucida* proffers us a model of how to think that conundrum—in spite or, perhaps, because of the fact that its author's legacy is written in terms of neither an irrecuperable subjectivism nor an unredeemable objectivism. I close, then, with the hope that my promise of an account of "lived experience" was not strangled before it left the ethnographer's throat. By the same token, if ethnography is to live on, it can only do so by capitalizing on its missed chances: the ones taken, no less than the ones yet to be.

Notes

Introduction

My thanks to Crystal Bartolovich, Tim Brennan, Eric Clarke, and Xiaoying Wang, both for their patience in wading through many versions of what passes here as a "statement of purpose" as well as their invaluable suggestions for its improvement.

1. The original French title of Michel de Certeau's book is *L'invention du quotidien/Arts de faire* (Paris: Union Generale d'Editions, 1980). Its English translation as *The Practice of Everyday Life*, trans. Steven Rendall (Berkeley and Los Angeles: University of California Press, 1984), connotes some of the ambiguity between "invention" and "modification."

2. Michel de Certeau, Luce Giard, and Pierre Mayol, *The Practice of Everyday Life*, vol. 2: *Living and Cooking*, trans. Timothy J. Tomasik (Minneapolis: University of Minnesota Press, 1998), 9, original emphasis.

3. Theodor W. Adorno, *The Jargon of Authenticity*, trans. Knut Tarnowski and Frederic Will (Evanston, Ill.: Northwestern University Press, 1973 [1964]), 25.

4. If the lag between the reception of French theory and its importation into cultural anthropology is any indication, it will be a while before the discipline is able to work out a useful relation to critical theory. For a current and colorless rendition of the supposed handicaps of Frankfurt school thinking, see George E. Marcus, *Ethnography through Thick and Thin* (Princeton: Princeton University Press, 1998). In this revaluation of ethnography, Marcus quite reductively characterizes Adorno's vision as clad in an " 'iron-cage' pessimism" (61).

5. Stuart Hall's essay "The Local and the Global" is something of a departure from this trend, although it should be pointed out that Hall's writings throughout the 1990s have affirmed "post-Marxist" accounts of "new social movements" that emphasize the primacy of discourse (over considerations of force or domination). See Stuart Hall, "The Local and the Global: Globalization and Ethnicity," in *Culture, Globalization, and the World System*, ed. Anthony D. King (London: Macmillan, 1991), 19–39.

6. The necessity of distinguishing between the terms "exile" and "immigration" is given a moral charge by Aijaz Ahmad in *In Theory: Classes, Nations, Literatures*

(London: Verso, 1992). Ahmad points out that there is a world of difference between "personal convenience" (often the motive force behind immigration, especially petit bourgeois immigration of the sort exemplified by the migration of Indians to the United States) and the absolute lack of choice imposed upon subjects—e.g., Palestinians—who not only "cannot speak" but also "cannot be" inside what are "their ancestral boundaries" (85). In addition, given that Indian immigration to this country has been overwhelmingly techno-managerial, there is also a contrast to be drawn between migrant laborers (who remain outside the circuit of production and consumption and who therefore never manage to break through to the embrace of bourgeois existence) and professionally and economically privileged immigrants. The gap between "cosmopolitan" and "proletarian" movements of populations is also specified in Timothy Brennan, *Salman Rushdie and the Third World: Myths of the Nation* (London: Macmillan, 1989), 23–24. I am also grateful to Brennan for pointing me to Edward Said's "The Mind of Winter," *Harper's Magazine*, 269 (September 1984), 47–55, which serves as a poignant and useful caution against hypostatizing the notion of the "diaspora."

7. See, particularly, Max Weber, "Asceticism and the Spirit of Capitalism" in his *The Protestant Ethic and the Spirit of Capitalism* (New York: Charles Scribner's Sons, 1958), 155–83.

8. My thanks to Cesare Casarino for pointing out to me that in the original Italian, *fenomeni morbosi* connotes varieties of murky, almost perverse phenomena.

9. The work of the Subaltern Studies group has made significant contributions to the historical analysis of postcolonial consciousness. In particular, the writings of Ranajit Guha have been very useful in describing links between the dominating economic imperatives of British colonialism in India and the failures of capitalism to realize itself *as a mode of thought or history*. See, for instance, Guha's "Dominance without Hegemony and Its Historiography," *Subaltern Studies* 4 (1992): 222–26.

10. Cited in J. Laplanche and J.-B. Pontalis, *The Language of Psycho-Analysis*, trans. Donald Nicholson-Smith (New York: W. W. Norton, 1973), 112, original emphases.

11. Jacques Derrida, "Freud and the Scene of Writing," in *Writing and Difference*, trans. Alan Bass (Chicago: University of Chicago Press, 1978), 196–231, quote at 211, original emphases.

12. Needless to say, I am not alone in questioning the historical and categorical specificity of the term "postcolonial." See, for their elaborations, Anne McLintock, "The Angel of Progress: Pitfalls of the Term 'Post-Colonialism,'" *Social Text* 31/32 (1992): 84–98, and Ella Shohat, "Notes on the Post-Colonial," *Social Text* 31/32 (1992): 99–113.

13. Stuart Hall has formulated the same question in another echo of Williams, although Hall's question has less to do with the politics of postcoloniality than it does with reviewing how the problem of postcoloniality has been addressed by poststructuralist critiques. See Hall's essay, "When Was 'the Post-Colonial'? Thinking at the Limit," in *The Post-Colonial Question: Common Skies, Divided Horizons*, ed. Iain Chambers and Lidia Curti (London: Routledge, 1996), 242–60. Let me also note that Williams's formulation, "When Was Modernism?" is itself an adaptation, as he tells us, from Gwynn Williams's essay "When Was Wales?"—a question addressing itself to the ideologically selective ways that particular traditions get constructed. See Raymond Williams, "When Was Modernism?" in his *The Politics of Modernism: Against the New Conformists* (London: Verso, 1989), 31–35.

14. See V. Y. Mudimbe on "gnosis" and ethnocentric constructions in his *The Invention of Africa: Gnosis, Philosophy, and the Order of Knowledge* (Bloomington: Indiana University Press, 1988), especially 1–23.

15. Gayatri Chakravorty Spivak, "Can the Subaltern Speak?" in *Marxism and the Interpretation of Culture*, ed. Cary Nelson and Lawrence Grossberg (Urbana: University of Illinois Press, 1988), 271–313. Marianna Torgovnick's *Gone Primitive* (Durham, N.C.: Duke University Press, 1991) is a symptom of what can happen when liberal feminist discourse tries, "consumptively," to coax "the primitive" into line with its own political preoccupations with inclusion. As an instance of repetition compulsion, Torgovnick's focus on the ethnic-as-object is caught up in the same politics of sanctioned ignorance that Spivak denounces.

16. This is a theme explored with great facility by V. S. Naipaul in *The Mimic Men* (London: Andre Deutsch, 1967; reprinted, Harmondsworth, England: Penguin Books, 1969). See also Homi K. Bhabha's adaptation of the theme of the "mimic man" in "Of Mimicry and Man: The Ambivalence of Colonial Discourse," in *The Location of Culture* (London: Routledge, 1994), 85–92.

17. Raymond Williams, *Culture and Society, 1780 to 1950* (London: Chatto and Windus, 1958), 376.

18. See Sigmund Freud, *The Psychopathology of Everyday Life*, trans. James Strachey (London: Hogarth Press, 1960 [1901]), passim.

19. The *Random House Dictionary*, 2nd ed., unabridged, defines "anomaly" as "(1) a deviation from the common rule, type, arrangement, or form; (2) an odd, peculiar, or strange condition, situation, quality, etc.; (3) an incongruity or inconsistency; (4) in astronomy, it is a quantity measured in degrees defining the position of an orbiting body with respect to the point at which it is nearest to or farthest from its primary. In meteorology, the amount of deviation of a meteorological quantity from the *accepted normal value* of that quantity. In grammar, an irregularity" (emphasis added). The question of the production of "normal" and "exceptional" values is central to my concerns in this book.

20. The reference is from the title of Marcus, *Ethnography through Thick and Thin.*

21. Lacan's formulation of the "mirror stage" (which is, of necessity, pre- or at least protosocial) renders it the motive force for a universalizing identity machine. I have argued this point in "Nationalist Emergence and Diasporic Knowledges," *Mediations* 18, no. 1 (Spring 1994): 53–59.

22. Walter Benjamin, "Theses on the Philosophy of History," in his *Illuminations*, trans. Harry Zohn (New York: Schocken Books, 1968), 256.

23. Walter Benjamin, *Gesammelte Schriften*, ed. Rolf Tiedemann (Frankfurt: Suhrkamp, 1982), vol. 2, 219.

24. See Jean-François Lyotard, *The Postmodern Condition: A Report on Knowledge*, trans. Geoff Bennington and Brian Massumi (Minneapolis: University of Minnesota Press, 1984).

25. See Jacques Derrida, "The Violence of the Letter," in his *Of Grammatology*, trans. Gayatri Chakravorty Spivak (Baltimore: Johns Hopkins University Press, 1974 [1967]), 101–40.

26. In a book that relies heavily on a Lacanian model of subject formation, Rey Chow formulates the problem of reading "between West and East." As Chow puts it, the relation between Western "theory" and non-Western "ethnicity" is not determined by elusive differences of exoticism or cultural arcaneness but, rather, is premised on

"the foundations on which the West constructs its patterns of domination and hegemony." See Rey Chow, *Woman and Chinese Modernity: The Politics of Reading between West and East* (Minneapolis: University of Minnesota Press, 1991), xvi. But the model for thinking domination is prefigured through the categories of the Symbolic and the Imaginary, an "etiology" that is asserted rather than justified.

27. Arjun Appadurai has commented on one such tendency within anthropology in which the realities of mundane existence are "relocated," as it were, to the more appealing (and thus orientalized) venues providing the stock-in-trade of anthropological field sites. See his "Introduction: Place and Voice in Anthropological Theory," *Cultural Anthropology* 3, no. 1 (1988): 16–20.

28. See, for example, Kamala Visweswaran, *Fictions of Feminist Ethnography* (Minneapolis: University of Minnesota Press, 1994).

29. Varying inflections to the problematic of "shock" in Benjamin can be found in, for example, Howard Caygill, *Walter Benjamin: The Colour of Experience* (London and New York: Routledge, 1998), especially 114–15, 143; Miriam Bratu Hansen, "Benjamin and Cinema: Not a One-Way Street," *Critical Inquiry* 25 (Winter 1999): 306–43; and Susan Buck-Morss, "Aesthetics and Anaesthetics: Walter Benjamin's Artwork Essay Reconsidered," *New Formations* 20 (Summer 1993): 123–43. Despite some differences in inflection, these discussions—to which I am greatly indebted—seem to me to be true to Benjamin's own materialist emphasis on matters of bodily perception/subjection and are more persuasive than, say, the ideas of Michel Foucault and his followers).

30. On the point of Benjamin's source influences, see Hansen, "Benjamin and Cinema," 316–17. Here it is sufficient to note that the ideas of Soviet film theorists such as Sergei Eisenstein were very much at work in Benjamin's thinking about the process of innervation. Eisenstein, it may be recalled, sought to theorize the conditions of transmitting emotion in the film spectator through the deployment of montage. See the 1923 essay "The Montage of Attractions," in his *Selected Works*, trans. Richard Taylor (Bloomington: Indiana University Press, 1988), 1–33.

31. A much longer consideration of Simmel's impact on twentieth-century German philosophy and literary theory (desperate to lose its idealistic precedents while remaining true to the Hegelian tradition) is necessary, but I cannot provide it here. Fredric Jameson has started this conversation in his recent (not altogether unproblematic) essay "The Theoretical Hesitation: Benjamin's Sociological Predecessor," *Critical Inquiry* 25 (Winter 1999): 267–88. Among other things, Jameson betrays his aestheticist investments when, for example, he claims that Benjamin "had a signal literary advantage over Simmel, namely, that he could draw on Baudelaire, whose characteristic language on these matters [of urban life and mental conditions]—not unrelated, to be sure, to that nascent psychology contemporaneous with him—is certainly far more elegant" (274). It could equally be said that Benjamin's tooclose affinities with the likes of Baudelaire is what makes him more of a participant in than a critic of ennui.

32. Georg Simmel, *The Philosophy of Money*, trans. Tom Bottomore and David Frisby (Boston: Routledge and Kegan Paul, 1978).

33. See David Frisby's introduction in David Frisby and Mike Featherstone, eds., *Simmel on Culture: Selected Writings* (London: Sage Publications, 1997), 18.

34. Georg Simmel, "The Metropolis and Mental Life," in his *On Individuality and Social Forms*, ed. Donald N. Levine (Chicago: University of Chicago Press, 1971), 324–39, quotations at 325, 329.

35. Benedict Anderson, *Imagined Communities: Reflections on the Origins and Spread of Nationalism* (London: Verso and New Left Books, 1983), is the standard reference even if, despite's Anderson's familiarity with Benjamin, "imagination" is basically a technologized capacity in this work. See also Ranajit Guha's criticism of Anderson's argument in "Nationalism Reduced to 'Official Nationalism,' "*Asian Studies Association of Australia Review* 9, no. 1 (1985): 103–8.

36. In this respect, I must mark my distance from such influential positions as that of Stuart Hall in his essay "Minimal Selves," in *Identity: The Real Me*, ICA Documents 6 (London: Institute of Contemporary Arts, 1988), 44–46.

37. See Patrick McGee, *Telling the Other: The Question of Value in Modern and Postcolonial Writing* (Ithaca, N.Y.: Cornell University Press, 1992), 43, 15, 9.

38. Theodor W. Adorno, *Negative Dialectics*, trans. E. B. Ashton (New York: Continuum, 1973 [1966]), 3.

39. James Clifford provides an authoritative discussion of modes of "salvage ethnography" in his essay "On Ethnographic Allegory," in *Writing Culture: The Poetics and Politics of Ethnography*, ed. James Clifford and George E. Marcus (Berkeley and Los Angeles: University of California Press, 1986), 98–121.

40. Benjamin, *Illuminations*, 257.

1. Writing the Field

1. Edward Said, "Opponents, Audiences, Constituencies, and Community," in *The Anti-Aesthetic*, ed. Hal Foster (Port Townsend, Wash.: Bay Press, 1983), 135–59.

2. I am referring here to Edward Said's by now classic formulation of "Traveling Theory," in his *The World, the Text, and the Critic* (Cambridge, Mass.: Harvard University Press, 1983), 226–47. Said's injunctions against the too-easy appropriation of theoretical frames (elaborated in the relay from Georg Lukács to Lucien Goldmann to Raymond Williams) have gone largely unheeded in eclectic versions of cultural studies. It is unfortunate, for example, that some poststructuralist approaches (literary and otherwise) reveal a renewed romanticization of the now "decentered" subject—exemplified by the return of the native who speaks as the "voice from the margins," the "postorientalist," the "passing" subject, and so on. The problem was never only that the center spoke on behalf of its other; it was also that speech acts, as Gayatri Chakravorty Spivak argued, are not adequate to the situation of knowledge. See "Can the Subaltern Speak?" in *Marxism and the Interpretation of Culture*, ed. Cary Nelson and Lawrence Grossberg (Urbana: University of Illinois Press, 1988), 271–313. Examples of the tendency to elevate subject-positional politics into "theories" of nonidentitarian knowledge can be found in disparate places: e.g., Judith Butler's *Gender Trouble: Feminism and the Subversion of Identity* (New York: Routledge, 1990); Joan Scott's "The Evidence of Experience," in *The Lesbian and Gay Studies Reader*, ed. Henry Abelove, Michèle Aina Barale, and David M. Halperin (New York: Routlege, 1993), 397–415; and, most exorbitantly, Iain Chambers's *Migrancy, Culture, Identity* (London: Routledge, 1994). Also, with a few notable exceptions, in James Clifford and Vivek Dhareshwar, eds., "Traveling Theory, Traveling Theorists," *Inscriptions* 5 (1989).

3. The sign of the native informant seems to predesignate scholars whose origins (as well as academic interests) lie in the ex-colonies or other parts of the non-

Western world; they are, as it were, "always already" native informants. For these sorts of moves, Spivak has rebuked postcolonialism as "just totally bogus," and I would like to take her criticism of disciplinary legitimation very seriously. See Gayatri Chakravorty Spivak, "Neocolonialism and the Secret Agent of Knowledge," *Oxford Literary Review* 13, nos. 1–2 (1991): 24. It should be understood that I do not take postcolonialism to be a field or subdiscipline of English studies, chiefly because some of the best work in its purview is done by scholars and critics outside the discipline, e.g., historians and comparatists.

4. Clifford Geertz, *Local Knowledge: Further Essays in Interpretive Anthropology* (New York: Basic Books, 1983), 55–70.

5. Gayatri Chakravorty Spivak, "Scattered Speculations on the Question of Cultural Studies," in her *Outside in the Teaching Machine* (New York: Routledge, 1993), 255–84. For some of the terms of the debate over essentialism, see the special issue of the journal *differences* 1, no. 2 (Fall 1989).

6. From Fredric Jameson, *Marxism and Form* (Princeton: Princeton University Press, 1971), 308.

7. Always highly instructive in his theoretical elaborations, Jameson here takes his cue from Adorno and offers the provocative statement that "dialectical thinking presents itself as the perversely hairsplitting, as the overelaborate and the oversubtle, reminding us that the simple is in reality only a simplification, and that the self-evident draws its force from hosts of buried presuppositions." Ibid.

8. I want to note that the term "praxis" has belonged to the dialectical tradition since the time of the Young Hegelians. It was not used by Hegel, certainly, and was intended by his successors precisely to wrest thought away from a contemplative unfolding. In the scheme of the philosophy of history, then, "praxis" belongs to "dialectics" only within a modern conception and gets its most acute elaboration in the writings of Georg Lukács.

9. Robert Sokolowski, "Edmund Husserl," in *The Cambridge Dictionary of Philosophy*, general editor Robert Audi (Cambridge: Cambridge University Press, 1995), 349.

10. Theodor W. Adorno, "Opinion Delusion Society," in his *Critical Models: Interventions and Catchwords*, trans. Henry W. Pickford (New York: Columbia University Press, 1998), 108.

11. Said, "Opponents, Audiences, Constituencies, and Community," 136, original emphasis.

12. The only reason to trouble the reader with German equivalents of words is to mark the influential legacy of German philosophy—from Kant and Marx to the work of the Frankfurt school (as well as prior to that). In the present context, the German equivalents notate some important differences in the meaning of "representation" and their corollary implications for theorizing its practice. Obviously, there are other Continental traditions of debate over the concept of representation, from Aristotle's to Auerbach's ideas about *mimesis*, for instance. The specificity of these debates aside, the point is not to indulge philological anxieties, which, for the most part, keep intact the privilege of European languages and philosophical systems rather than to open up the ground for thinking seriously about the genealogy of terms. In the context of postcolonial scholarship, linguistic and translative problems are hardly innocent, and I want as much to draw attention to the conventions of scholarly disputation as to justify a knowledge of German (or Latin or Greek).

13. Roland Barthes's brilliant reading of *S/Z* reinscribes some conventional assumptions about the constitution of objects even though he successfully prises semiosis away from structure. For a highly original critique of disciplinary objects, see John Mowitt, *Text: The Genealogy of an Anti-Disciplinary Object* (Durham, N.C.: Duke University Press, 1994).

14. Multiculturalism is one of the general rubrics under which postcolonial discourse and scholarship is sometimes accommodated. Other labels include minority discourse, Third World studies, emergent cultural economies, and global literatures.

15. Said, *The World, the Text, and the Critic*, 149.

16. Spivak contends that avowals of "secularity" are themselves products of an Enlightenment critique of Western monotheism. Against this product of a Western secular imaginary (whose elevation she questions on the ex-colonial intellectual's part), she offers the possibility, speaking as a subcontinental skeptic, of a Vedantic commitment to an already split conceptualization of knowledge as *dvaita* (crudely, "dual" or "twofold"). The breadth of Spivak's (or Said's) scholarship cannot of course be marshaled by, in Aijaz Ahmad's deathless phrase, "lesser and later critics." Suffice it to say, then, that in the context of living and working in the metropolitan academy, it is precisely a Western secularism that will have to be engaged—and undone dialectically. See Gayatri Chakravorty Spivak, "Not Virgin Enough to Say That [She] Occupies the Place of the Other," in her *Outside in the Teaching Machine*, 173–78.

17. Jameson, *Marxism and Form*, 309.

18. Although I have learned a great deal from the work of Third World feminists and anthropologists, their continuing reliance on "first principles"—of their own subject positions, their disciplinary formations (psychoanalytic criticism, anthropology, deconstructionism)—keeps them locked into an epistemology of identity and difference. My own project is, both by virtue of this methodological elision and also because it takes its impetus from the philosophy of the Frankfurt school, quite discontinuous with these varying feminist critiques of representation. Readers may want to look up Gloria Anzaldua, "Speaking in Tongues: A Letter to Third World Women," in *This Bridge Called My Back: Writings of Radical Women of Color*, ed. Cherrie Moraga and Gloria Anzaldua (Watertown, Mass.: Persephone Press, 1981); Rey Chow, *Women and Chinese Modernity* (Minneapolis: University of Minnesota Press, 1991); and Kamala Visweswaran, *Fictions of Feminist Ethnography* (Minneapolis: University of Minnesota Press, 1994). I am also compelled to suggest that although the deconstructive edge of Gayatri Chakravorty Spivak's work has energized many feminist scholars, her integrally Marxist insights have pretty much fallen by the wayside. This makes for a form of feminist theory claiming the name of "materialist feminism" that, to borrow Said's phraseology, has not traveled very well. In a welcome direction for postcolonial analysis, Spivak moves us to think about the international division of labor and its displacements of "reason." See her *A Critique of Postcolonial Reason: Toward a History of the Vanishing Present* (Cambridge, Mass.: Harvard University Press, 1999). I have not been able to take into account her important arguments in this recent book within the space of my intervention here.

19. Eve Kosofsky Sedgwick, "Queer Performativity: Henry James's *The Art of the Novel*," lecture delivered at the University of Pittsburgh, January 1993; later published under the same title in *GLQ* 1, no. 1 (1993): 1–16.

20. The allusion is to Jacques Derrida, *Spectres of Marx*, trans. Peggy Kamuf (New York: Routledge, 1994).

21. Even in his quite conventional capacity as chair of the 1992 commission appointed to report on "standards" to the American Comparative Literature Association, the late Charles Bernheimer remarked that deconstructionism counterposes itself to traditional New Criticism *not* as a fundamentally transformative critical enterprise but, rather, as a matter of showing "values to be delusive, cognition to be erroneous, agency to be illusory, and motivations to be aberrant." He continues: "The appeal of deconstruction can partially be understood, I think, in relation to the prevailing post-Vietnam mood of cynicism and distrust. Deconstruction as a technique of demystificatoin requires systematic suspicion.... Comparison in this high-theoretical practice collapses the distinctions on which the comparative process relies and demonstrates how each element is contaminated by the other. When applied in the political arena, for instance on the Cold War rhetoric of opposition, this strategy has a strong subversive effect, undermining the moral claims of both sides, showing that the two opponents are both engaged in deceit masking violence. Deconstructors argue that this demonstration is itself a political intervention. But it is so, in my view, only in a very limited sense. *The intervention is basically inert.* It amounts to saying, 'a plague on both your houses.' Viewed from the deconstructive abyss, engagement on either side involves mystification and blindness. *Abysmal wisdom resides in disengagement and reading.*" Charles Bernheimer, ed., *Comparative Literature in the Age of Multiculturalism* (Baltimore: Johns Hopkins University Press, 1995), 4–5, emphases added.

22. That the critique of empire is made possible by, among other things, imperial languages and concepts has been a powerful argument since the appearance of Chinua Achebe's *Morning Yet on Creation Day* (New York: Doubleday, 1975). See also the writings of Stuart Hall collected in *Stuart Hall: Critical Dialogues in Cultural Studies,* ed. David Morley and Kuan-Hsing Chen (New York: Routlege, 1996). It seems relevant to suggest that one is no more obliged to believe that Marxism is passé than to assume that the West is the best—especially since many of our experiences attest to the contrary. It has been a historical characteristic of Western capitalist cultures to attempt to universalize themselves with the ideological ruse that what you see is what you get.

23. Jameson, *Marxism and Form,* 160–61.

24. See Barbara Herrnstein Smith, *Contingencies of Value: Alternative Perspectives for Critical Theory* (Cambridge, Mass.: Harvard University Press, 1988).

25. Jameson, *Marxism and Form,* 311.

26. Ibid., 309.

27. Although I am in general sympathy with Asha Varadharajan's excellent book *Exotic Parodies: Subjectivity in Adorno, Said, and Spivak* (Minneapolis: University of Minnesota Press, 1995), I take issue with her characterization of postcolonial intellectual work. Varadharajan casts herself (as well as other notable scholars) in the following light: "My interest in this traffic of selves and others, colonizers and colonized, men and women, color and whiteness, is that of a member of the familiar, if still anomalous, breed of intellectual émigrés, or, as they are now called, 'native informants'" (xv). The irony, if any is intended, is lost in subsequent pages, in which the predicament of the postcolonial academic is read as continuous with that of the native informant.

28. Butler, *Gender Trouble,* x. Butler's demystification of the "compulsory order of sex/gender/desire" leads her to an important critique of the circularity of the category "women," but her own analysis confuses means and ends. She rightly states that "[i]f a stable notion of gender no longer proves to be the foundational premise of feminist politics, perhaps a new sort of feminist politics is now desirable to contest the very reifications of gender and identity, one that will take the variable construction of identity as both a methodological and normative prerequisite, if not a political goal" (*Gender Trouble,* 5). Precisely because the construction of identity is a *methodological* question, it is not obviated by recourse to de facto delegations of it as performativity. This too is circular reasoning (of the sort that Butler warns against).

29. Theodor W. Adorno, *Negative Dialectics,* trans. E. B. Ashton (New York: Continuum, 1973 [1966]), 149.

30. Following on the heels of the problem of subjectivism, a too-hasty replacement of masculinist objectivism with a supposedly feminist nativism reproduces its own philosophical difficulties. But a certain nativism does indeed seem to be valorized for the ways that it supposedly "complicates" objectivism. I am thinking here of the reinscription of ontological thinking in discussions of, for example, "hyphenated ethnographers" in Visweswaran, *Fictions of Feminist Ethnography* or "subalternization" in Trinh T. Minh-ha, *Woman, Native, Other: Writing Postcoloniality and Feminism* (Bloomington: Indiana University Press, 1989).

31. Eve Sedgwick makes this point well in *Epistemology of the Closet* (Berkeley and Los Angeles: University of California Press, 1990), 1–63. In the context of her separate and distinct analysis of the shortcomings of differential thinking, Varadharajan notes the unresolved difficulties even in the powerful work of Gayatri Spivak: "Spivak's analysis often assumes that the interaction between subject and object poles in the dialectic is analogous to the failure of a force to move a simply resistant object. She collapses the poles of the dialectic because theory's capacity to be 'off the mark' is matched by the insubstantiality of the object it seeks to theorize. It is difficult to escape the tautological conclusion that theory is its own (insubstantial) object" (Varadharajan, *Exotic Parodies,* xxiii).

32. If he is cited in anthropological literature at all, Benjamin is evoked in an elliptical fashion for his "theses" on history, for the Baudelairean flavor of his ideas about modernity or (more commonly) on the decline of aura in art, and sometimes as a latter-day champion of surrealism. By and large, such appropriations of Benjamin's work miss its dialectical force and ignore his hard-fought attempts to maintain a balance between an "anthropological materialism" and a historical materialist concern with "a revolutionary society." But since anthropologists, like historians, seem to prefer the exoticism of apocalypse ("lost" societies) to revolution, this is consistent with my point about the reception of Marxist ideas in an anodyne culture of criticism. See, for instance, James Clifford, "On Ethnographic Surrealism," in his *The Predicament of Culture* (Cambridge, Mass.: Harvard University Press, 1988), 117–51; Michael Fischer, "Ethnicity and the Post-Modern Arts of Memory," and Stephen Tyler, "Post-Modern Ethnography: From Document of the Occult to Occult Document," both in *Writing Culture: The Poetics and Politics of Ethnography,* ed. James Clifford and George E. Marcus (Berkeley and Los Angeles: University of California Press, 1986), 194–233 and 122–40.

33. See also the celebratory semantic maneuvers of Michael Taussig in his *The Nervous System* (New York: Routledge, 1992) and *Mimesis and Alterity* (New York:

Routledge, 1993). Taussig replaces the exoticism of place with the exoticism of writing. Regardless of the much-needed critique of the hypothesis-mongering tradition of Boasian and Malinowskian anthropology, this rather unproblematized turn to Foucauldianism is less than salutary. Such a tendency to follow the primrose path of textualism can also be found in emergent versions of postcolonial history. For a critique of anthropological thinking, see Paul Smith, *Discerning the Subject* (Minneapolis: University of Minnesota Press, 1988), especially 83–99.

34. See the influential readings of Bhabha and Henry Louis Gates Jr. in Homi K. Bhabha, "Interrogating Identity: Frantz Fanon and the Postcolonial Prerogative," in his *The Location of Culture* (New York: Routledge, 1994), 40–65; and Henry Louis Gates Jr., "Critical Fanonism," *Critical Inquiry* 17, no. 3 (1991): 457–70.

35. Frantz Fanon, *The Wretched of the Earth,* trans. Constance Farrington (New York: Grove Press, 1963 [1961]).

36. Ibid., 199, emphasis added.

37. Ibid., 200.

38. I am greatly indebted to Neil Lazarus and John Mowitt for their differing but absolutely crucial rereadings of the continuities between Fanon's analysis of the relation of intellectuals to political, particularly nationalist, consciousness and the (as-yet unrealized) contestatory potential of postcolonial intellectual production. Lazarus, in particular, has helped me recognize the myriad difficulties inhering in Bhabha's readings of postcoloniality as "supplementary." See Neil Lazarus, "Disavowing Decolonization: Fanon, Nationalism, and the Problematic of Representation in Current Theories of Colonial Discourse," *Research in African Literatures* 24, no. 4 (1993): 70–98; and John Mowitt, "Algerian Nation: Fanon's Fetish," *Cultural Critique* 22 (Fall 1992): 165–86.

39. Fanon, *The Wretched of the Earth,* 153, emphasis added.

40. It may be pertinent to note, amid the effluent appropriations of Lacanian theories of subjectivity, Susan Buck-Morss's important suggestion that Lacan's theory of the subject models a theory of the fascist subject. See her "Aesthetics and Anaesthetics: Walter Benjamin's Artwork Essay Reconsidered," *New Formations* 20 (Summer 1993): 123–43.

41. Fanon, *The Wretched of the Earth,* 163.

42. Homi K. Bhabha, "Remembering Fanon: Self, Psyche, and the Colonial Condition," in *Remaking History,* ed. Barbara Kruger and Phil Mariani (Seattle, Wash.: Bay Press, 1989); and Christopher Miller, *Theories of Africans: Francophone Literature and Anthropology in Africa* (Chicago: University of Chicago Press, 1990).

43. Fanon, *The Wretched of the Earth,* 311, emphasis added. Lazarus, "Disavowing Decolonization," demonstrates the disparity between Fanon's argument about the need for reformulating the terrain of thought and Bhabha's "back to front" rendition of this imperative as bespeaking a disavowal, a "fearfulness" on behalf of its own radical and antihumanist insights (88–89).

44. These comments are enabled by Mowitt's "Algerian Nation," although I am skeptical about the extent to which the discourse of fetishism, with its emphasis on displacement, can coordinate the antagonisms of postcolonial enunciation. Even if Fanon's psychic relation to the Algerian revolution contained fetishistic elements, it seems debatable that this supplementary dynamic accords with an oppositional cultural politics in postmodernity.

45. For thoroughgoing critiques of Geertz's views (and their influence on contemporary cultural analysis even outside the boundaries of anthropology), see Edward Said, "Representing the Colonized: Anthropology's Interlocutors," *Critical Inquiry* 15, no. 2 (1989): 202–25; and Vincent Pecora, "The Limits of Local Knowledge," in *The New Historicism,* ed. H. Aram Veeser (New York: Routledge, 1989), 243–76.

46. Clifford Geertz, *Works and Lives* (Stanford, Calif.: Stanford University Press, 1988), 139.

47. Geertz, *Local Knowledge,* 57.

48. Ibid., 58.

49. In his attempt to work through the "obviousness" with which pragmatism offers its explanations of ideological truths, Althusser offers the following reproof: [P]ragmatism sets out in search of a *de facto* guarantee: *success* in practice, which often constitutes the sole content assignable to what is called the 'practice criterion.' At any rate, we are served with a *guarantee* which is the irrefutable index of an *ideological* question and answer, whereas we are in search of a *mechanism*! The proof of the pudding is in the eating! So what! We are interested in the *mechanism* that ensures that it really is a pudding we are eating and not a poached baby elephant, though we *think* we are eating our daily pudding!" In Louis Althusser and Étienne Balibar, *Reading Capital* (London: Verso, 1970), 57, original emphases.

50. Geertz, *Local Knowledge,* 58.

51. Althusser and Balibar, *Reading Capital,* 21, original emphases.

52. Althusser and Balibar, *Reading Capital,* 22.

53. A quick gloss on the concept of contradiction may be found in the glossary of *Reading Capital:* "A term for the articulation of a practice into the complex whole of the social formation. Contradictions may be antagonistic or non-antagonistic according to whether their state of over-determination is one of fusion or condensation, or one of displacement" (ibid., 311).

54. Althusser and Balibar, *Reading Capital,* 24.

55. See James Clifford, "Power and Dialogue in Ethnography: Marcel Griaule's Initiation," in *Observers Observed: Essays in Ethnographic Fieldwork,* ed. George Stocking (Madison: University of Wisconsin Press, 1983), 121–56. Even my undergraduates who read Griaule's *Conversations with Ogotomelli* were able to discern that the longer Griaule engaged the Dogon elder in his so-called conversations, the more clearly the structure of Griaule's preoccupations emerged as defining the "reality." See Marcel Griaule, *Conversations with Ogotomelli: An Introduction to Dogon Religious Ideas* (London: Published for the International African Institute by Oxford University Press, 1965).

56. Althusser and Balibar, *Reading Capital,* 105.

57. The phrase is taken from Mary E. John, "Postcolonial Feminists in the Western Intellectual Field: Anthropologists *and* Native Informants?" in Clifford and Dhareshwar, *Inscriptions* 5: 49–73. My own preoccupations as a postcolonial scholar have taken a direction away from location and topography in the strict sense that, understandably for anthropologists, underpins the notion of the "field." I might suggest that this is an artifact of, as Althusser argued about classical political economy, "the determination of the visible as visible" and one which requires a "change of terrain" (Althusser and Balibar, *Reading Capital,* 25, 27).

58. The term "traveling cultures" is derived from the essay of the same name by James Clifford, in *Cultural Studies,* ed. Lawrence Grossberg, Cary Nelson, and Paula Treichler (New York: Routledge, 1992), 96–116.

59. Clifford, "Traveling Cultures," 97.

60. I am grateful to Tim Brennan for his knowledgeable observations about the specificity of the Frankfurt school's relationship to Surrealism.

61. See, for instance, Celeste Olalquiaga, *Megalopolis: Contemporary Cultural Sensibilities* (Minneapolis: University of Minnesota Press, 1992).

62. See Arjun Appadurai, "Disjuncture and Difference in the Global Cultural Economy," *Public Culture* 2, no. 2 (1990): 1–24. It should be said that my perspective is quite discontinuous from that of Appadurai. I thank Tim Brennan for illuminating a more rigorously materialist view of "globalization."

63. Clifford, "Traveling Cultures," 97, quote at 98.

64. Ibid., 97.

65. Ibid., 110.

66. Lazarus, "Disavowing Decolonization," 83.

67. Roland Barthes, "Change the Object Itself" (1971), in his *Image, Music, Text,* trans. Stephen Heath (New York: Hill and Wang, 1977), 167, 168, original emphasis.

68. For more on Barthes's "second enlargement" of semiology, see his *Image, Music, Text,* particularly the 1971 essay "Change the Object Itself" reprinted there.

69. Althusser and Balibar, *Reading Capital,* 29, 188, original emphases.

70. Ania Loomba makes the same point in "Overworlding the 'Third World,'" in *Colonial Discourse and Postcolonial Theory: A Reader,* ed. Patrick Williams and Laura Chrisman (New York: Columbia University Press, 1994), 307.

71. See Theodor W. Adorno, "The Meaning of Working Through the Past," in his *Critical Models: Interventions and Catchwords,* trans. Henry W. Pickford (New York: Columbia University Press, 1998), 89–103. Of particular relevance to the question of "working through" is the translator's note 1 (337–38), which tells us that "'*Aufarbeitung*' is here translated as 'working through' and requires clarification since it does not wholly coincide with the psychoanalytical term 'working through' *(Durcharbeitung),* though it is related. Its common meaning is that of working through in the sense of dispatching tasks that have built up and demand attention, catching up on accumulated paperwork, etc. It thus conveys the sense of getting through an unpleasant obligation, clearing one's desk, etc., and some politicians and historians with less sensitivity to language than Adorno began using the term in reference to the need to reappraise, or 'master' the past (the German for the latter being *Vergangenheitsbewältigung,* which connotes both confrontation and overcoming). At the outset of the essay Adorno contrasts 'working through' *(aufarbeiten)* with a serious 'working upon' *(verarbeiten)* of the past in the sense of assimilating, coming to terms with it.'"

72. I should like to note the differences between thematizing shock-experience as a *defense* against trauma and regarding trauma as a reaction to shock. The former position traces its currency from Henri Bergson and Freud to its aesthetic and sociological elaboration by Aragon and Benjamin. Taussig, in *The Nervous System,* emphasizes the latter in his discussions of the shock of montage and modern discourses of culture and control. Though his citation of anthropological exotica is undoubtedly interesting, his theoretical case about the traumatic bent of everyday

experience is not well sustained because he misunderstands the specificity of Benjamin's argument that shock relates to the subject's *management* of affect (as opposed to a deployment of nervous energy). As a result of this misunderstanding, *The Nervous System* contains some oddly decontextualized discussions confusing terror and shock, neurosis and psychosis.

73. These highly condensed arguments about the fully situated nature of the encounter between capitalism and modernity receive their elaboration in Benjamin's essays "The Storyteller" and "On Some Motifs in Baudelaire." My own reading was clarifed tremendously by Buck-Morss, "Aesthetics and Anaesthetics," 130–31.

74. The idea that in the context of a modern social and penal order, the awareness of the subjected body is transferred to the subjectivity of the "condemned" is enlarged throughout Michel Foucault's *Discipline and Punish*, trans. Alan Sheridan (New York: Vintage Books, 1979 [1975]).

75. I want to distinguish this proposition from arguments spun out of a loosely Deleuzian model, which abstract the experience of postcoloniality into a sort of global Brownian motion. But as more careful interpreters of theories of *chock*-experience (shock-experience) contend, mechanisms of breakdown or dispersal are in fact attended by a dialectical reversal that articulates a sensibility that is more invested in consolidating identity as a cognitive rather than locational project. For Deleuzian readings, see the essays in Iain Chambers and Lidia Curti, eds., *The Post-Colonial Question: Common Skies, Divided Horizons* (New York: Routledge, 1996), especially Lawrence Grossberg's "The Space of Culture, the Power of Space," 169–88.

76. Benjamin on Baudelaire, quoted in Buck-Morss, "Aesthetics and Anaesthetics," 131. As I hope this indicates, my reading inflects the argument about postcolonial subjectivity very differently from Bhabha's influential propositions, which (as Lazarus, "Disavowing Decolonization," 89, has convincingly shown) apply only rather narrowly to "colonized elitism" (than to the actual constituencies of colonized subalterns, with whom he evinces very little acquaintance). See Homi K. Bhabha, "Sly Civility," in his *The Location of Culture*, 93–101. Benita Parry has also commented critically on Bhabha's tendency to conflate localized readings to a generalized theory of postcolonial positionality. See her early and cogent intervention "Problems in Current Theories of Colonial Discourse," *Oxford Literary Review*, nos. 1–2 (1995): 9, 27–58.

77. Bhabha, "Sly Civility." Whatever the value of this trope for examining the construction of the "litigious, lying native" of nineteenth-century colonial regulation in India, it cannot justifiably be extended (as Bhabha does elsewhere) to explain the postcolonial native's subjective mode of address.

78. Gayatri Chakravorty Spivak has commented on the difference between postcolonial intellectuals (like herself or Said) and other postcolonial subjects in terms of the exigencies of being "wild anthropologists." According to her, "we [i.e., postcolonial intellectuals] have decided to look at the scandal of our production [as Westernized subjects]." Her distinction is useful, though it is of course the case that even nonintellectuals think about their "production," even if they do not think of it as scandalous. In any case, as Spivak herself has maintained in other places, if the upwardly mobile aspirations of postcolonial intellectuals is part and parcel of the process of entering the metropolitan academy, obviously mere reflexivity does not exempt us from the bourgeois scandal. See Gayatri Chakravorty Spivak, "The New

Historicism: Political Commitment and the Postmodern Critic," in *The New Historicism*, ed. H. Aram Veeser (New York: Routledge, 1989), 290.

79. Anannya Bhattacharjee suggestively describes the practices of "ex-nomination," whereby bourgeois ideology is naturalized in the self-production of an immigrant Indian identity. Bhattacharjee's critique of the coming-to-consciousness of the Indian bourgeoisie in the First World centers on its radical disavowal of social problems within the community, particularly of violence against women. See her essay "The Habit of Ex-Nomination: Nation, Woman, and the Indian Immigrant Bourgeoisie," *Public Culture* 5, no. 1 (Fall 1992): 19–44.

80. Bayes' Theorem in statistics, named after the Reverend Thomas Bayes, an eighteenth-century mathematician who posited the role of a loaded dice in all games of inference.

81. By the descriptive conventions of interpretive anthropology, my ethnographic field would have been far more convincing had it been located in a more picturesque "there." Witness, for example, Geertz's retelling of Raymond Firth's "classic" beginning to *We, the Tikopia* (1936): "In the cool of the early morning, just before sunrise, the bow of the *Southern Cross* headed towards the eastern horizon, on which a tiny dark blue outline was faintly visible. Slowly it grew into a rugged mountain mass, standing up sheer from the ocean; then as we approached within a few miles it revealed around its base a narrow ring of low, flat land, thick with vegetation. The sullen grey day with its lowering cloud strengthened my grim impression of a solitary peak, wild and stormy, upthrust in a waste of waters. . . . Vahihaloa, my 'boy,' looked over the side from the upper deck, 'My word, me fright too much,' he said with a quavering laugh; 'me tink this fella man he savvy kaikai me.' *Kaikai* is the pidgin-English term for 'eat.'. . . Later we went ashore in one of the canoes. . . . We were surrounded by crowds of naked chattering youngsters, with their pleasant light-brown velvet skins and straight hair, so different from the Melanesians we had left behind. They darted about splashing like a shoal of fish, some of them falling bodily into pools in their enthusiasm." And so on (cited in Geertz, *Works and Lives*, 11–12). Then Geertz confidently tells us, "There can be little doubt from this that Firth was, in every sense of the word, 'there.' All the fine detail, marshaled with Dickensian exuberance and Conradian fatality—the blue mass, lowering clouds, excited jabberings, velvet skins, shelved beach, needle carpet, enstooled chief—conduce to a conviction that what follows, five hundred pages of resolutely objectified description of social customs—the Tikopia do this, the Tikopia believe that—can be taken as fact" (13). Here is the self-deception of anthropological hermeneutics writ large: If by virtue of his occasional lapse into pidgin or the descriptive fetishization of velvet skins and native jabberings, we take as *fact* that Firth was "there," then so was Edgar Rice Burroughs.

82. As with any venture of this sort, this group was only a small fraction of the total immigrant Indian population in southern New Jersey. This does not make it less representative or set it apart from other ethnographic studies, in which the reliance on translators and informants, as well as intensive observation, also only produces synecdochic rather than numerically representative interpretations. In fact, examples abound of ethnographic studies in which the "sample" of informants is far fewer. Marjorie Shostak's *Nisa: The Life and Words of a !Kung Woman* (Cambridge, Mass.: Harvard University Press, 1981) is among the better-known examples of an account that is mostly based on a single informant. In my own case,

the problem is less one of "numbers" than it is of the imposition on all the people who had consented to be my ethnographic subjects.

83. For example, the problem of caste and its retooled structures in the indigenous context of postcolonial India is rather complicated and quite distinct from my own interests in this study. For sociohistorical analyses of the problem of caste, see Louis Dumont's anthropological classic, *Homo Hierarchicus: The Caste System and Its Implications,* trans. Mark Sainsbury, Louis Dumont, and Basia Gulati (Chicago: University of Chicago Press, 1980 [1966]). For an account of the interplay between caste and colonialism, see Nicholas Dirks, "Castes of Mind," *Representations,* no. 37 (Winter 1992), 56–78.

84. See Smith, *Discerning the Subject,* 87–95.

85. Ibid., 97.

86. I rely here on Smith's rendering of Freud's gloss on the difference between the neurotic analysand and the paranoiac (ibid., 95).

2. The Antinomies of Everyday Life

1. Raymond Williams, "Literature and Sociology," in his *Problems in Materialism and Culture* (London: Verso, 1980), 17.

2. Ibid., 23. Williams comments wryly on the textualist conceits for making assumptions about the consciousness of a social group: "The idea of a world-view, a particular organized way of seeing the world, is of course familiar to us in our own studies. Indeed I myself had to spend many years getting away from it, in the ordinary form in which I found it presented. The Elizabethan world-picture, I came to believe, was a thing fascinating in itself, but then it was more of a hindrance than a help in seeing the full substance of Elizabethan drama. Again, I learned the Greek world-picture and was baffled by Greek drama; the Victorian world-picture and found the English nineteenth-century novel amazing" (ibid., 24).

3. The implicit target of my critique here is Homi Bhabha, whose influence on poststructuralist versions of postcolonial critique has been significant though problematic. Many of his notions turn on a "time-consciousness" that produces both otherness and a deferred truth (premised as it is on the irruption of "mimetic" subjectivities). One gets the sneaking suspicion that we ought to be interested in the stuff of postcolonial "dissemination" because it bends the rule of the game: "Feelings" of mimicry subvert the "structure" of colonial domination, as it were. Bhabha's method is not only syncretic but associative, and it relies for impact on a blurring of the distinction between consciousness and oppositional consciousness that is, bluntly put, egregious. See his essay "DissemiNation: Time, Narrative, and the Margins of the Modern Nation," in Homi K. Bhabha, ed., *Nation and Narration* (London: Routledge, 1990), 291–322.

4. Raymond Williams, "The Welsh Industrial Novel," in his *Problems in Materialism and Culture* (London: Verso, 1980), 213–29.

5. Ibid., 222.

6. Ibid., 214.

7. Edward Said, "Traveling Theory," in his *The World, the Text, and the Critic* (Cambridge, Mass.: Harvard University Press, 1983), 226–47, quotation at 231.

8. Ibid., 240.

9. Ibid.

10. Georg Lukács, *History and Class Consciousness: Studies in Marxist Dialectics,* trans. Rodney Livingstone (Cambridge: MIT Press, 1971 [1968]), 178.

11. Ibid., 179.

12. Said, "Traveling Theory," 232.

13. Lukács, *History and Class Consciousness,* 105.

14. Said, "Traveling Theory," 232.

15. Emphasis added. This definition is taken from the *Random House Dictionary of the English Language,* 2nd ed. unabridged.

16. Lukács, *History and Class Consciousness,* 83–222.

17. Ibid., 83.

18. Ibid., 84, original emphasis.

19. Ibid., 95–99, passim. This "ghostly" disarticulation that "stamps its imprint upon the whole consciousness of man" is, according to Lukács, given its most heightened example in Kant's description of marriage. Here is Lukács quoting Kant: "Sexual community [...] is the reciprocal use made by one person of the sexual organs and faculties of another.... marriage is the union of two people of different sexes with a view to the mutual possession of each other's sexual attributes for the duration of their lives" (ibid., 100).

20. Walter Benjamin, "Capitalism as Religion" (1921), in *Walter Benjamin: Selected Writings* (Cambridge, Mass.: Harvard University Press, 1996), 288–91.

21. Lukács, *History and Class Consciousness,* 185.

22. Homi K. Bhabha, *The Location of Culture* (New York: Routledge, 1994), 244.

23. See Ernst Bloch, "Nonsynchronism and the Obligation to Its Dialectics" (1932), trans. Mark Ritter, *New German Critique* 11 (Spring 1977): 22–38.

24. Ibid., 22, emphasis added.

25. Ibid., 33, original emphasis.

26. Ibid., 35.

27. Theodor W. Adorno, *The Jargon of Authenticity,* trans. Knut Tarnowski and Frederic Will (Evanston, Ill.: Northwestern University Press, 1973 [1964]), 34.

28. Ibid., 26.

29. Lukács, *History and Class Consciousness,* 204, emphasis added.

30. The falseness with which experience is reified—so that it appears, simultaneously, as detached from the objective conditions of capitalism and as affirming a self-evident identity—has been rendered with great complexity in Theodor W. Adorno, *Negative Dialectics,* trans. E. B. Ashton (New York: Continuum, 1973 [1966]). In Adorno's thinking, "The [exchange principle], the reduction of human labour to the abstract universal concept of average working hours, is fundamentally akin to the principle of identification" (146). The terrain of everyday life subtends the reified poles of "work" and "life"; that is to say, it is where the abstraction of human labor both denies and requires the messiness of daily life practices. I have been helped to think along these lines by Susan Willis's pioneering study of the domestic as commodity, *A Primer for Daily Life* (London: Routledge, 1991).

31. Lukács, *History and Class Consciousness,* 204.

32. Fredric Jameson, "The Antinomies of Postmodernity," in his *The Seeds of Time* (New York: Columbia University Press, 1994), 1–71.

33. Lukács, *History and Class Consciousness,* 205. These points were also made explicitly by Marx in *The Holy Family* and *The German Ideology,* where it should be

recalled that the object of critique was less the capitalist mode of production than a theoretical scene intoxicated by a language of dialectical reversal: one that by an internal logic of its own transported the critic far from an experiential realm, including a specific kind of realm that Marx, in a famous early letter to Arnold Ruge, called "politics."

34. Georges Bataille, "Sacrificial Mutilation and the Severed Ear of Vincent van Gogh," in his *Visions of Excess: Selected Writings, 1927–1939*, trans. Allan Stoekl with Carl R. Lovitt and Donald M. Leslie Jr. (Minneapolis: University of Minnesota Press, 1985), 62.

35. The phrase "fantasy bribe" is Jameson's. He uses it to hypothesize that even the most degraded aspects of mass culture contain implicitly or explicitly utopian elements because "[they] cannot manipulate unless they offer some genuine shred of content as a fantasy bribe to the public about to be so manipulated." See Fredric Jameson, "Reification and Utopia in Mass Culture," *Social Text* 1 (Winter 1979): 130–48, quotation at 144.

36. Louis Marin, "Disneyland: A Degenerate Utopia," *Glyph* 1 (1977): 50–66.

37. Jameson, "Reification and Utopia in Mass Culture," 144.

38. Ibid., 131, emphasis added.

39. Henri Lefebvre, *Introduction to Modernity*, trans. John Moore (London: Verso, 1995 [1962]), 1 (paragraph break suppressed).

40. Lefebvre also takes up the problematic of everyday life in two other texts: *Everyday Life in the Modern World* (New Brunswick, N.J.: Transaction Publishers, 1990 [1984]) and *Critique of Everyday Life* (London: Verso, 1991), vol. 1.

41. See Paul Willis, with Simon Jones, Joyce Canaan, and Geoff Hurd, *Common Culture: Symbolic Work at Play in the Everyday Cultures of the Young* (Boulder, Colo.: Westview Press, 1990), 10, original emphasis.

42. Ibid., 6.

43. Ibid., 137.

44. Terry Eagleton, "Capitalism, Modernism, and Postmodernism," in *Modern Criticism and Theory: A Reader*, ed. David Lodge (London: Longman, 1988), 385–98. Originally published in *New Left Review* (1985).

45. For his phenomenology, see Hans-Georg Gadamer, *Truth and Method*, 2nd rev. ed., trans. Joel Weinsheimer and Donald G. Marshall (New York: Crossroad, 1991 [1965]).

46. Ibid., 60.

47. Ibid., 61, emphasis added.

48. A somewhat different argument about the necessity of working through the Western archive (both of knowledge and historical consciousness) is proposed in Partha Chatterjee's *Nationalist Thought and the Colonial World: A Derivative Discourse?* (London: Zed Press, 1986). Chatterjee demonstrates that the historical scenario of the development of Indian nationalism, though derived from categories of Enlightenment thought, can by no means be seen as merely contained within the restrictive horizons of European experience or history. Modular conceptions of historical existence (such as the idea of nationhood) are produced, but not exhausted, in their definition by the West. Such a perspective (which I share) refuses the nativism that would require rejecting everything Western. A more historicized appropriation of the West's ideological and philosophical claims does not just allow a re-

sponsible rejoinder to its systematic hegemony over the rest of the world; it also reflects the constitutively specular or reflective dimensions of theory (derived from the Greek, *theoria*—"a thing viewed").

49. Hannah Arendt, "Walter Benjamin: 1892–1940," introduction to *Illuminations*, by Walter Benjamin, trans. Harry Zohn (New York: Schocken Books, 1968), 1–51.

50. Franz Kafka, in a letter to Max Brod, cited by Arendt in her introduction to Benjamin, *Illuminations*, 31.

51. Walter Benjamin, "The Storyteller" (1936) and "On Some Motifs in Baudelaire" (1939), both in his *Illuminations*, 83–109 and 155–200.

52. Referring to the life and work of Eric Auerbach, Edward Said has advanced the thesis that exilic consciousness produces extraordinary perceptions into problems of culture and location. See Said, *The World, the Text, and the Critic*, especially 1–30.

53. Walter Benjamin, "A Berlin Childhood" (1932), trans. Mary-Jo Leibowitz, *Art and Literature: An International Review* 4 (1965): 37–45.

54. I want, through this coinage, to resist the overused notion of a "discursive economy," which stresses the afflatus of the discursive while capitalizing on the materialist appeal of the economic.

3. Personal Memory and the Contradictions of Selfhood

1. The category of the "future anterior"—from Ernst Bloch's image of an "anticipatory illumination" *(Vor-Schein)* and Benjamin's ideas about a profane redemption, to Siegfried Kracauer's version of theological materialism—is immensely relevant here, though I cannot do justice to the complex dialecticization of this category in a brief gloss. By the same token, in adducing this conceptual category I, want to maintain my distance from the tendentious reading of nostalgia as a "social disease," as "the desire for desire," or as an open-ended (but simultaneously prelapsarian) narrative of a future-past—found, for example, in Susan Stewart's rendering. See her *On Longing: Narratives of the Miniature, the Gigantic, the Souvenir, the Collection* (Durham, N.C.: Duke University Press, 1993), especially 23–24.

2. The status of the "subject," whether in contemporary critical theory or in modes of ethnographic representation, has been problematized thoroughly. For examples, see James Clifford and George E. Marcus, eds., *Writing Culture: The Poetics and Politics of Ethnography* (Berkeley and Los Angeles: University of California Press, 1986); Paul Smith, *Discerning the Subject* (Minneapolis: University of Minnesota Press, 1988); and Gayatri Chakravorty Spivak, "Can the Subaltern Speak?" in *Marxism and the Interpretation of Culture*, ed. Cary Nelson and Lawrence Grossberg (Urbana: University of Illinois Press, 1988), 271–313. The terms "subject" and "self," "subjectivity" and "selfhood," have discontinuous valences that vary with usage. I use them synonymously to indicate the relations that variously enable and constrain the agency of historical actors, that is, to indicate the shifting movements between a sense of the subject/self as determined or interpellated and as, at the same time, self-authorizing, bearing agency.

3. Peter Stallybrass and Allon White, *The Politics and Poetics of Transgression* (Ithaca, N.Y.: Cornell University Press, 1986).

4. Ibid., 3.

5. The resemblance between dream and possibility, and between banality and enigma, is at the crux of Benjamin's arguments when he says, "The similarity of one thing to another which we are used to, which occupies us in a wakeful state, reflects only vaguely the deeper resemblance of the dream world in which everything that happens appears not in identical but in similar guise, opaquely similar one to another. Children know a symbol of this world: the stocking which has the structure of this dream world." This is the active work of symbolization—which, insofar as it is active, is also futural. (Why else would any labor be expended?) See Walter Benjamin, "The Image of Proust," in his *Illuminations,* trans. Harry Zohn (New York: Schocken Books, 1968), 204–5.

6. See Howard Caygill's impressive book *Walter Benjamin: The Colour of Experience* (London and New York: Routledge, 1998), especially 66–69.

7. Benjamin, "The Image of Proust," 203, emphasis added.

8. Ibid.

9. This problem has been explored by Johannes Fabian in *Time and the Other: How Anthropology Makes Its Object* (New York: Columbia University Press, 1983).

10. Evidence of the tendency to semanticize the other can be found in James Clifford, "Introduction: Partial Truths," In Clifford and Marcus, *Writing Culture,* 1–26; Vincent Crapanzano, *Tuhami: Portrait of a Moroccan* (Chicago: University of Chicago Press, 1980); and Stephen A. Tyler, "Post-Modern Ethnography: From Document of the Occult to Occult Document," in Clifford and Marcus, *Writing Culture,* 122–45. The standard critique of anthropologism remains Edward Said, "Representing the Colonized: Anthropology's Interlocutors," *Critical Inquiry* 15 (1989): 205–25.

11. Antonio Gramsci, *Selections from the Prison Notebooks,* trans. Quintin Hoare and Geoffrey Nowell Smith (New York: International Publishers, 1971); see especially "The Study of Philosophy," 323–77, quotation at 324. It should be noted that the Italian formulation, *mode bizarre,* connotes more of the contradictions of a worldview than the standard English translation gives it. This point is elaborated by Wolfgang Fritz Haug in *Commodity Aesthetics, Ideology, and Culture* (New York: International General, 1987), 68.

12. Ibid., 324.

13. Richard Johnson, Gregor McLennan, Bill Schwarz, and David Sutton, *Making Histories: Studies in History Writing and Politics* (Minneapolis: University of Minnesota Press, 1982).

14. Ibid., 211.

15. Michel de Certeau, Luce Giard, and Pierre Mayol, *The Practice of Everyday Life,* vol. 2: *Living and Cooking,* trans. Timothy J. Tomasik (Minneapolis: University of Minnesota Press, 1998), 147.

16. Stallybrass and White, *The Politics and Poetics of Transgression,* 4.

17. These numbers are based on rough estimates of membership in various regional organizations and from a report in the *Philadelphia Inquirer,* March 25, 1999, which cites 1990 U.S. census figures to the effect that there are 25,000 South Asians in the Delaware Valley area, which includes southern New Jersey and Philadelphia. About 20,000 people of South Asian descent live close to the city of Philadelphia; the rest in the suburbs of southern New Jersey.

18. Jenny Sharpe, "Is the United States Postcolonial? Transnationalism, Immigration, and Race," *Diaspora* 4, no. 2 (1995): 181–99.

19. Ibid., 193.

20. Procedural considerations have been described in chapter 1. Here I wish only to convey that early in my fieldwork I decided not to enter every social occasion with the paraphernalia of observation: tape recorder, notebook, or camera. Though far from resulting in genuinely spontaneous interactions with my ethnographic interlocutors, this was indeed less disruptive and made for better maintenance of "rule-governed behavior." Moreover, I was able to keep within sight of my interest in how narratives get produced in taken-for-granted interactions (rather than through more self-consciously calculated measures).

21. Certeau, Giard, and Mayol, *The Practice of Everyday Life,* vol. 2, 24, original emphasis.

22. Ibid., 25, original emphasis.

23. The advantages and particularities of "insider knowledge" have been explored in other ways by Lila Abu-Lughod in *Veiled Sentiments: Honor and Poetry in a Bedouin Society* (Berkeley and Los Angeles: University of California Press, 1986), see especially 1–35.

24. The names of my informants are pseudonyms. I have tried to maintain the "spirit" of people's names: to be consistent, for instance, on matters such as whether people were addressed habitually by their initials ("Deejay" or "P. C."), by a recognizable "pet name" (such as "Botu"), or by their first names (such as "Sudhir"). Names are, of course, crucial in the construction of identity; Indian names, in particular, connote specific meanings that, whether Hindu or Muslim, derive from Persian, Sanskrit, or Urdu roots (e.g., Sudhir, "the calm one"; Ajit, "the unconquerable"). The suffixes -*da/dada* or -*di/didi* in Bengali and -*bhai* or -*didi* in Hindi, when attached to names, designate age differences between men and women who were older than I.

25. Stallybrass and White, *The Politics and Poetics of Transgression,* 191, original emphasis.

26. Ibid., 176.

27. The trope of recovering the self—connoting, as it does, an image of disease—is expanded upon by Ashis Nandy in his *The Intimate Enemy: Loss and Recovery of Self under Colonialism* (Delhi: Oxford University Press, 1983).

28. See Gayatri Chakravorty Spivak, *The Post-Colonial Critic: Interview, Strategies, Dialogues,* ed. Sarah Harasym (New York: Routledge, 1990); and Partha Chatterjee, *Nationalist Thought and the Colonial World: A Derivative Discourse?* (London: Zed Books, 1986).

29. Mrinalini Sinha has argued that the ideology of the "effeminate" Bengali was an integral part of the British colonial system in India, which propagated an overt myth of civilization while concealing its covert purposes of exploitation. Rendering the educated Bengali as excessively emotional and feminized was a way of justifying the rule of the Raj and of withholding power from educated and Anglicized natives (who might otherwise be regarded as competent to govern themselves). See Mrinalini Sinha, *Colonial Masculinity: The "Manly Englishman" and the "Effeminate Bengali" in the Late Nineteenth Century* (Manchester, England: Manchester University Press, 1995).

30. Stallybrass and White, *The Politics and Poetics of Transgression,* 193, original emphases.

31. The neologistic formulation "the inappropriate/d other" is from Trinh T.

Minh-ha. It draws on the idea that the subaltern woman is an "inappropriate" subject within the dominant culture as well as in mainstream feminist or anthropological discourses (which continue to presume and dissimulate the white woman as their point of interest). The other woman is also an absent representation *tout court* and in this sense is "un-appropriated." The neologism, then, is a condensation. See Trinh T. Minh-ha, *Woman, Native, Other: Writing Postcoloniality and Feminism* (Bloomington: Indiana University Press, 1989).

32. Anthony Cohen, *The Symbolic Construction of Community* (London: Verso, 1985), 86.

33. Ibid., 87.

34. Ibid., emphasis in original.

35. Satya Mohanty, "Us and Them: On the Philosophical Bases of Political Criticism," *Yale Journal of Criticism* 2, no. 2 (1989): 1–31.

36. Clifford Geertz, *Local Knowledge: Further Essays in Interpretive Anthropology* (New York: Basic Books, 1983), 80.

37. Pratibha Parmar, "Gender, Race, and Class: Asian Women in Resistance," in *The Empire Strikes Back: Race and Racism in 70s Britain*, Centre for Contemporary Cultural Studies (London: Hutchinson, 1982), 236–75.

38. Homi K. Bhabha, "The Commitment to Theory," *New Formations* 5 (1988): 5–23.

39. Ibid., 19.

4. Food and the Habitus

1. Pierre Bourdieu is usually credited with the concept of the habitus, but Bourdieu borrowed from Norbert Elias's early (1939) use of it to distinguish between the old-fashioned notion of "national character" and the accumulated weight of "the fortunes of a nation...sedimented into the habitus of its individual members." For more on Elias's laying out of the concept, see his *The Germans: Power Struggles and the Development of Habitus in the Nineteenth and Twentieth Centuries*, trans. Eric Dunning and Stephen Mennell (New York: University Press, 1996 [1989]), especially, the preface, ix, and notes to the preface, 438n3. We may note that Benjamin also refers to "the habitus of a lived life" (in drafts of the *Arcades Project*), but as I understand it, he does not elevate the term to identify a concept.

2. Erving Goffman, *The Presentation of Self in Everyday Life* (New York: Anchor Books, 1959).

3. Ibid., 192.

4. Ibid., 191–92.

5. Ibid., 192, quoted from Col. J. L. Sleeman, *Thugs, or A Million Murders* (London: Sampson Low, 1933 [1920]), 79.

6. Pierre Bourdieu, *Distinction: A Social Critique of the Judgement of Taste*, trans. Richard Nice (Cambridge, Mass.: Harvard University Press, 1984 [1979]), 173.

7. Ibid., 174, emphasis added.

8. Both quotations in this paragraph are taken from Theodor W. Adorno, "Vandalism," in his *Minima Moralia: Reflections from Damaged Life* (London: Verso, 1974 [1951]), 138–39.

9. My thanks to Prabhakara Jha for recalling an occasion when, on being introduced, a woman gushed at him, "You're Indian? I *love* Indian food." To which he

responded, "On behalf of Indian food, I thank you." I continue to appreciate his insights into and witticisms about the Western reception of "postcoloniality."

10. See Roland Barthes, *Mythologies*, trans. Annette Lavers (New York: Hill and Wang 1972 [1957]), 62–64.

11. Ibid., 63, original emphasis.

12. Ibid., 63–64.

13. To give a couple of examples, nationalist aspirations of formerly colonized countries cannot be equated with (or seen as equivalents to) those of imperial nations any more than "women's studies" can be said to have the same scholarly agenda as that of various conservative-sponsored "men's studies" programs. In other words, history is not (and has never been) a level playing field in which all positions are formally equivalent.

14. Tautology, Barthes argues, is among the features of myth. See his "Myth Today," in his *Mythologies*, 152–53. In this context, his distinction between the mythologist and the "myth-consumer" is also worth remembering. The former is "condemned to live in a theoretical sociality" (157), whereas the latter lives with and speaks about the "proverbial," *existential* quality of life. Crucially, this difference leads Barthes to focus on the bourgeois, which is to say class-determined, nature of myth; it is also what prevents his analysis from becoming preoccupied with culturalist explanations of mythological *doxa*. For an overwhelmingly existentialist account of the commonplaces and mythologies of Soviet Russia, see Svetlana Boym's *Common Places: Mythologies of Everyday Life in Russia* (Cambridge, Mass.: Harvard University Press, 1994).

15. In Bourdieu's words, "the social agents whom the sociologist classifies are producers not only of classifiable acts but also of acts of classification which are themselves classified." See his *Distinction*, 467.

16. For a nuanced treatment of the conceits of poststructuralist criticism and their materialist correctives in the work of Adorno in particular, see Peter Dews's excellent essay "Adorno, Poststructuralism, and the Critique of Identity," in *The Problems of Modernity: Adorno and Benjamin*, ed. Andrew Benjamin (London: Routledge, 1989), 1–22.

17. Friedrich Nietzsche, *The Will to Power*, ed. Walter Kaufman (New York: Random House, 1967), 272.

18. Susan Stewart, *On Longing: Narratives of the Miniature, the Gigantic, the Souvenir, the Collection* (Durham, N.C.: Duke University Press, 1993), 23.

19. Ibid., x, original emphasis.

20. Rosalind Coward and John Ellis, *Language and Materialism* (London: Routledge, Kegan, Paul, 1977).

21. Stewart, *On Longing*, xi.

22. To be a bit more careful than Stewart, we might think of the difference between *transcendence* and the *transcendental*. They are connected but not identical: Whereas the former is concerned with overcoming human suffering and is premised on the idea that human life is transitory, belief in the latter implies an idealist and pathos-filled sense of human nature, seen as stemming from the void and having no purpose. The one is sociohistorical in orientation; the other, metaphysical. (The poststructuralist haste to condemn Marxist thinking as a supposedly degraded universalism has led to some conflationary accounts of the two.)

23. Jameson has suggested that the hostility to the concept of totality stems from

"[t]he misconception [that] seems to be based on the idea that if you talk about something repeatedly, you must like it; to point something out insistently turns into the advocacy of the thing, very much on the principle of messengers who bring bad news (and suffer the consequences)." See his *Late Marxism: Adorno, or The Persistence of the Dialectic* (London and New York: Verso, 1990), 230.

24. Theodor W. Adorno, "Die Aktualitat der Philosophie" (1973), translated as "The Actuality of Philosophy," trans. Benjamin Snow, *Telos* 31 (Spring 1977): 120–33.

25. See Shierry Weber Nicholsen, *Exact Imagination, Late Work: On Adorno's Aesthetics* (Cambridge: MIT Press, 1997), 4.

26. Ibid.

27. Trent Schroyer, foreword to *The Jargon of Authenticity*, by Theodor W. Adorno, trans. Knut Tarnowski and Frederic Will (Evanston, Ill.: Northwestern University Press, 1973 [1964]), viii, emphasis added.

28. Schroyer, foreword to Adorno, *The Jargon of Authenticity*, xiv.

29. Adorno, *The Jargon of Authenticity*, 30.

30. Ibid., 163.

31. Theodor W. Adorno, *Negative Dialectics*, trans. E. B. Ashton (New York: Continuum, 1973 [1966]), 207.

32. Jameson, *Late Marxism*, 119.

33. Adorno, quoted in ibid.

34. Jameson, *Late Marxism*, 261n20.

35. Adorno, *Negative Dialectics*, 207.

36. See especially Walter Benjamin, "Epistemo-Critical Prologue," in his *The Origin of German Tragic Drama*, trans. John Osborne (London: Verso, 1977 [1928]), 27–56.

37. See, for instance, the extremely problematic rendering of Benjamin's ideas on death and narrative in Rey Chow, "Walter Benjamin's Love Affair with Death," *New German Critique* 48 (Fall 1989): 63–86, and in Eduardo Cadava's conflation of the "click of history" with the mediated click of the camera estranging "man and his surroundings" in his *Words of Light: Theses on the Photography of History* (Princeton: Princeton University Press, 1997), especially 5–7. Though Cadava offers suggestive epigrams with which to think about the metaphor of photography as a form of historiography in Benjaminian terms, he forgets (unlike Benjamin himself) that metaphors are not reality and, therefore, cannot exhaust the task of the "materialist historian."

38. From Walter Benjamin's unfinished *Arcades Project (Das Passagenwerk)*, cited in Richard Sieburth, "Benjamin the Scrivener," in *Benjamin: Philosophy, Aesthetics, History*, ed. Gary Smith (Chicago, University of Chicago Press, 1983), 23.

39. Despite Benjamin's scattered references to *Beyond the Pleasure Principle* and *The Psychopathology of Everyday Life*, that he was relatively skeptical toward Freud's ideas is proposed by both Jameson in *Late Marxism*, and Rolf Wiggershaus in his authoritative overview of the Frankfurt school, *The Frankfurt School: Its History, Theories, and Political Significance*, trans. Michael Robertson (Cambridge: MIT Press, 1994).

40. It may be recalled that among his various proposals about the nature of media, Marshall McLuhan distinguished between "hot" and "cool" media; hot media (face-to-face, oral, performative) depend upon the quality of immediacy for their effect, whereas cool media (radio, television, film) retain their effectivity over space and time. See his *Understanding Media: The Extensions of Man* (New York: Signet Books, 1964).

41. Michel de Certeau, Luce Giard, and Pierre Mayol, *The Practice of Everyday Life,* vol. 2: *Living and Cooking,* trans. Timothy J. Tomasik (Minneapolis: University of Minnesota Press, 1998).

42. Ibid., ix.

43. Ibid., 181.

44. Ibid., 183.

45. Ibid., 184.

46. Approaches that fit food into binaristic and functionalist accounts have been very influential in cultural studies, though the underlying methodological difficulties have been studiously ignored. However, on the assumption that such problems are (and should be) easily detected in the source material, let me direct the reader to Mary Douglas, *Purity and Danger: An Analysis of Concepts of Pollution and Taboo* (London: Routledge and Kegan Paul, 1966); Louis Dumont, *Homo Hierarchicus: The Caste System and Its Implications,* trans. Mark Sainsbury, Louis Dumont, and Basia Gulati (Chicago: University of Chicago Press, 1980 [1966]); and Claude Lévi-Strauss, *The Raw and the Cooked: Mythologiques* (Chicago: University of Chicago Press, 1969). Contrasting examples of voluntaristic explanations of symbolic processes abound in the literature, particularly in New Historicist approaches to culture and history. Let me cite the most obvious influences of anthropological voluntarism on literary criticism: the work of Victor Turner, e.g., *Dramas, Fields, and Metaphors: Symbolic Action in Human Society* (Ithaca, N.Y.: Cornell University Press, 1974) and *The Forest of Symbols: Aspects of Ndembu Ritual* (Ithaca, N.Y.: Cornell University Press, 1967), and above all, Clifford Geertz, *The Interpretation of Cultures* (New York: Basic Books, 1973).

47. Bourdieu, *Distinction,* 194.

48. Ibid.

5. The Dialectics of Ethnic Spectatorship

It should be understood that I use the terms "ethnic," "immigrant," and "postcolonial" somewhat interchangeably here. I do not think this compromises the specficity of my "object," since a generalized visibility of otherness is exactly what is at stake in understanding how postcolonial subjects fit within a scheme of specularity and representation.

1. See Ernst Bloch, *Literary Essays,* trans. Andrew Joron and others (Stanford: Stanford University Press, 1998), especially 239–46.

2. Ibid., 240.

3. Ibid.

4. Ibid.

5. Ibid., emphasis added.

6. Ibid., 241.

7. Ibid.

8. Theodor W. Adorno, "The Meaning of Working Through the Past," in his *Critical Models: Interventions and Catchwords,* trans. Henry W. Pickford (New York: Columbia University Press, 1998), 89. Adorno is here rehearsing his comments from an earlier debate on the validity of the Frankfurt Institute's research into the "authoritarian personality" in the light of its highly critical appraisal by Peter R. Hof-

statter, a conservative psychologist. Also see the translator's notes to *Critical Models*, 338n2.

9. Bloch, *Literary Essays*, 241.

10. The contradictions of "cosmopolitanism," as an ethic of U.S. imperial self-assurance retooled in terms of a global expansiveness, are explored in detail by Timothy Brennan, *At Home in the World: Cosmopolitanism Now* (Cambridge, Mass.: Harvard University Press, 1998).

11. In "Modernity and Narration—in Feminine Detail," in *Women and Chinese Modernity* (Minneapolis: University of Minnesota Press, 1991), 84–120, Rey Chow defines details as "the sensuous, trivial, and superflous textual presences that exist in an ambiguous relation with some larger 'vision' such as reform and revolution, which seeks to subordinate them but which is displaced by their surprising returns. As such, details are also the vital joints—produced in the process of reading—at which the coherence of certain modes of narration can be untied" (85). Although I am not as convinced of the value of investing the detail with the hermeneutic power to tie or untie the social as is Chow, her emphasis on "the social as detail" is useful for thinking about the inscription of an incomplete, political affect in textual presences (which are not always or even predominantly literary).

12. Theodor W. Adorno, "Culture and Administration," trans. Wes Blomster, *Telos* 37 (Fall): 93–112.

13. See Stuart Hall, "Cultural Identity and Diaspora," in *Identity: Community, Culture, Difference*, ed. Jonathan Rutherford (London: Lawrence and Wishart, 1990), 222–37.

14. The reference is to Fredric Jameson's discussion of the "split" between Western machineries of representation and the dynamics of Third World texts in "Third-World Literature in the Era of Multinational Capitalism," *Social Text* 5 (Fall 1986): 69.

15. See, for instance, the wholly constitutive influence of Freud (as well as Lacan) on discussions of subject formation in the work of critics such as Teresa de Lauretis, *Alice Doesn't: Feminism, Semiotics, Cinema* (Bloomington: Indiana University Press, 1984); Kaja Silverman, *The Acoustic Mirror: The Female Voice in Psychoanalysis and Cinema* (Bloomington: Indiana University Press, 1988); and Chow, *Women and Chinese Modernity*. A typical example of the inflationary rhetoric surrounding the discourse of the unconscious can also be found in the essays in *Screen* 29, no. 4 (1998). Because of her parallel interest in theorizing "ethnic spectatorship," let me refer specifically to Chow's discussion, "Seeing Modern China: Toward a Theory of Ethnic Spectatorship," in her *Women and Chinese Modernity*, 3–33. She suggests that apparatuses of seeing have become very important in demarcating boundaries between self and other and that such boundaries go to the heart of understanding power relations governing the identification of subjects (and objects). But her proposals about *ethnic* spectatorship provide little more than a "reading against the grain" of psychoanalytic propositions about "suture," "interpellation," and so on, with no consideration of the materialities governing the relationship between image and spectator or history and interpretation. The problem is exemplified, above all, in Chow's reference to Gayatri Chakravorty Spivak's analysis of the British justification of anti-*sati* laws in terms of "white men saving brown women from brown men" as being analogous to Bernardo Bertolucci's allegorizing of "China-as-woman" in his film *The Last Emperor*. The obvious distinction between Bertolucci's utterances (cinematic and verbal) and Spivak's paraphrasing of British legal doc-

trine in India is that the former is in the realm of fantasy whereas the latter represents a very different—and concrete—relay between enunciation and effect. So although I find her investigation of processes of identification amid (and because of) the illusion of an "invisible gaze" interesting (and hence worth citing at some length), I remain unconvinced that Chow establishes her case for an ethnic form of spectatorship.

16. This meaning of the conjunctural can be derived (even if it militates against his own penchant for the "symptomatic reading") from Louis Althusser's propositions in *Reading Capital,* particularly where Althusser notes that a rigorous understanding of "historical time" requires one to think of the historical present as irreversibly traversed by unevenness—that is, by something other than the narrative logic of the psychoanalytic "moment." See Louis Althusser and Étienne Balibar, *Reading Capital* (London: Verso, 1979 [1968]), especially 105–7.

17. The stage productions of *The Mahabharata* were performed at the Brooklyn Academy of Music in New York and at the Kennedy Center in Washington, D.C. Southern New Jersey's major local newspaper, the *Philadelphia Inquirer,* took its cue from its prestigious counterparts, the *New York Times* and the *Washington Post,* in bestowing lavish praise on Brook's product.

18. *New York Times,* March 20, 1991.

19. Unless otherwise noted, all quotations from *The Mahabharata* are from my transcription of the televised version.

20. In the preface to *The Order of Things,* Michel Foucault parodies the arbitrariness of the classificatory impulses of Western forms of knowledge. He quotes Borges's reference to a "certain Chinese encyclopedia" in which "animals are divided into: (a) belonging to the Emperor, (b) embalmed, (c) tame, (d) sucking pigs, (e) sirens, (f) fabulous, (g) stray dogs, (h) included in the present classification, (i) frenzied, (j) innumerable, (k) drawn with a very fine camelhair brush, (l) *et cetera,* (m) having just broken the water pitcher, (n) that a long way off look like flies." See Michel Foucault, *The Order of Things: An Archeology of the Human Sciences* (New York: Vintage, 1973), xv.

21. In fact, the serialized broadcasts on the Indian national television network, Doordarshan, of the home-grown spectacular "mythologicals"—the *Ramayana* and the *Mahabharata*—speak to very different problems emerging from the misappropriation of literary texts and traditions. The intractabilities of the Indian state's narrowly constructed vision of Hindu nationalism as the totality of Indian culture remains an issue that is quite distinct from those that I pursue here, since in terms of genre, intention, and effect, the Indian productions are fundamentally dissimilar to Brook's Eurocentric concerns.

22. See Walter Benjamin, "On Some Motifs in Baudelaire," in his *Illuminations,* trans. Harry Zohn (New York: Schocken Books, 1968), 155–200.

23. I should say that Mishra is less critical than I am of Brook's "postmodern" effort at representing the epic. But he draws our attention to some very important thematic and conceptual complexities of the text that for the most part are missed in the Brook production. See Vijay Mishra, "The Great Indian Epic and Peter Brook," in *Peter Brook and the "Mahabharata": Critical Perspectives,* ed. David Williams (London: Routledge, 1991), 195–205.

24. Ibid., 196.

25. See Rustom Bharucha, "A View from India," in Williams, *Peter Brook and the "Mahabharata,"* 230.

26. Ibid., 250.

27. Ibid., 238.

28. Gautam Dasgupta, "Peter Brook's 'Orientalism,'" in Williams, *Peter Brook and the "Mahabharata,"* 265.

29. See Howard Caygill's extraordinarily lucid mapping of Benjamin's work in his *Walter Benjamin: The Colour of Experience* (London: Routledge, 1998), 102–3, emphasis added.

30. Walter Benjamin, "The Storyteller" in his *Illuminations*, 87.

31. Caygill, *Walter Benjamin*, 98, original emphasis.

32. Benjamin, "The Storyteller," in his *Illuminations*, 89.

33. The implications of this distinction in Benjamin's work are explored in more detail by Andrew Benjamin in his essay "Tradition and Experience: Walter Benjamin's 'On Some Motifs in Baudelaire,'" in *The Problems of Modernity: Adorno and Benjamin*, ed. Andrew Benjamin (London: Routledge, 1989), 122–40. Of particular interest is the author's discussion of the forms of symbolization or correspondence that attest to the plenitude of identity and representation prior to its sealing off in the present. Forms of experience given in modernity *(Erlebnis)* require "redemption" so that a lost experience *(Erfahrung)*—associated with the continuity of tradition—may be resolved.

34. Bharucha also comments on the ethnocentric undertones of Brook's claims about universality: "One cannot agree with the premise that '*The Mahabharata* is Indian but it is universal.' The 'but' is misleading. *The Mahabharata*, I would counter, is universal *because* it is Indian. One cannot separate the culture from the text" ("A View from India," 231).

35. In a few remarks on Brook, R. Radhakrishnan also attests to the problems with *The Mahabharata*'s "modernist irony and cerebral posturing, its shallow United Nations–style internationalism, its casting of an African American male in a manner that endorse[s] certain black male stereotypes, and finally of a certain western/ Eurocentric arrogance that commodifies the work of a different culture and decontextualizes it in the name of a highly skewed and uneven globalism." See his "Is the Ethnic 'Authentic' in the Diaspora?" in *The State of Asian America: Activism and Resistance in the 1990s*, ed. Karim Aguilar-San Juan (Boston: South End Press, 1994), 231.

36. Bharucha, "Peter Brook's 'Orientalism'" in Williams, *Peter Brook and the "Mahabharata,"* 265.

37. Naomi Schor, *Reading in Detail: Aesthetics and the Feminine* (New York: Methuen, 1987).

38. At the time I was a postdoctoral fellow at the Pembroke Center, working on issues of cultural translation and the acquisition of cultural literacy among second-generation children of Indian immigrants.

39. In the entire party (including myself), there was only one non-Bengali woman. She was from a neighboring state in India (Bihar), spoke Bengali fluently, and, given the regional dynamics of eastern India, was also interpellated by the imperialist status of Bengal in cultural matters.

40. A long-time collaborator of Brook's, Michael Kustow was, at the time of this production, the commissioning editor (arts) for Channel 4 Television and a co–

executive producer of *The Mahabharata* film. Kustow is not alone among Western critics in his praise of Brook's "truly grand goal—the exploration of what theatre can do that communicates globally, across cultural boundaries" (261). One supposes that it is the undeniable virtue of such a goal that led Kustow to draw an affirmative line between Brook's vision of the *Mahabharata* and prior European attempts to discover the wisdom of the East and put it to the ends of bourgeois art. Kustow's own words are revealing in this regard: "French culture has rarely been confined by xenophobia. Artaud is one of many French artists—Paul Claudel, Victor Segalen, Henry Michaux, René Dumal—who have opened themselves to and been transformed by India and Asia. And the anthropological riches of the Musée de l'Homme and Musée Guimet have nourished modern artists as nowhere else. All colonization may be barbaric, but some ends of empire are more civilized than others" (257). These and other gems of Eurocentric presumptuousness can be found in Michael Kustow, "Something More Volcanic," in Williams, *Peter Brook and the "Mahabharata,"* 253–61. Originally published in *London Review of Books,* October 3, 1985.

41. See Peter Brook, "The Language of Stories," interviewed by Georges Banu, trans. David Williams, in Williams, *Peter Brook and the "Mahabharata,"* 46, emphasis added.

42. Quoted in Bharucha, "A View from India," 246.

43. From Peter Brook's foreword to the printed text, in *The Mahabharata,* by Jean-Claude Carrière, trans. Peter Brook (New York: Harper and Row, 1987 [1985]), xvi.

Afterword

1. The phrase is Judith Butler's, uttered a few months before she avowed her own left-leaning, but necessarily less conservative, allegiances to Marx and Adorno in the pages of the *New York Times,* after having been called a "bad writer."

2. Patrick McGee, *Telling the Other: The Question of Value in Modern and Postcolonial Writing* (Ithaca, N.Y.: Cornell University Press, 1992).

3. Ibid., 20.

4. The idea of a general economy draws on the authority of Georges Bataille's specification of it, but Derrida makes it interchangeable with *différance* on the grounds that value must be related to the "nonbasis" of expenditure and therefore on the tendentious terms of the indifference of value and nonvalue. This view is proposed in Jacques Derrida, *Writing and Difference,* trans. Alan Bass (Chicago: University of Chicago Press, 1978), see especially, 271. McGee gives the idea his own spin in *Telling the Other,* 20.

5. Adorno's critique of the ways that such a faith dissimulates a nihilism that has "turn[ed] into farce, into mere method" is still the most brilliant critique of an idealist and impressionist linguistic philosophizing. See Theodor W. Adorno, *The Jargon of Authenticity,* trans. Knut Tarnowski and Frederic Will (Evanston, Ill.: Northwestern University Press, 1973 [1964]), 28. The phrase "splendor of the simple" is Heidegger's (quoted in Adorno, 50). For Heidegger's own meditations on the problem of the "worldly," see Martin Heidegger, *Being and Time,* trans. John Macquarrie and Edward Robinson (San Francisco: Harper and Row Publishers, 1962), especially part 3, "The Worldhood of the World," 91–148.

6. McGee, *Telling the Other,* 20.

7. Ibid., 23.

8. Ibid., 22.

9. Ibid., 23.

10. Ibid., 152.

11. Guy Debord, *The Society of the Spectacle,* trans. Donald Nicholson-Smith (New York: Zone Books), 130, original emphasis.

12. Ibid., 43–44.

13. McGee fuses Williams with Baudrillard, but it is the latter whom he cites approvingly for having transcended a productivist emphasis: "Production merely accumulates and is never diverted from its end. It replaces all illusions with just one: its own, which has become the reality principle" (McGee, *Telling the Other,* 45).

14. Raymond Williams, "Base and Superstructure in Marxist Cultural Theory," in his *Problems in Materialism and Culture* (London: Verso, 1980), 38, emphasis added.

15. See McGee, *Telling the Other,* particularly 202, where he inadvertently reveals how the "seduction" of and by otherness ultimately devolves into an utter solipsism: "This fascination [with the other] directs us to a revelation. It makes apparent, or brings to the surface, *the voice of the other within us*" (emphasis added). I have trained so much of my attention on McGee's writing in this afterword in order to underscore the self-indulgent direction of poststructuralist ruminations on postcolonial otherness in which the focus on "subjectivity" dissimulates a narcissism. Baudrillard's views on the problematic of signification or subjectivity (both subsumed under the category of symbolic exchange) are instructive in their excessiveness, but by no means are they irreconcilable with the poststructuralist project in general.

16. Roland Barthes, *Camera Lucida: Reflections on Photography* (New York: Hill and Wang, 1981 [1980]).

17. Martin Jay, *Downcast Eyes: The Denigration of Vision in Twentieth-Century French Thought* (Berkeley and Los Angeles: University of California Press, 1994), 437.

18. Fredric Jameson, "Pleasure: A Political Issue," in his *The Ideologies of Theory: Essays, 1971–1986,* vol. 2: *The Syntax of History* (Minneapolis: University of Minnesota Press, 1988), 65.

19. Naomi Schor, *Reading in Detail: Aesthetics and the Feminine* (New York and London: Methuen, 1987), 88.

20. Ibid., 88.

21. This is how Schor reads Barthes's investments in the Orient: in Japan, haiku poetry, and the "insignificant" detail. Ibid., 88–89.

Index

adquation, 29, 30

Adorno, Theodor W., 3, 4, 12, 16, 21, 23, 28–29, 37, 43, 73, 122, 132–33, 135, 142, 146, 178

aesthetic: aestheticism, 47; aesthetics, 145, 157; conventions, 161, 165; experience, 145, 152; form, 47, 68, 132, 156, 169; value, 142

alienation, 4, 15, 49, 52–54, 76, 81, 84–85, 91, 111, 142, 144, 153, 158, 169, 171, 173

Althusser, Louis, 45–46, 50, 59, 82, 149

Anderson, Benedict, 17

anomaly, 10, 13, 23

anthropology, 13, 19, 23–24, 39, 43, 47, 177

antinomy, 68–69, 75, 79

Aragon, Louis, 47, 52

Arendt, Hannah, 83–85

authenticity, 20, 32, 122, 129, 130, 132–34, 143, 151–52, 154; and inauthentic, 5; and inauthenticity, 13, 130–31, 133

Barthes, Roland, 49–50, 124–27, 155, 178–80

Bataille, Georges, 77

Baudelaire, Charles, 52–53, 157

Baudrillard, Jean, 22, 172, 174, 176

Bayes, Thomas, 58

Beethoven, Ludwig van, 145

belatedness, 10, 52, 83, 88

Benjamin, Walter, 12–13, 15–17, 21, 24–25, 28, 36, 48, 52–54, 71, 78, 83–86, 90–91, 120, 133–35, 149, 153, 157–58, 170, 174–76

Bhabha, Homi K., 11, 38, 41, 52, 114

Bharucha, Rustom, 154–55

Bloch, Ernst, 16, 73, 141–42, 151, 158, 169

Bond, James, 144

Borges, Jorge Luis, 150–51, 154

Bourdieu, Pierre, 21, 49, 97, 118, 120–21, 127, 129, 137–39

bourgeois, 5; context, 104; desire, 99; experience, 16, 57; history, 71; humanism, 41; ideology, 127; life, 20, 72, 117; normativity, 57; practices, 99, 140; self-consolidation, 47; thought, 70, 74; values, 62, 135, 139, 157. *See also* embourgeoisement

Brecht, Bertolt, 142, 150

Breton, André, 52

Brook, Peter, 21, 143, 147–48, 152–53, 155, 158, 161, 166

Buck-Morss, Susan, 15

Butler, Judith, 37

capital: capitalism, 11, 13, 17, 53, 74, 93, 122, 149, 173, 177; capitalist: exchange, 150; as crisis, 69–70, 72, 171; existence, 73, 177; ideologies, 20; logic of, 5–6, 11, 149, 172; as religion, 71; societies, 14

carnivalesque, 99

Carrière, Jean-Claude, 166

caste, 60, 93, 100

Keya Ganguly is associate professor in the Department of Cultural Studies and Comparative Literature at the University of Minnesota. She is coeditor (with John Mowitt and Jochen Schulte-Sasse) of the journal *Cultural Critique.*